EVALUATING AND IMPROVING
UNDERGRADUATE TEACHING

IN SCIENCE, TECHNOLOGY, ENGINEERING, AND MATHEMATICS

Committee on Recognizing, Evaluating, Rewarding, and Developing
Excellence in Teaching of Undergraduate Science, Mathematics,
Engineering, and Technology

Marye Anne Fox and Norman Hackerman, Editors

Center for Education
Division of Behavioral and Social Sciences and Education

NATIONAL RESEARCH COUNCIL
OF THE NATIONAL ACADEMIES

The National Academies Press
Washington, D.C.
www.nap.edu

THE NATIONAL ACADEMIES PRESS   500 Fifth Street, N.W.   Washington, DC 20001

NOTICE: The project that is the subject of this report was approved by the Governing Board of the National Research Council, whose members are drawn from the councils of the National Academy of Sciences, the National Academy of Engineering, and the Institute of Medicine. The members of the committee responsible for the report were chosen for their special competences and with regard for appropriate balance.

This study was conducted under an award from the Presidents of the National Academies. Any opinions, findings, conclusions, or recommendations expressed in this publication are those of the author(s) and do not necessarily reflect the views of the organizations or agencies that provided support for the project.

Library of Congress Cataloging-in-Publication Data

Evaluating and improving undergraduate teaching in science, technology, engineering, and mathematics / Marye Anne Fox and Norman Hackerman, editors ; Committee on Recognizing, Evaluating, and Rewarding Undergraduate Teaching, Center for Education, Division of Behavioral and Social Sciences and Education National Research Council.
    p. cm.
Includes index.
 ISBN 0-309-07277-8 (pbk.)
 1. Science—Study and teaching—Evaluation. 2. College teaching—Evaluation. I. Fox, Marye Anne, 1947- II. Hackerman, Norman. III. National Research Council (U.S.). Committee on Recognizing, Evaluating, and Rewarding Undergraduate Teaching.
 Q181 .E93 2003
 507.1—dc21

                          2002013890

Additional copies of this report are available from the National Academies Press, 500 Fifth Street, N.W., Lockbox 285, Washington, DC 20055; (800) 624-6242 or (202) 334-3313 (in the Washington metropolitan area); Internet, http://www.nap.edu

Printed in the United States of America

Suggested citation: National Research Council. (2003). *Evaluating and improving undergraduate teaching in science, technology, engineering, and mathematics.* Committee on Recognizing, Evaluating, Rewarding, and Developing Excellence in Teaching of Undergraduate Science, Mathematics, Engineering, and Technology, M.A. Fox and N. Hackerman, Editors. Center for Education, Division of Behavioral and Social Sciences and Education. Washington, DC: The National Academies Press.

BK
$35.56

THE NATIONAL ACADEMIES
Advisers to the Nation on Science, Engineering, and Medicine

The **National Academy of Sciences** is a private, nonprofit, self-perpetuating society of distinguished scholars engaged in scientific and engineering research, dedicated to the furtherance of science and technology and to their use for the general welfare. Upon the authority of the charter granted to it by the Congress in 1863, the Academy has a mandate that requires it to advise the federal government on scientific and technical matters. Dr. Bruce M. Alberts is president of the National Academy of Sciences.

The **National Academy of Engineering** was established in 1964, under the charter of the National Academy of Sciences, as a parallel organization of outstanding engineers. It is autonomous in its administration and in the selection of its members, sharing with the National Academy of Sciences the responsibility for advising the federal government. The National Academy of Engineering also sponsors engineering programs aimed at meeting national needs, encourages education and research, and recognizes the superior achievements of engineers. Dr. Wm. A. Wulf is president of the National Academy of Engineering.

The **Institute of Medicine** was established in 1970 by the National Academy of Sciences to secure the services of eminent members of appropriate professions in the examination of policy matters pertaining to the health of the public. The Institute acts under the responsibility given to the National Academy of Sciences by its congressional charter to be an adviser to the federal government and, upon its own initiative, to identify issues of medical care, research, and education. Dr. Harvey V. Fineberg is president of the Institute of Medicine.

The **National Research Council** was organized by the National Academy of Sciences in 1916 to associate the broad community of science and technology with the Academy's purposes of furthering knowledge and advising the federal government. Functioning in accordance with general policies determined by the Academy, the Council has become the principal operating agency of both the National Academy of Sciences and the National Academy of Engineering in providing services to the government, the public, and the scientific and engineering communities. The Council is administered jointly by both Academies and the Institute of Medicine. Dr. Bruce M. Alberts and Dr. Wm. A. Wulf are chair and vice chair, respectively, of the National Research Council.

www.national-academies.org

COMMITTEE ON RECOGNIZING, EVALUATING, REWARDING, AND DEVELOPING EXCELLENCE IN TEACHING OF UNDERGRADUATE SCIENCE, MATHEMATICS, ENGINEERING, AND TECHNOLOGY

MARYE ANNE FOX (*Co-chair*) North Carolina State University
NORMAN HACKERMAN (*Co-chair*) The Robert A. Welch Foundation, TX
TRUDY BANTA, Indiana University-Purdue University at Indianapolis
JOHN CENTRA, Syracuse University, NY
BARBARA GROSS DAVIS, University of California-Berkeley
DENICE DENTON, University of Washington
DIANE EBERT-MAY, Michigan State University
TIMOTHY GOLDSMITH, Yale University, CT
MANUEL GOMEZ, University of Puerto Rico
EILEEN LEWIS, University of California-Berkeley
JEANNE L. NARUM, Project Kaleidoscope, Washington, DC
CORNELIUS J. PINGS, University of Southern California
MICHAEL SCRIVEN, Claremont Graduate University, CA
CHRISTINE STEVENS, St. Louis University, MO
DENNIS WEISS, The Richard Stockton College of New Jersey

JAY B. LABOV (*Study Director*)
TERRY K. HOLMER (*Senior Project Assistant*)

COMMITTEE ON UNDERGRADUATE SCIENCE EDUCATION
JULY 1999

Preface

Americans have long appreciated the need for high-quality education and have invested accordingly, at levels from preschool through graduate education. Because of the impact of science and technology on the nation's economic growth, these fields have received substantial government and private research funding at colleges and universities. Indeed, since World War II, federal funding through peer-reviewed grants and contracts has placed in the hands of university faculty the primary responsibility for more than half of the nation's basic research in these fields. This investment has contributed significantly to making the United States a world leader in the discovery and application of new knowledge and has produced a well-respected system for graduate training in science and engineering. In recent years, additional financial support from industry and nonprofit organizations has provided new opportunities for graduate and undergraduate students at many universities to participate in original research projects. Recognition of the importance of original peer-reviewed research in institutions of higher learning is clearly laudable. As Robert Gavin noted in the 2000 publication *Academic Excellence: The Role of Research in the Physical Sciences at Undergraduate Institutions*, "research activity plays a central role in keeping the faculty up to date in the field and improves their teaching."

Because of the key role of science, technology, engineering, and mathematics (STEM), mechanisms for careful scrutiny and evaluation of the quality of research in these fields are highly developed, and academic scientists and engineers often derive reward and recognition from their research achievements. As is the case with most scholarship, the criteria used in these evaluations differ from one discipline to another, and faculty evaluations at research-intensive universities generally solicit the candid judgments of national or international peers from outside the home institution when a faculty member or program is to be evaluated. Reliance on one's disciplinary colleagues for a critique of the merits of one's research accomplishments and proposals is widely accepted as a necessary investment of faculty time and effort.

In contrast, the evaluation of teaching accomplishments has been more haphazard and less rigorous, particularly at research universities. Some faculty are not convinced of the objectivity of techniques used for describing the effectiveness of teaching and learning, especially at institutions at which competing demands on faculty time make it challenging to balance all of the normal faculty responsibilities and to focus on classroom and laboratory instruction.

Even though the dominant values, beliefs, culture, and missions of many U.S. higher education institutions often emphasize high-quality instruction, particularly in lower division undergraduate teaching, a common perception is that teaching is less closely scrutinized and less clearly rewarded than is research. Given the variety of goals among the many different sizes and types of American colleges and universities, it is not surprising that substantial differences exist in capability

and achievements in the balance between teaching and research. However, if the broad teaching missions of colleges and universities are to be attained, rigorous evaluation to improve teaching and learning must become integral to STEM departmental culture. If so, faculty and administration must be convinced that objective and comprehensive methods exist for performing such evaluations and that these techniques can be used without imposing undue burden or impossible time commitments on already busy faculty. Our study points out ways in which the fair evaluation of teaching and learning in STEM disciplines can be institutionalized as the basis for allocating rewards and promotions, at a level of effort consistent with a department's or college's educational mission.

Over the past several years, the National Research Council (NRC) has assumed an aggressive role in strengthening STEM education. The NRC's Committee on Undergraduate Science Education has coordinated this effort in colleges and universities. This study, undertaken by the Committee on Evaluating Undergraduate Teaching, examines the crucial issue of how best to evaluate the effectiveness of undergraduate instruction to improve student learning and to enhance faculty teaching skills. The committee members included faculty and administrators in science, mathematics, and engineering; experts in assessment and evaluation; and representatives of several higher education organizations dedicated to the improvement of education. (See Appendix D for biographical sketches of the committee members.)

This is a timely undertaking. Pressures are mounting from within and beyond academe (e.g., state boards of regents and legislatures, business and industry) to improve learning, particularly in introductory and lower-division courses. These calls also request accountability of academic departments, including a new emphasis on improved teaching and enhanced student learning through curriculum revision and collegial peer mentoring.

It is the committee's view that a well-structured evaluation of teaching can be meaningful to those being evaluated and to those who must render personnel decisions based on these evaluations. Conducted appropriately, such evaluations would be crucial components of the institution's efforts to improve education. Indeed, progress in educational research has clarified the effectiveness of new methods, linking them with demonstrable outcomes: improved student learning and academic achievement. It is the committee's hope that the recent research findings presented in this report will be incorporated into existing evaluative practice.

Marye Anne Fox, *Co-chair*
Norman Hackerman, *Co-chair*
Committee on Recognizing, Evaluating, Rewarding, and Developing Excellence in Teaching of Undergraduate Science, Mathematics, Engineering, and Technology

Acknowledgments

The committee members and staff acknowledge the contributions of a number of people for providing presentations, additional data, and valuable insight to the committee both during and between committee meetings: John V. Byrne, President Emeritus, Oregon State University and Director, Kellogg Commission on the Future of State and Land-Grant Universities; Barbara Cambridge, Director, Teaching Initiatives, American Association for Higher Education, and Director, Carnegie Academy Campus Program; R. Eugene Rice, Director, Assessment Forum, American Association for Higher Education; Alan H. Schoenfeld, Professor of Education, University of California-Berkeley, and Chair, Joint Policy Board on Mathematics Task Force on Educational Activities.

At the National Research Council (NRC), we also would like to acknowledge Michael J. Feuer, former director of the NRC's Center for Education (CFE) and currently executive director of the NRC's Division of Behavioral and Social Sciences and Education, for providing critical support and leadership during the writing and report review phases of this study; Kirsten Sampson Snyder, CFE Reports Officer, for her support and guidance in shepherding this report through report review and in working on the final stages of production; Rona Briere and Kathleen (Kit) Johnston for their editing skills and insight; Eugenia Grohman and Yvonne Wise, for their assistance and support in revising the report at several stages of its development; and also Rodger W. Bybee, former executive director of the NRC's Center for Science, Mathematics, and Engineering Education, and current Executive Director of the Biological Sciences Curriculum Study. Dr. Bybee helped conceive this study and offered support and guidance for it during the time that he was affiliated with the NRC.

This report has been reviewed in draft form by individuals chosen for their diverse perspectives and technical expertise, in accordance with procedures approved by the NRC's Report Review Committee. The purpose of this independent review is to provide candid and critical comments that will assist the institution in making the published report as sound as possible and to ensure that the report meets institutional standards for objectivity, evidence, and responsiveness to the study charge. The review comments and draft manuscript remain confidential to protect the integrity of the deliberative process. We wish to thank the following individuals for their participation in the review of this report:

David F. Brakke, Dean, College of Science and Mathematics, James Madison University

Brian P. Coppola, Department of Chemistry, University of Michigan

James Gentile, Dean, Natural Science Division, Hope College, Holland, Michigan

Melvin D. George, Department of Mathematics, University of Missouri

Daniel Goroff, Associate Director, Derek Bok Center for Teaching and Learning and Department of Mathematics, Harvard University

Peter D. Lax, Courant Institute of Mathematical Sciences, New York University

Susan B. Millar, College of Engineering, University of Wisconsin, Madison

Robert E. Newnham, Department of Materials Science and Engineering, Pennsylvania State University

Sheri D. Sheppard, Associate Professor of Mechanical Engineering, Stanford University, and

Michael J. Smith, Education Director, American Geological Institute.

Although the reviewers listed above have provided many constructive comments and suggestions, they were not asked to endorse the conclusions or recommendations nor did they see the final draft of the report before its release. The review of this report was overseen by Frank G. Rothman, Brown University, and Pierre C. Hohenberg, Yale University. Appointed by the NRC, they were responsible for making certain that an independent examination of this report was carried out in accordance with institutional procedures and that all review comments were carefully considered. Responsibility for the final content of this report rests entirely with the authoring committee and the institution.

Contents

EVALUATING AND IMPROVING

UNDERGRADUATE TEACHING

IN SCIENCE, TECHNOLOGY, ENGINEERING, AND MATHEMATICS

Executive Summary

This report recommends a set of strategies to evaluate undergraduate teaching and learning in science, technology, engineering, and mathematics (STEM[1]). It is based on a study conducted by a National Research Council (NRC) committee charged with synthesizing relevant research in pedagogy and practice as a basis for developing resources to help postsecondary STEM faculty and administrators evaluate and reward effective teaching. The study committee was a subcommittee of the NRC's Committee on Undergraduate Science Education.

The committee's principal goal was to determine whether fair and objective methods exist for the evaluation of teaching and learning, and if so, how such methods could be used as a basis for the professional advancement of faculty. The committee found that many such methods exist, and that their utility deserves wider appreciation and application in the evaluation of both individuals and departments.

The committee found that *summative* evaluations of teaching, such as those used in some faculty promotion and tenure decisions, often do not rely on evidence of student learning, and this relationship needs to be strengthened and formalized. The committee also found that *formative* evaluations (e.g., ongoing informal feedback from students and colleagues) can serve several important educational goals: (1) coupling candid teaching evaluation with opportunities for ongoing professional development; (2) supporting faculty

---

[1] This abbreviation for science, technology, engineering, and mathematics education, taken from the official designation of the National Science Foundation for education in the disciplines, is used as shorthand throughout the report.

who wish to explore the scholarship of teaching and learning; and (3) applying such formative evaluation techniques to departmental programs, not only to individual faculty.[2]

Four fundamental premises guided the committee's deliberations:

(1) Effective postsecondary teaching in science, mathematics, and technology should be available to *all* students, regardless of their major.

(2) The design of curricula and the evaluation of teaching and learning should be collective responsibilities of faculty in individual departments or, where appropriate, through interdepartmental arrangements.

(3) Scholarly activities that focus on improving teaching and learning should be recognized as bona fide endeavors that are equivalent to other scholarly pursuits. Scholarship devoted to improving teaching effectiveness and learning should be accorded the same administrative and collegial support that is available for efforts to improve other research and service endeavors.

(4) Faculty who are expected to work with undergraduates should be given support and mentoring in teaching

throughout their careers; hiring practices should provide a first opportunity to signal institutions' teaching values and expectations of faculty.

Underlying these premises is the committee's recognition that science, mathematics, and engineering instructors face a number of daunting challenges: the need to apply principles of human learning from research in cognitive science to the assessment of learning outcomes, to teach and advise large numbers of students with diverse interests and varying reasons for enrolling, to prepare future teachers, to provide faculty and students with engaging laboratory and field experiences, and to supervise students who undertake original research. Simultaneously addressing these challenges requires knowledge of and enthusiasm for the subject matter, familiarity with a range of appropriate pedagogies, skill in using appropriate tests, ease in professional interactions with students within and beyond the classroom; and active scholarly assessment to enhance teaching and learning.

Yet the committee found that most faculty who teach undergraduates in the STEM disciplines have received little formal training in teaching techniques, in assessing student learning, or in evaluating teaching effectiveness. Formal programs aimed at improving

---

[2]Detailed definitions of formative and summative evaluation can be found in Chapter 5.

teaching are still rare. A firm commitment to open intradepartmental communication about teaching effectiveness is therefore critical to any convincing evaluation of teaching based on these premises. And because considerable variation exists across institutions and disciplines, there is no single formula or pathway to effective evaluation of teaching.

The research literature suggests that some *combination of the following kinds of formative and summative evidence* about student learning can be helpful in evaluating and improving a faculty member's teaching:

Departmental and other colleagues can provide informed input about teaching effectiveness through direct observation, analysis of course content and materials, or information about the instructor's effectiveness in service and interdisciplinary courses. *Undergraduates and graduate teaching assistants* could offer useful information based on their experiences in the instructor's courses and laboratories, the instructor's supervision of research, and the quality of academic advising. Additionally, *graduate students* could comment on the supervision and mentoring they have received as they prepare for teaching. The *faculty member being evaluated* could provide self-assessment of his or her teaching strengths and areas for improvement; this assessment

could be compared with the other independent evidence. The *instructor's willingness to seek external support to improve teaching and learning* also is evidence of her or his commitment to effective undergraduate teaching.

Effective evaluation also emerges from a *combination of sources* of evidence. *Current students*, those who had taken a course in previous years, and *graduating seniors and alumni* could provide evidence about the instructor's role in their learning. *Graduate teaching assistants* could discuss the instructor's approaches to teaching, levels of interactions with students, and the mentoring that they receive in improving their own teaching skills. *Departmental and other faculty colleagues*, both from within and outside the institution, could evaluate the currency of the materials the instructor presents and his or her level of participation and leadership in improving undergraduate education. The *faculty member being evaluated* can provide critical information about his or her teaching challenges and successes through self-reflection and other evidence of effective teaching, student learning, and professional growth. *Institutional data and records* offer insights about changes in enrollments in a faculty member's courses over time, the percentage of students who drop the instructor's courses, and the number of students who go on to take additional courses in the discipline and related subject areas.

Each of these criteria is subject to multiple interpretations and should be viewed with care. For example, research suggests that grade distributions are not as useful an indicator of teaching effectiveness as other types of indicators and should be used cautiously, if at all.

A central idea behind formative evaluation of teaching and learning is a two-way feedback system known as "outcomes assessment." Faculty need to set clear goals for their students and ascertain whether students are meeting those goals throughout the course. Students need to have a clear idea of what is expected of them and whether they are meeting those expectations. Chapter 5 describes in detail a variety of procedures that close these feedback loops, providing faculty with credible information about what students know and can do as a result of instruction while giving students information about how well they have mastered the course material. Whatever the means of outcomes assessment that are employed, measures of students' conceptual understanding are critically important in judging the success of a course.

Implementing such processes can be time-consuming and involve faculty other than the instructor in charge of the course. Departmental commitment to the shared goal of improving under-graduate education is critical to the success of such approaches. Improving summative evaluation also requires that the faculty at-large, academic administrators, and committees on promotion and tenure have confidence in the credibility of the process.

RECOMMENDATIONS

An undisputed strength of American higher education is that each institution has a unique mission. It is very unlikely that any general model for evaluating teaching and learning could pertain to all schools. Several broad recommendations, however, may be generally useful when adapted to local goals and visions.

1. Overall Recommendations

(1.1) Teaching effectiveness should be judged by the quality and extent of student learning. Many different teaching styles and methods are likely to be effective.

(1.2) Scholarly activities that focus on improving teaching and learning should be recognized and rewarded as a bona fide scholarly endeavor and accorded the types of institutional supports aimed at improving scholarship generally.

(1.3) Valid summative assessments of teaching should not only rely on student evaluations, but should include peer reviews and teaching portfolios used for promotion, tenure, and post-tenure review. Such assessments should be designed to provide fair and objective information to aid faculty in the improvement of their teaching. Building consensus among faculty, providing necessary resources, and relying on the best available research on teaching, learning, and measurement are critical for this approach to evaluation.

(1.4) Individual faculty—beginners as well as more experienced teachers—and their departments should be rewarded for consistent improvement of learning by both major and nonmajor students. All teaching-related activities—such as grading, reporting of grades, curriculum development, training of teaching assistants, and related committee work—should be included in evaluation systems adopted for faculty rewards.

(1.5) Faculty should accept the obligation to improve their teaching skills as part of their personal commitment to professional excellence. Departments and institutions of higher education should reinforce the importance of such professional development for faculty through the establishment and support of campus resources (e.g., centers for teaching and learning) and through personnel policies that recognize and reward such efforts. At the same time, institutions should recognize that disciplines approach teaching differently and that such differences should be reflected in evaluation procedures.

Much of this report offers recommendations to faculty about how they can use evaluation to improve their teaching. Accordingly, the following set of recommendations is directed toward policy makers, administrators, and leaders of organizations associated with higher education.

2. Recommendations for Presidents, Overseeing Boards, and Academic Officers

(2.1) Quality teaching and effective learning should be highly ranked institutional priorities. All faculty and departmental evaluations and accreditation reviews should include rigorous assessment of teaching effectiveness. University leaders should clearly assert high expectations for quality teaching to newly hired and current faculty.

(2.2) Campus-wide or disciplinary-focused centers for teaching and learning should be tasked with providing faculty with opportunities for ongoing professional development that include understanding how people learn, how to improve current instruction though student feedback (formative evaluation), and how educational research can be translated into improved teaching practice. Such centers should provide equipment and facilities required for innovative teaching.

(2.3) At least one senior university-level administrator should be assigned responsibility for encouraging departmental faculty to adopt effective means (as proven by research) to improve instruction.

(2.4) Faculty who have excelled in teaching should be publicly recognized and rewarded. Endowments should be established to recognize the serious contributions of faculty who have made a sustained contribution to quality teaching.

(2.5) Faculty should be encouraged to develop curricula that transcend disciplinary boundaries, through a combination of incentives (including funding), expectations of accountability, and development of standards for disciplinary and interdisciplinary teaching.

(2.6) Willingness to emphasize student learning and to make allocations of departmental resources in support of teaching should be an essential requirement in appointing deans, department chairs, and similar administrative positions.

(2.7) Graduate school deans should require that departments that employ graduate students in fulfilling their teaching mission should show evidence that their faculties are effectively mentoring graduate teaching assistants and advising them about their duties to undergraduate students.

3. Recommendations for Deans, Department Chairs, and Peer Evaluators

(3.1) Departments should periodically review a departmental mission statement that includes appropriate emphasis on teaching and student learning. These reviews should address not only the major curriculum, but also service offerings—such as courses designed for nonmajors and prospective teachers.

(3.2) Individual faculty members should be expected to contribute to a balanced program of undergraduate teaching. Participation of established faculty in lower-division, introductory, and general-education courses should be encouraged. Faculty who are most familiar with new developments in the discipline can provide leadership in departmental curricular review and revision. Not all faculty must contribute equally to instruction at every level, but it is a departmental responsibility to ensure that the instructional needs of all students are met by caring, responsible faculty.

(3.3) Departments should contribute to campus-wide awareness of the premium placed on improved teaching. They should build consensus among their own faculty about the suitability of the institution's procedures for summative evaluation of teaching, recognizing that the way that practitioners of a specific discipline approach learning will affect the ways that teaching should be evaluated.

(3.4) In addition to numerical data from end-of-course student evaluations and on participation in specific courses, effective peer reviews of teaching should provide a subjective assessment of a faculty member's commitment to quality teaching. Generally, this should include evaluation of a faculty member's knowledge and enthusiasm for the subject matter; familiarity with a range of appropriate pedagogical methods; skills in using appropriate tests and laboratory experiences; quality of advising and other professional interactions with students within and beyond the classroom; and active scholarly commitment to enhancing top-quality teaching and learning.

(3.5) Department heads, in submitting personnel recommendations, should provide separate ratings on teaching, research, and service, each with supporting evidence, as key components of their overall rating and recommendation.

(3.6) Normal departmental professional development activity should include informing faculty about research findings that can improve student learning.

(3.7) As appropriate for achieving departmental goals, departments should provide funds to faculty to enhance teaching skills and knowledge and encourage them to undertake or rely upon educational research that links teaching strategies causally to student learning. Additional funds should be made available to departments that adopt this strategy.

(3.8) Departments should recognize that in the course of their careers, some faculty may shift the balance of their departmental obligations to place a greater emphasis on instruction or educational leadership. These shifts should be supported, consistent with a departmental mission, so long as active engagement with innovative teaching is being addressed.

4. Recommendations for Granting and Accrediting Agencies, Research Sponsors, and Professional Societies

(4.1) Funding agencies should support programs to enable an integrated network of national and campus-based centers for teaching and learning. An important goal of such a network is to conduct and disseminate research on approaches that enhance teaching and learning in STEM. The network can also provide information on the use of formative and summative assessment for improving teaching and learning. To the extent possible, these investments should not be made at the expense of sponsored research.

(4.2) Funding agencies and research sponsors should undertake a self-examination by convening expert panels to examine whether agency policies might inadvertently compromise a faculty member's commitment to quality undergraduate teaching.

(4.3) Accreditation agencies and boards should revise policies to emphasize quality undergraduate learning as a primary criterion for program accreditation.

(4.4) Professional societies should offer opportunities to discuss undergraduate education issues during annual and regional meetings. These events might include sessions on teaching techniques and suggestions for overcoming disciplinary and institutional barriers to improved teaching.

(4.5) Professional societies should encourage publication of peer-reviewed articles in their general or specialized journals on evolving educational issues in STEM.

PART I

What Is Known:
Principles, Research Findings,
and Implementation Issues

1
Recent Perspectives on Undergraduate Teaching and Learning

This report addresses a crucial challenge to changing and improving undergraduate education in the United States: how to evaluate the effectiveness of undergraduate teaching in science, technology, engineering, and mathematics (STEM[1]) in ways that will enable faculty to enhance student learning, continually improve teaching in these fields, and allow faculty to develop professionally in the practice and scholarship of teaching and learning. Although many view higher education in the United States as among the best such systems in the world, there have been numerous calls for reform, particularly in the STEM disciplines. Top-ranking policy makers (e.g., Greenspan, 2000; Seymour, in press) have stated that globalization of the economy, significant advances in scientific discovery, and the ubiquity of information technologies make it imperative for all U.S. students (grades K–16) to understand the methods and basic principles of STEM if they are to succeed. Recent reports from the National Science Foundation ([NSF], 1996, 1998), the National Science Board (2000), the National Research Council (NRC), (1996b, 1999a), and others (e.g., Boyer Commission, 1998) have challenged the nation's colleges and universities to ensure that *all* undergraduates increase their knowledge and understanding of STEM and the relevance of these disciplines to other areas of learning and human endeavors.

---

[1]This abbreviation for science, technology, engineering, and mathematics education, taken from the official designation of the National Science Foundation for education in the disciplines, is used as shorthand throughout the report.

IMPETUS FOR AND CHALLENGES TO CHANGE

Calls for Accountability from Outside of Academe

The reforms within K–12 education that have been enacted in almost every state and many districts include systems for measuring achievement and accountability. State legislatures, departments of education, school boards, and the general public expect those responsible for educating students to be held specifically accountable for the quality of the outcomes of their work (Rice et al., 2000).

The call for accountability is also being clearly heard at the postsecondary level. State legislatures are demanding that public universities provide quantifiable evidence of the effectiveness of the academic programs being supported with tax dollars. Other bodies, including national commissions, institutional governing boards, and professional accrediting agencies, also have begun to recommend that universities and colleges be held more accountable for student learning (see, e.g., National Center for Public Policy and Higher Education, 2001; see also Chapter 3, this report).

One aspect of the call for accountability in higher education is particularly important for faculty in STEM. Corpo-rate leaders and the public alike are focusing on the need for a scientifically and technologically literate citizenry and a skilled workforce (Capelli, 1997; Greenspan, 2000; International Technology Education Association, 2000; Murnane and Levy, 1996; National Council of Teachers of Mathematics, 2000; NRC, 1996a, 1999a, 2000d). Corporate leaders also have made it increasingly clear that their workforce needs more than basic knowledge in science, mathematics, and technology. They expect those they hire to apply that knowledge in new and unusual contexts, as well as to communicate effectively, work collaboratively, understand the perspectives of colleagues from different cultures, and continually update and expand their knowledge and skills (Capelli, 1997; Greenspan, 2000; Rust, 1998).

Calls for Change from Within Academe

While public pressure for reforming undergraduate teaching and learning and holding educators accountable for such improvements is real and growing, recent surveys also suggest that increasing numbers of faculty are advocating strongly for quality teaching and are paying close attention to how effective teaching is recognized, evaluated, and rewarded within departments and at the institutional level (Ory, 2000). In a recent survey of doctoral students, for example, 83 percent indicated that teaching "is one of the most appealing aspects of faculty life, as well as its core undertaking" (Golde and Dore, 2001, p. 21).

In recent interviews with new faculty members, Rice et al. (2000)[2] reported that interviewees overwhelmingly expressed enjoyment of and commitment to teaching and working with students. However, early-career faculty expressed concerns about how their work is evaluated. They perceive that expectations for their performance are vague and sometimes conflicting. They also indicated that feedback on their performance often is insufficient, unfocused, and unclear. Many expressed concern about the lack of a "culture of collegiality" or a "teaching community" at their institutions (Rice et al., 2000).

During the past decade, there also has been increasing concern among senior faculty and administrators about improving undergraduate STEM education. These efforts have been spurred by reports from a variety of national organizations (e.g., Boyer, 1990; Boyer Commission, 1998; NRC, 1996b, 1997a; NSF, 1996; Project Kaleidoscope, 1991, 1994) calling for reform in these disciplines. Professional societies also are devoting serious attention to enhancing undergraduate teaching and learning in these disciplines (e.g., Council on Undergraduate Research <http://www.cur.org>; Doyle, 2000; McNeal and D'Avanzo, 1997; NRC, 1999b, 2000b; Howard Hughes Medical Institute <http://www.hhmi.org>; National Institute for Science Education <http://www.wcer.wisc.edu/nise>; Project Kaleidoscope <http://www.pkal.org>; Rothman and Narum, 1999; and websites and publications of increasing numbers of professional societies in the natural sciences, mathematics, and engineering).

---

[2]This report by Rice et al. (2000) is a product of the American Association for Higher Education's (AAHE's) ongoing Forum on Faculty Roles and Rewards. The report provides the results of structured interviews that were undertaken with 350+ new faculty members and graduate students aspiring to be faculty members from colleges and universities around the country. The aim of that study was to obtain perspectives from those who are just beginning their academic careers and to offer guidance for senior faculty, chairs, deans, and others in higher education who will be responsible for shaping the professoriate of the future. Rice et al. offer ten "Principles of Good Practice: Supporting Early-Career Faculty," accompanied by an action inventory to prompt department chairs, senior colleagues, and other academic leaders to examine their individual and institutional practices. These principles and specific action items are also available in a separate publication by Sorcinelli (2000), which is available at <http://www.aahe.org/ffrr/principles_brochure.htm>.

Challenges to Change

Although there are many pressures on postsecondary institutions to examine and change their practices and assumptions about teaching and learning, it also is clear that the circumstances in which such changes must occur are exceedingly complex. One challenge is the diversity of the U.S. higher education community. Institutions range from those that serve several hundred students to those that enroll many thousands. Institutional histories and academic missions vary widely, as do their sources of support, means of governance, and student populations. These differences inevitably result in varying expectations on the part of students, faculty, parents, and funders with respect to the relative balance among research, teaching, and service.

A second challenge is that some deeply entrenched aspects of university culture need to change if undergraduate teaching and learning are to improve (Mullin, 2001). One perception of the current culture is that more professional rewards and recognition accrue to those faculty who succeed at research than to those who devote their energies primarily to teaching (Brand, 2000). This perception persists because many postsecondary faculty and administrators believe that it is difficult to measure the effectiveness of an instructor's

teaching or a department's curriculum objectively (Glassick et al., 1997). This challenge becomes especially difficult when one of the measures is the amount students have learned.

Finally, perhaps the most significant challenge is that many undergraduate faculty in the STEM disciplines have received little or no formal training in techniques or strategies for teaching effectively, assessing student learning, or evaluating the effectiveness of their own teaching or that of their colleagues. Such training is not a firm requirement for being hired as a college-level faculty member. Formal, ongoing programs for professional development aimed at improving teaching are still rare at many postsecondary institutions. Faculty may discover what is known about assessing learning only by perusing the research literature, by participating in workshops on teaching and learning (e.g., Bloom, 1956; see also Anderson et al., 2001; Chickering and Gamson, 1987; and Osterlind, 1989), or by discussing problems with colleagues.

The ultimate goal of undergraduate education should be for individual faculty and departments to improve the academic growth of students. A considerable body of research now exists on how students learn (summarized in *How People Learn: Brain, Mind, Experience, and School*, NRC, 2000c); on the assessment of teaching and learning (e.g.,

Knowing What Students Know: The Science and Design of Educational Assessment, NRC, 2001); and on other research findings that relate closely to the responsibilities of undergraduate faculty and could lead to direct improvements in undergraduate education. Overviews and summaries of research on learning and the application of that scholarship to the assessment of learning are provided at the end of this chapter in Annex Boxes 1-1 and 1-2, respectively.

Many college faculty are not familiar with that literature, however, nor do they have the time, opportunity, or incentives to learn from it. Moreover, assessing whether students actually have learned what was expected requires that faculty rethink course objectives and their approaches to teaching. Extending the assessment of learning outcomes beyond individual courses to an entire departmental curriculum requires that faculty collectively reach consensus about what students should learn and in which courses that knowledge and those skills should be developed.

STATEMENT OF TASK AND GUIDING PRINCIPLES

The committee conducted its work according to the following statement of task from the NRC:

The goal of this project is to develop resources to help postsecondary science, technology, engineering, and mathematics (STEM) faculty and administrators gain deeper understanding about ways convincingly to evaluate and reward effective teaching by drawing on the results of educational research. The committee will prepare a National Research Council report on the evaluation of undergraduate STEM teaching, with a focus on pedagogical and implementation issues of particular interest to the STEM community. The report will emphasize ways in which research in human learning can guide the evaluation and improvement of instruction, and will discuss how educational research findings can contribute to this process.

In responding to this charge, the committee embraced four fundamental premises, all of which have implications for how teaching is honored and evaluated by educational institutions:

• Effective postsecondary teaching in STEM should be available to all students, regardless of their major.
• The design of curricula and the evaluation of teaching and learning should be collective responsibilities of faculty in individual departments or, where appropriate, performed through other interdepartmental arrangements.
• Scholarly activities that focus on improving teaching and learning should be recognized as bona fide endeavors that are equivalent to other scholarly pursuits. Scholarship devoted to im-

proving teaching effectiveness and learning should be accorded the same administrative and collegial support that is available for efforts to improve other research and service endeavors.

• Faculty who are expected to work with undergraduates should be given support and mentoring in teaching throughout their careers; hiring practices should provide a first opportunity to signal institutions' teaching values and expectations of faculty.

Thus, the central theme of this report is that teaching evaluation must be coupled with emphasis on improved student learning and on departmental and institutional support of improved teaching through ongoing professional development. Although the challenge is daunting, it is far from impossible. To the contrary, there is mounting evidence that colleges and universities of all types are embracing the challenge of improving undergraduate teaching and resolving these issues in innovative ways (Suskie, 2000). The committee was convinced by its examination of a wide range of literature that well-designed and implemented systems for evaluating teaching and learning can and do improve undergraduate education. Research on effective evaluation of teaching points to a number of principles that are increasingly well supported by evidence and embraced by a

growing segment of the higher education community. Accordingly, this report is organized according to six guiding principles:

(1) A powerful tool for increasing student learning is ongoing, informal assessment (formative assessment). Emerging research on learning shows that thoughtful and timely feedback informed by pedagogical content knowledge[3] is critical for developing among students at all levels a more advanced understanding of key concepts and skills in a discipline.

(2) Formative assessment has benefits for both students and faculty. Faculty

---

[3]Shulman (1986, p. 9) was the first to propose the concept of *pedagogical content knowledge*, stating that it ". . . embodies the aspects of content most germane to its teachability. . . . [P]edagogical content knowledge includes . . . the most powerful analogies, illustrations, examples, explanations, and demonstrations—in a word, the ways of representing and formulating the subject that makes it comprehensible to others. . . .[It] also includes an understanding of what makes the learning of specific concepts easy or difficult: the conceptions and preconceptions that students of different ages and backgrounds bring with them to the learning." Thus, teachers use pedagogical content knowledge to relate what they know about what they teach (subject matter knowledge) to what they know about effective teaching (pedagogical knowledge). The synthesis and integration of these two types of knowledge characterize pedagogical content knowledge (Cochran, 1997).

who use formative assessment effectively also benefit because the feedback loop that is established as they obtain information about student learning enables them to determine rapidly and accurately how to adjust their teaching strategies and curricular materials so their students will learn more effectively (see Chapter 5, this report, for additional details).

(3) Appropriate use of formative evaluation facilitates the collection and analysis of information about teaching effectiveness for more formal personnel decisions (summative evaluation). If formative evaluation is employed regularly, faculty also generate information they can use for purposes of documenting the effectiveness of their teaching when they are involved with personnel decisions such as continuing contracts, salary increases, tenure, promotion, or professional awards. Departments and institutions also can use data compiled by individual faculty to examine student learning outcomes and to demonstrate what and how students are learning.

(4) The outcomes of effective formative and summative assessments of student learning by individual faculty can be used by other faculty to improve their own teaching, as well as by departments to strengthen existing academic programs or design new ones. Faculty can integrate such information with their own course materials, teaching philosophy, and so on to produce portfolios and other materials that make their work visible to wider communities in reliable and valid ways. Producing such materials demonstrates the accomplishments of faculty in fostering student learning, in developing themselves as scholars, and in contributing to their fields.

(5) Embracing and institutionalizing effective evaluation practices can advance the recognition and rewarding of teaching scholarship and communities of teaching and learning. By adopting policies and practices that inform and support the effective use of formative evaluation, departments, institutions, and professional societies can develop effective criteria for evaluating summatively the teaching effectiveness and educational scholarship of faculty.

(6) Effective and accepted criteria and practices for evaluating teaching enable institutions to address the concerns of those who are critical of undergraduate teaching and learning. As links between formative and summative student assessment and between summative student assessment and faculty evaluation become part of everyday practice, higher education leaders will be able to respond more effectively to criticisms about the low visibility and value of teaching in higher education.

In applying these principles, individual faculty, academic departments, and institutions of higher education can benefit from an overview of existing research on effective practices for evaluating faculty and academic programs. They also need practical guidance about how to initiate the process or advance it on their campuses. Meeting these needs is the primary purpose of this report.

ORGANIZATION OF AND INTENDED AUDIENCES FOR THIS REPORT

Report Organization

In this report, the six organizing principles stated above are used to provide an overview of the current status of research on evaluating teaching and learning. The report also provides a set of guidelines, based on emerging research, for evaluating the teaching of individuals and the academic programs of departments. Faculty and administrators can adapt these ideas for evaluating teaching and programs to the needs of their departments and campuses as appropriate for their institutional mission and identity.

Part I (Chapters 1 through 4) presents principles and research findings that can support improvements in the evaluation of undergraduate teaching in STEM and reviews implementation

issues. **Chapter 2** reviews characteristics of effective undergraduate teaching and summarizes challenges that faculty may encounter in trying to become more effective teachers. By comparing the "cultures" of teaching and disciplinary research, **Chapter 3** examines barriers associated with making undergraduate teaching and learning a more central focus through effective systems for teaching evaluation. This chapter also provides suggestions for better aligning these cultures within the university. **Chapter 4** presents key research findings on how to evaluate undergraduate teaching in STEM more effectively.

Part II (Chapters 5 through 8) applies the principles, research findings, and recommendations set forth in Part I, providing an overview of specific methodologies and strategies for evaluating the effectiveness of undergraduate teaching in STEM. **Chapter 5** reviews a variety of methodologies that can be used to evaluate teaching effectiveness and the quality of student learning. Some of these methods also can be applied to evaluate teaching, course offerings, and curriculum at the departmental level. Indeed, it is the committee's conviction that similar expectations and criteria can and should apply to academic departments and institutions as a whole. **Chapters 6 and 7** provide practical strategies for using the methodologies presented in Chapter 5 to evaluate individual teachers and departmental undergraduate programs, respectively. Finally, all of these findings serve as the basis for a set of recommendations aimed at improving evaluation practices, presented in **Chapter 8**.

Four appendixes also are provided. Because student evaluations of teaching occupy a place of prominence in current evaluation processes, **Appendix A** provides an in-depth examination of research findings on the efficacy and limitations of input from undergraduate students. Based on concerns of many faculty about the design and analysis of student evaluations of teaching, colleges and universities across the United States have begun to revise such forms. **Appendix B** offers specific examples, used by a variety of types of institutions that comport with the six guiding principles of this report; these examples can serve as models for other institutions that are looking to revamp their student evaluation forms. Similarly, as peer review of teaching gains greater prominence in the instruments for both formative and summative evaluations of teaching, faculty and administrators will require assistance on ways to undertake this process fairly and equitably. **Ap-pendix C** includes examples of peer evaluation forms that are consistent with the findings and recommendations of this report. Finally, **Appendix D** provides biographical sketches of the committee members.

This report also provides readers with links to a wealth of additional information and guides available at numerous websites. These links are found primarily in footnotes or in the list of References. All of these links were tested prior to the release of the report and were found to be operable as of July 20, 2002.

Intended Audiences

A primary audience for this report is the individual STEM faculty members who teach disciplinary and interdisciplinary courses at colleges and universities, especially at the introductory level. This report also is directed to departmental and institutional leaders in higher education, including college and university presidents and chancellors, provosts, academic deans, and department chairs—those who can best promote a culture and community of teaching and learning and can encourage faculty collaboration in improving student learning and academic success.

Annex Box 1-1. Seven Principles of Learning

Research in the cognitive, learning, and brain sciences has provided many new insights about how humans organize knowledge, how experience shapes understanding, how individuals differ in learning strategies, and how people acquire expertise. From this emerging body of research, scientists and others have been able to synthesize a number of underlying principles of human learning. That knowledge can be synthesized into the following seven principles of learning:

1. Learning with understanding is facilitated when new and existing knowledge is structured around the major concepts and principles of the discipline.
Proficient performance in any discipline requires knowledge that is both accessible and usable. Experts' content knowledge is structured around the major organizing principles, core concepts, and "big ideas" of the discipline. Their strategies for thinking and solving problems are closely linked to their understanding of such core concepts. Therefore, knowing many disconnected facts is not sufficient for developing expertise. Understanding the big ideas also allows disciplinary experts to discern the deeper structure and nature of problems and to recognize similarities between new problems and those previously encountered. Curricula that emphasize breadth of coverage and simple recall of facts may hinder students' abilities to organize knowledge effectively because they do not learn anything in depth, and thus are not able to structure what they are learning around the major organizing principles and core concepts of the discipline.

2. Learners use what they already know to construct new understandings.
College students already possess knowledge, skills, beliefs, concepts, conceptions, and misconceptions that can significantly influence how they think about the world, approach new learning, and go about solving unfamiliar problems. They often attempt to learn a new idea or process by relating it to ideas or processes they already understand. This prior knowledge can produce mistakes as well as new insights. How these links are made may vary in different subject areas and among students with varying talents, interests, and abilities. Learners are likely to construct interpretations of newly encountered problems and phenomena in ways that agree with their own prior knowledge even when those interpretations conflict with what a teacher has attempted to teach. Therefore, effective teaching involves gauging what learners already know about a subject and finding ways to build on that knowledge. When prior knowledge contains misconceptions, effective instruction entails detecting those misconceptions and addressing them, sometimes by challenging them directly.

3. Learning is facilitated through the use of metacognitive strategies that identify, monitor, and regulate cognitive processes.

Metacognition is the ability of people to predict and monitor their current level of understanding and mastery of a subject or performance on a particular task and decide when it is not adequate (NRC, 2000e). Metacognitive strategies include (1) connecting new information to former knowledge; (2) selecting thinking strategies deliberately; and (3) planning, monitoring, and evaluating thinking processes. To be effective problem solvers and learners, students need to reflect on what they already know and what else they need to know for any given situation. They must consider both factual knowledge—about the task, their goals, and their abilities—and strategic knowledge about how and when to use a specific procedure to solve the problem at hand. Research indicates that instructors can facilitate the development of metacognitive abilities by providing explicit instruction focused on such skills, by providing opportunities for students to observe teachers or other content experts as they solve problems, and by making their thinking visible to those observing.

4. Learners have different strategies, approaches, patterns of abilities, and learning styles that are a function of the interaction between their heredity and their prior experiences.

Individuals are born with a potential to learn that develops through their interaction with their environment to produce their current capabilities and talents. Among learners of the same age, there are important differences in cognitive abilities (such as linguistic and spatial aptitudes or the ability to work with symbolic representations of the natural world), as well as in emotional, cultural, and motivational characteristics. Thus, some students will respond favorably to one kind of instruction, whereas others will benefit more from a different approach. Educators need to be sensitive to such differences so that instruction and curricular materials will be suitably matched to students' developing abilities, knowledge base, preferences, and styles. Students with different learning styles also need a range of opportunities and ways to demonstrate their knowledge and skills. Using one form of assessment will work to the advantage of some students and to the disadvantage of others; multiple measures of learning and understanding will provide a better picture of how well individual students are learning what is expected of them.

5. Learners' motivation to learn and sense of self affect what is learned, how much is learned, and how much effort will be put into the learning process.

Both internal and external factors motivate people to learn and develop competence. Regardless of the source, learners' level of motivation strongly affects their willingness to persist in the face of difficulty or challenge. Intrinsic motivation is enhanced when students perceive learning tasks as interesting and personally meaningful, and presented at an appropriate level of difficulty. Tasks that are too difficult can frustrate; those that are too easy can lead to boredom. Research also has revealed strong

continued on next page

Annex Box 1-1. Continued

connections between learners' beliefs about their own abilities in a subject area and their success in learning that subject. For example, some students believe their ability to learn a particular subject or skill is predetermined, whereas others believe their ability to learn is substantially a function of effort. The use of instructional strategies that encourage conceptual understanding is an effective way to increase students' interest and enhance their confidence about their abilities to learn a particular subject.

6. The practices and activities in which people engage while learning shape what is learned.

Research indicates that the way people learn a particular area of knowledge and skills and the context in which they learn it become a fundamental part of what is learned. When students learn some subject matter or concept in only a limited context, they often miss seeing the applicability of that information to solving novel problems encountered in other classes, in other disciplines, or in everyday life situations. By encountering a given concept in multiple contexts, students develop a deeper understanding of the concept and how it can be used and applied to other contexts. Faculty can help students apply subject matter to other contexts by engaging them in learning experiences that draw directly upon real-world applications, or exercises that foster problem-solving skills and strategies that are used in real-world situations. Problem-based and case-based learning are two instructional approaches that create opportunities for students to engage in practices similar to those of experts. Technology also can be used to bring real-world contexts into the classroom.[4]

7. Learning is enhanced through socially supported interactions.

Learning can be enhanced when students have opportunities to interact and collaborate with others on instructional tasks. In learning environments that encourage collaboration, such as those in which most practicing scientists and mathematicians work, individuals have opportunities to test their ideas and learn by observing others. Research demonstrates that providing students with opportunities to articulate their ideas to peers and to hear and discuss others' ideas in the context of the classroom is particularly effective in enhancing conceptual learning. Social interaction also is important for the development of expertise, metacognitive skills (see learning principle #3), and formation of the learner's sense of self (see learning principle #5).

------

[4]Specific techniques for structuring problem-based learning and employing technology in college classrooms are discussed on the website of the National Institute for Science Education. Suggestions for creative uses of technology are available <http://www.wcer.wisc.edu/nise/cl1/ilt/default.asp>. Each site also provides further references. Additional resources on problem-based learning are found in Allen and Duch (1998).

SOURCE: Excerpted and modified from NRC (2002b, Ch. 6). Original references are cited in that chapter.

Annex Box 1-2. Overview of Research on Effective Assessment of Student Learning

• Although assessments used in various contexts and for differing purposes often look quite different, they share common principles. Assessment is always a process of reasoning from evidence. Moreover, assessment is imprecise to some degree. Assessment results are only estimates of what a person knows and can do. It is essential to recognize that one type of assessment is not appropriate for measuring learning in all students. Multiple measures provide a more robust picture of what an individual has learned.

• Every assessment, regardless of its purpose, rests on three pillars: a model of how students represent knowledge and develop competence in the subject domain, tasks or situations that allow one to observe students' performance, and an interpretation method for drawing inferences from the performance evidence thus obtained.

• Educational assessment does not exist in isolation. It must be aligned with curriculum and instruction if it is to support learning.

• Research on learning and cognition indicates that assessment practices should extend beyond an emphasis on skills and discrete bits of knowledge to encompass more complex aspects of student achievement.

• Studies of learning by novices and experts in a subject area demonstrate that experts typically organize factual and procedural knowledge into schemas that support recognition of patterns and the rapid retrieval and application of knowledge. Experts use metacognitive strategies to monitor their understanding when they solve problems and perform corrections of their learning and understanding (see Annex Box 1-1, principle 3, for additional information about metacognition). Assessments should attempt to determine whether a student has developed good metacognitive skills. They should focus on identifying specific strategies that students use for problem solving.

• Learning involves a transformation from naïve understanding into more complete and accurate comprehension. Appropriate assessments can both facilitate this process for individual students and assist faculty in revising their approaches to teaching. To this end, assessments should focus on making students' thinking visible to both themselves and their instructors so that faculty can select appropriate instructional strategies to enhance future learning.

• One of the most important roles for assessment is the provision of timely and informative feedback to students during instruction and learning so that their practice of a skill and its subsequent acquisition will be effective and efficient.

• Much of human learning is acquired through discourse and interactions with others. Knowledge is often associated with particular social and cultural contexts, and it encompasses understanding about the meaning of specific practices, such as asking and answering questions. Effective assessments need to determine how well students engage in communicative practices that are appropriate to the discipline being

continued on next page

Annex Box 1-2. Continued

assessed. Assessments should examine what students understand about such practices and how they use tools appropriate to that discipline.

• The design of high-quality assessments is a complex process that involves numerous iterative and interdependent components. Decisions made at a later stage of the design process can affect those occurring at an earlier stage. Thus, as faculty develop assessments of student learning, they must often revisit their choices of questions and approaches and refine their designs.

• Although reporting of results occurs at the end of an assessment cycle, assessments must be designed from the outset to ensure that reporting of the desired types of information will be possible. Providing students with information about particular qualities of their work and about what they can do to improve is crucial for maximizing learning.

• For assessment to be effective, students must understand and share the goals for learning that are assessed. Students learn more when they understand and, in some cases, participate in developing the criteria by which their work will be evaluated, and when they engage in peer and self-assessment during which they apply those criteria. Such practices also help students develop metacognitive abilities, which, in turn, improve their development of expertise in a discipline or subject area.

SOURCE: Excerpted and modified from NRC (2001, pp. 2–9). References to support these statements are provided in that report.

2

Characterizing and Mobilizing Effective Undergraduate Teaching

In a recent address, Zimpher (1998) offered the following predictions:

1. **Teaching will be more public than it ever has been before.** It will be open to inspection, discussion, and increasing accountability.

2. **The nature and quality of assessment will change.** Faculty will teach within a culture of evidence that will place great importance on demonstrating learning outcomes.

3. **Evaluation and documentation of teaching will change.** It will be done more systematically and rigorously and will involve multiple methods and sources.

4. **Teaching will become technologically enabled.** Instructional technology will be used within the classroom as well as for anytime, anyplace learning.

5. **Content transmission will not be the focus of teaching.** As information continues to grow and be readily available in many forms, the focus will be on helping learners to know how to access information, evaluate it critically, and use it to solve problems.

6. **Curriculum and program design will be inseparable from teaching and learning.** Coordination, integration, and teamwork will be hallmarks in the future.

7. **Diversity will be seen as asset-based.** Higher education will realize that all benefit when different perspectives and cultures are included.

8. **Different pedagogies that students have experienced prior to college will change their expectations about good teaching.** They will come with values for collaborative and active learning, and for contextual, experiential approaches, such as service learning.

9. **Higher education facilities will have to look different.** Rooms will have to be flexible to accommodate the new pedagogies and they will have to be technologically sophisticated.

10. **A new scholarship of teaching will occur.** Value will be placed on systematically exploring teaching issues and researching experiments with new approaches and conditions affecting student learning.

In light of these predictions, what steps are institutions of higher education and supporting organizations taking to mobilize faculty and resources to enhance learning for undergraduate students?

Graduate students, faculty, and administrators from all types of postsecondary institutions in the United States are increasingly interested in the revamping of teaching practices to enhance student learning in science, technology, engineering, and mathematics (STEM) (see Rothman and Narum, 1999). In part, this increased interest has stemmed from observations by faculty that their approaches to teaching may not result in the expected levels of student learning (e.g., Hestenes, 1987; Hestenes and Halloun, 1995; Mazur, 1997; Wright et al., 1998). Some faculty and departments are confronting the pedagogical and infrastructural challenges of offering smaller classes (e.g., the need for additional instructors to teach more sections), especially for introductory courses. Others are using innovative approaches to teaching based on emerging research in the cognitive and brain sciences about how people learn (e.g., National Research Council [NRC], 2000c). Still others are experimenting with the effectiveness of different learning strategies to accommodate the broader spectrum of stu-

dents who now enroll in STEM courses as undergraduates.

Many individual faculty and departments are actively engaged in moving undergraduate education from a faculty-centered teaching model to a student-centered learning model (Barr and Tagg, 1999). Moreover, numerous campuses in the United States and abroad are establishing teaching and learning centers.[1] As these centers evolve, they are supporting new pedagogies and more efficient methods of assessing teaching and learning, and are serving as focal points for efforts to advance the scholarship of teaching and learning (Boyer, 1990; Glassick et al., 1997; Ferrini-Mundy, personal communication). Many of these centers are increasingly tailoring their assistance to faculty to reflect differences in approaches and emphases among disciplines. Experts in these discipline-based centers are often disciplinary faculty with expertise in pedagogical content knowledge, assessment of learning, and other issues specific to their disciplines (see also Huber and Morreale, 2002).

---

[1]A list of websites of teaching and learning centers of colleges and universities in Asia, Australia and New Zealand, Europe, and North America is available at <http://www.ku.edu/~cte/resources/websites.html>.

Many of the professional organizations and disciplinary societies with which university and college faculty affiliate are making the improvement of teaching and learning in undergraduate STEM a component of their missions and programs. Higher education organizations, government agencies, and private foundations are sponsoring workshops on student learning and supporting summer workshops on new teaching methods. They are engaging graduate students in programs that can better prepare them to become stimulating future faculty and encouraging faculty to present papers or posters on their teaching or research in education at professional meetings.[2] These organizations also are publishing books, reports, and journal articles that address teaching and learning (e.g., Boyer Commission, 1998; Herron, 1996; Ireton et al., 1996; Landis et al., 2001; National Institute for Science Education, 2001c; NRC, 1991, 1995b, 1996b, 1997a, 1999a; Uno, 1997).

The remainder of this chapter reviews the key characteristics of effective

teaching, as well as challenges faced by those seeking to become more effective instructors.

CHARACTERISTICS OF EFFECTIVE TEACHING

If teaching and student learning are to improve, faculty and those who evaluate them must recognize the characteristics of effective teaching. The research literature contains many examples of successful standards and practices for effective teaching that are based on evidence of enhanced student learning (e.g., Braskamp and Ory, 1994; Centra, 1993; Davis, 1993: Lowman, 1995; McKeachie, 1999; Neff and Weimer, 1990; Perry and Smart, 1997; references in NRC 2000c, 2001, and 2002b). On the basis of that literature, the committee articulates five characteristics of effective teaching that can be used as a starting point for improving teaching. In Chapter 6, these characteristics are elaborated as criteria that could serve as the basis for evaluating teaching effectiveness.

1. Knowledge of Subject Matter

Although it appears obvious, any list of characteristics of high-quality teaching of STEM that is centered on desired student outcomes must begin with the premise that faculty members must be

---

[2]Examples are *Microbiology Education,* published by the American Society of Microbiology; *Journal of Chemical Education,* published by the Division of Chemical Education of the American Chemical Society; and *Physics Today,* published by the American Institute of Physics.

well steeped in their disciplines. They must remain active in their areas of scholarship to ensure that the content of their courses is current, accurate, and balanced, especially when presenting information that may be open to alternative interpretation or disagreement by experts in the field. They also should allow all students to appreciate ". . . interrelationships among the sciences and the sciences' relationship to the humanities, social sciences, and the political, economic, and social concerns of society" (NRC, 1999a, p. 26).

Knowledge of subject matter can be interpreted in other ways. For example, several recent reports (e.g., Boyer Commission, 1998; NRC, 1999a; National Science Foundation [NSF], 1996) have emphasized that the undergraduate experience should add value in tangible ways to each student's education. Faculty must teach subject matter in ways that encourage probing, questioning, skepticism, and integration of information and ideas. They should provide students with opportunities to think more deeply about subject matter than they did in grades K–12. They should enable students to move intellectually beyond the subject matter at hand.

Faculty who possess deep knowledge and understanding of subject matter demonstrate the following characteristics:

- They can help students learn and understand the general principles of their discipline (e.g., the processes and limits of the scientific method).
- They are able to provide students with an overview of the whole domain of the discipline (e.g., Coppola et al., 1997).
- They possess sufficient knowledge and understanding of their own and related sub-disciplines to answer most students' questions and know how to help students find appropriate information.
- They stay current through an active research program or through scholarly reading and other types of professional engagement with peers.
- They are genuinely interested in what they are teaching.
- They understand that conveying the infectious enthusiasm that accompanies original discovery, application of theory, and design of new products and processes is as important to learning as helping students understand the subject matter.

2. Skill, Experience, and Creativity with a Range of Appropriate Pedagogies and Technologies

Deep understanding of subject matter is critical to excellent teaching, but not sufficient. Effective teachers also understand that, over the course of their educational experiences, undergraduates develop different strategies for maximizing their individual abilities to learn, reason, and think critically about complex issues (King and Kitchener, 1994; National Institute for Science Education, 2001c; NRC, 1997a, 1999a). To be most effective, teachers need to employ a variety of learning strategies and contextually appropriate pedagogies[3] that serve the range of students' learning styles (see, e.g., Annex Box 1-1, Chapter 1). Faculty who are effective in this regard demonstrate the following characteristics:

- They are organized and communicate clearly to students their expectations for learning and academic achievement.
- They focus on whether students are learning what is being taught and view the learning process as a joint venture between themselves and their students.
- They encourage discussion and promote active learning strategies (see Annex Box 1-1, Chapter 1).
- They persistently monitor students' progress toward achieving learning

goals through discussions in class, out-of-class assignments, and other forms of assessment.

- They have the ability to recognize students who are not achieving to their fullest potential and then employ the professional knowledge and skill necessary to assist them in overcoming academic difficulties.

Along with these characteristics, an increasingly important component of pedagogy is the appropriate use and application of information technologies to enhance learning. Electronic networking, the Internet, remote sensing, distance learning, and databases and digital libraries (e.g., NRC, 1998b, 2000c; NSF, 1998)[4] are changing fundamentally the ways in which teaching and learning take place in higher education. Although no one would suggest that top-quality instruction cannot be attained without the use of networking resources, instructional changes made possible through information technology are profound and have already imbued research communities in the natural sciences, mathematics, and

---

[3]"Contextually appropriate pedagogies" is also known in the research literature as "pedagogical content knowledge" (defined earlier in note).

[4]For further discussion of digital libraries and their importance in undergraduate STEM education, see Borgman et al. (1996) and NRC (1998b). NSF is now engaged in developing a digital national library for undergraduate STEM education (additional information is available at <http://www.ehr.nsf.gov/ehr/due/programs/nsdl>.

engineering. Professional development can assist faculty in deciding whether and how they might use these tools most effectively for enhancing learning. The role of information technology in undergraduate classrooms, laboratories, and field environments is an important area for continued investigation (e.g., American Association for Higher Education [AAHE], 1996; Collis and Moonen, 2001; National Institute for Science Education, 2001a).

As information and other technologies become more pervasive in teaching and learning of the natural sciences, mathematics, and engineering, a faculty member's use of such resources is likely to become an increasingly important component of teaching evaluations. As with other areas of pedagogy in which college-level faculty have had little formal training or professional development, they will have to learn appropriate and effective uses of hardware and software that are coupled with new ways of viewing teaching and learning.

3. Understanding of and Skill in Using Appropriate Assessment Practices

In part, proficiency in assessment involves a faculty member's skill in evaluating student learning. This skill is evident when teachers:

- Assess learning in ways that are consistent with the objectives of a course and integrate stated course objectives with long-range curricular goals.

- Know whether students are learning what is being taught. This requires that faculty be persistent in collecting and analyzing assessments of student learning and committed to using the data collected as a tool for improving their own teaching skills (see, e.g., principle 5 in Astin et al., 1996).

- Determine accurately and fairly students' knowledge of the subject matter and the extent to which learning has occurred throughout the term (not just at the end of the course).

4. Professional Interactions with Students Within and Beyond the Classroom

Teaching responsibilities extend beyond designing and offering courses. Faculty are expected to direct original student research and involve students as collaborators in their own research, advise and mentor students, participate in departmental and campus curricular committees, and sometimes supervise teaching assistants. Students may also view their teachers as role models for life as responsible, educated citizens. For example, beyond helping students learn scientific principles or technological processes, faculty can help them open their eyes to the ethical issues and political decisions that often affect science and technology (e.g., Coppola and Smith, 1996).

Professionalism in a faculty member's relationships and interactions with students also should be based on criteria such as the following:

• Faculty meet with all classes and assigned teaching laboratories, post and keep regular office hours, and hold exams as scheduled.

• They demonstrate respect for students as individuals; this includes respecting the confidentiality of information gleaned from advising or student conferences.

• They encourage the free pursuit of learning and protect students' academic freedom.

• They address sensitive subjects or issues in ways that help students deal with them maturely.

• They contribute to the ongoing intellectual development of individual students and foster confidence in the students' ability to learn and discover on their own.

• They advise students who are experiencing problems with course material and know how to work them in venues besides the classroom to help them achieve. On those occasions when students clearly are not prepared to undertake the challenges of a particular course, faculty should be able to counsel them out of the course or suggest alternative, individualized approaches for learning the subject matter.

• They uphold and model for students the best scholarly and ethical standards (e.g., University of California Faculty Code of Conduct).[5]

5. Involvement with and Contributions to One's Profession in Enhancing Teaching and Learning

Effective teaching needs to be seen as a scholarly pursuit that takes place in collaboration with departmental colleagues, faculty in other departments in the sciences and engineering, and more broadly across disciplines (Boyer, 1990; Glassick et al., 1997; Kennedy, 1997). Faculty can learn much by working with colleagues both on and beyond the campus, thereby learning to better integrate the materials they present in their own courses with what is being taught in other courses (Hutchings, 1996; NRC, 1999a).

---

[5]The University of California System's *Faculty Code of Conduct Manual* is available at <http://www.ucop.edu/acadadv/acadpers/apm/>.

CHALLENGES TO EFFECTIVE TEACHING

Faculty in the STEM disciplines face a number of challenges in seeking to become more effective teachers. Some of these challenges are common to all teaching and learning, while others are more endemic to these disciplines. Some of the more general challenges include improving the assessment of learning outcomes and preparing future teachers. More discipline-specific challenges include teaching a broad range and large numbers of students, providing engaging laboratory and field experiences, and encouraging students to undertake original research that increasingly is highly sophisticated and technical.

Improving the Assessment of Learning Outcomes

The committee took particular note of Astin et al.'s (1996) *Assessment Forum: Nine Principles of Good Practice for Assessing Student Learning.* Because these authors articulate succinctly the position the committee has taken in this report, their principles are presented verbatim in Box 2-1. These principles also could be applied in evaluating departmental programs.

Preparing Future Teachers

Scientists have an obligation to assist in science teachers' professional development. Many scientists recognize the obligation and are ready to get involved. Scientists can provide opportunities for teachers to learn how the scientific process works, what scientists do and how and why they do it. They can provide research opportunities for practicing teachers; act as scientific partners; provide connections to the rest of the scientific community; assist in writing grant proposals for science-education projects; provide hands-on, inquiry-based workshops for area teachers (e.g., NRC, 2000a); and provide teachers access to equipment, scientific journals, and catalogs not usually available in schools. They can help teachers to review educational material for its accuracy and utility.

When scientists teach their undergraduate classes and laboratories, potential science teachers are present. Scientists should recognize that as an opportunity to promote and act as a model of both good process and accurate content teaching and so strive to improve their own teaching (NRC, 1996c, p. 3).

Box 2-1. Nine Principles of Good Practice for Assessing Student Learning

1. The assessment of student learning begins with educational values. Assessment is not an end in itself but a vehicle for educational improvement. Its effective practice, then, begins with and enacts a vision of the kinds of learning we most value for students and strive to help them achieve. Educational values should drive not only what we choose to assess but also how we do so. Where questions about educational mission and values are skipped over, assessment threatens to be an exercise in measuring what's easy, rather than a process of improving what we really care about.

2. Assessment is most effective when it reflects an understanding of learning as multidimensional, integrated, and revealed in performance over time. Learning is a complex process. It entails not only what students know but what they can do with what they know; it involves not only knowledge and abilities but values, attitudes, and habits of mind that affect both academic success and performance beyond the classroom. Assessment should reflect these understandings by employing a diverse array of methods, including those that call for actual performance, using them over time so as to reveal change, growth, and increasing degrees of integration. Such an approach aims for a more complete and accurate picture of learning and therefore firmer bases for improving our students' educational experience.

3. Assessment works best when the programs it seeks to improve have clear, explicitly stated purposes. Assessment is a goal-oriented process. It entails comparing educational performance with educational purposes and expectations—those derived from the institution's mission, from faculty intentions in program and course design, and from knowledge of students' own goals. Where program purposes lack specificity or agreement, assessment as a process pushes a campus toward clarity about where to aim and what standards to apply; assessment also prompts attention to where and how program goals will be taught and learned. Clear, shared, implementable goals are the cornerstone for assessment that is focused and useful.

4. Assessment requires attention to outcomes but also and equally to the experiences that lead to those outcomes. Information about outcomes is of high importance; where students "end up" matters greatly. But to improve outcomes, we need to know about student experience along the way—about the curricula, teaching, and kind of student effort that lead to particular outcomes. Assessment can help us understand which students learn best under what conditions; with such knowledge comes the capacity to improve the whole of their learning.

continued on next page

Box 2-1. Continued

5. Assessment works best when it is ongoing not episodic. Assessment is a process whose power is cumulative. Though isolated, "one-shot" assessment can be better than none, improvement is best fostered when assessment entails a linked series of activities undertaken over time. This may mean tracking the progress of individual students, or of cohorts of students; it may mean collecting the same examples of student performance or using the same instrument semester after semester. The point is to monitor progress toward intended goals in a spirit of continuous improvement. Along the way, the assessment process itself should be evaluated and refined in light of emerging insights.

6. Assessment fosters wider improvement when representatives from across the educational community are involved. Student learning is a campus-wide responsibility, and assessment is a way of enacting that responsibility. Thus, while assessment efforts may start small, the aim over time is to involve people from across the educational community. Faculty play an especially important role, but assessment's questions can't be fully addressed without participation by student-affairs educators, librarians, administrators, and students. Assessment may also involve individuals from beyond the campus (alumni/ae, trustees, employers) whose experience can enrich the sense of appropriate aims and standards for learning. Thus understood, assessment is not a task for small groups of experts but a collaborative activity; its aim is wider, better informed attention to student learning by all parties with a stake in its improvement.

7. Assessment makes a difference when it begins with issues of use and illuminates questions that people really care about. Assessment recognizes the value of information in the process of improvement. But to be useful, information must be connected to issues or questions that people really care about. This implies assessment approaches that produce evidence that relevant parties will find credible, suggestive, and applicable to decisions that need to be made. It means thinking in advance about how the information will be used, and by whom. The point of assessment is not to gather data and return "results"; it is a process that starts with the questions of decision-makers, that involves them in the gathering and interpreting of data, and that informs and helps guide continuous improvement.

8. Assessment is most likely to lead to improvement when it is part of a larger set of conditions that promote change. Assessment alone changes little. Its greatest contribution comes on campuses where the quality of teaching and learning is visibly valued and worked at. On such campuses, the push to improve educational performance is a visible and primary goal of leadership; improving the quality of undergraduate education is central to the institution's planning, budgeting, and personnel decisions. On such campuses, information about learning outcomes is seen as an integral part of decision making, and avidly sought.

9. Through assessment, educators meet responsibilities to students and to the public. There is a compelling public stake in education. As educators, we have a responsibility to the public that supports or depends on us to provide information about the ways in which our students meet goals and expectations. But that responsibility goes beyond the reporting of such information; our deeper obligation—to ourselves, our students, and society—is to improve. Those to whom educators are accountable have a corresponding obligation to support such attempts at improvement.

SOURCE: Astin et al. (1996); see <http://www.aahe.org/principl.htm>.

This committee agrees with the conclusions expressed by other NRC committees (NRC 1999a, 2000b) that science faculty in the nation's universities should, as one of their primary professional responsibilities, model the kinds of pedagogy that are needed to educate both practicing and prospective teachers. Those NRC reports provide a series of recommendations for how chief academic officers and faculty can work together to promote more effective education for teachers of mathematics and science. These recommendations include developing courses that provide all students with a better understanding of the relationships among the sciences, that integrate fundamental science and mathematics, and that help students understand how these areas of knowledge relate to their daily lives and

to the world economy. Standards for teacher education and professional development for teachers are an integral component of the *National Science Education Standards* (NRC, 1996a); much useful information can be found in that document to help postsecondary faculty understand their role in promoting more effective teacher education. Contributing authors in Siebert and Macintosh (2001) offer advice and numerous examples of how the principles contained in the *National Science Education Standards* can be applied to higher education settings.

An impending shortage of qualified K–12 teachers over the next decade (National Center for Education Statistics, 1999) will compound the shortage that already exists for elementary and secondary school science and mathematics teachers. It should be noted that impending teacher shortages do not apply only to K–12 education. Declining graduate student enrollments in some disciplines suggest that having enough people who are qualified to teach undergraduate students, including those who may go on to become K–12 teachers, may become problematic in the future (e.g., Lovitts and Nelson, 2000).

Even if the number of graduate students were to remain sufficient, it is important to recognize that most college-level faculty who currently teach in the STEM disciplines have never received formal preparation for teaching *any* students, let alone those who aspire to be teachers at either the precollege or university level. Institutions of higher education need to develop collaborative strategies for addressing this problem (Gaff et al., 2000; NRC 2000b).

Teaching a Broad Range and Large Numbers of Students

As science and technology play ever more pervasive roles in society, it is imperative that all students, not just those planning careers in these fields, develop an appreciation for and understanding of these subjects. This understanding must involve more than knowledge of some specific set of content. Faculty in the STEM disciplines have a special obligation to plan and conduct their courses in ways that make these disciplines relevant to the wide range of students who now enroll in them and often constitute the majority of students in lower division courses (Greenspan, 2000; NRC, 1999a). As numerous reports have suggested, this responsibility applies equally to academic departments (NRC, 1996b, 1999a; NSF, 1996; Project Kaleidoscope, 1995).

Courses and programs offered to nonmajors in STEM can be very different from similar courses and programs in other disciplines. Introductory courses and programs (and sometimes more advanced courses) in the social sciences and humanities typically are geared toward any student who wishes to enroll in them. For mathematics and science, however, departments and institutions sometimes insist on offering separate introductory courses for prospective majors and nonmajors. In too many instances, faculty and departments view the offerings for nonmajors, especially at the introductory level, as "service courses" that may impose additional staffing and resource demands not found in other sectors of the university. As a result, many of these courses for nonmajors (and in some cases, those for majors as well) tend to have large numbers of students enrolled and are offered in large lecture halls. These kinds of facilities do not conform with the design of classroom and laboratory space that has been recommended for optimal teaching and learning by undergraduates (e.g., Project Kaleidoscope, 1995). Accumulating evidence suggests that nonmajors often fare better in smaller courses and inquiry-based laboratory experiences where they become actively engaged with the subject matter.[6] Constraints on staff and limited financial resources may preclude science departments from offering these kinds of experiences, however. Such limitations may lead students to become disenfranchised, and the students may evaluate the courses and the instructors that teach them accordingly.

---

[6]Recent reports suggest that at least some barriers and limitations can be overcome by emphasizing inquiry-based approaches to learning during classroom instruction (e.g., Ebert-May et al., 1997). As defined by the *National Science Education Standards,* "Inquiry is a multifaceted activity that involves making observations; posing questions; examining books and other sources of information to see what is already known; planning investigations; reviewing what is already known in light of experimental evidence; using tools to gather, analyze and interpret data; proposing answers, explanations, and predictions; and communicating the results. Inquiry requires identification of assumptions, use of critical and logical thinking, and consideration of alternative explanations" (NRC, 1996a, p. 23). Additional detail on inquiry-based approaches to teaching and learning (focused on grades K–12 but applicable in many ways to higher education) can be found in NRC (2000a).

Providing Engaging Laboratory and Field Experiences

A number of national commissions and organizations have emphasized the importance of laboratory-rich teaching environments for undergraduates in the natural sciences (NSF, 1996; Project Kaleidoscope, 1991, 1994, 1998). Large amounts of time are needed to organize and oversee teaching laboratories and field experiences for undergraduates. Providing such experiences also requires effective programs to train graduate or undergraduate teaching assistants. If the laboratory experience is tied to a specific course, instructors also must commit time and effort to integrating the laboratory exercises with classroom work or to organizing the laboratory in ways that provide students with learning experiences not covered in class. Teaching laboratories that are independent from other courses (e.g., a technical skills laboratory) must respond to needs of both students and instructors in other courses. The exercise or experiment selected should be appropriate for the topic at hand. The design and execution of laboratory work, especially in courses with large numbers of students, also must emphasize safety and reflect consideration of potential impacts on the local environment.

If laboratory and field experiences (particularly in introductory courses and courses for nonscience majors) are to become integral components of undergraduate science and engineering education, the effectiveness with which these additional demands for teaching are met should be specifically recognized and evaluated in the reviews of individual instructors. Appropriate professional development should be made available to those faculty not familiar with inquiry-based laboratory experiences, who as a consequence may not have structured laboratory and field experiences to meet this important learning objective.

Engaging Students in Original Research

"Education through research" is becoming an increasingly popular and effective way for undergraduates to learn about science firsthand. With the increasing emphasis on engaging undergraduates in original or applied research, the one-on-one mentoring that takes place in supervised undergraduate research is one of the best predictors of students' professional success (e.g., Doyle, 2000; NRC, 1999a; NSF, 1996).

To properly oversee and mentor undergraduate students who undertake original research, faculty must have sufficient time to help students appreciate the scope and significance of their projects. Supervising faculty members may need to spend large amounts of time working with students to introduce them to the relevant literature, to use appropriate instrumentation and research protocols, and to understand laboratory safety protocols.

It also is important for faculty supervisors to help undergraduates grow as researchers. Part of that supervision should include providing the training and experiences that all undergraduate students need to learn effective communication skills that ultimately will allow them to publish successfully in the scholarly literature or to deliver an appropriate presentation to colleagues. Failure is a routine part of research, and students should be allowed to experience it as appropriate.

Students also should be given greater responsibility for overseeing projects and for working with other students as they demonstrate increasing maturity and research prowess. Involving graduate students or senior undergraduate students as cosupervisors of projects can provide important and effective introductory training for those who ultimately will seek teaching positions. It also may entail the integration of undergraduate research projects with those of graduate students or postdoctoral fellows working in closely related areas in the laboratory or the field.

Supervision of undergraduate research should be viewed positively when evaluating a faculty member's teaching *and* research. This is especially the case if a student's work merits publication as a coauthor in the original literature or in a presentation at a professional conference.

It is critical for faculty and administrators to understand that the criteria for evaluating teaching in these environments may be very different than is the case for more traditional classroom or laboratory situations. Department- or institution-wide instruments for evaluating and comparing teaching quality across disciplines may not reflect the different kinds of preparation and presentation that are required for these kinds of activities in the natural sciences and engineering. Thus, efforts should be made to adopt or adapt some of the newer instruments that are more appropriate for these kinds of teaching.

Limitations on Faculty Knowledge of Research on Effective Teaching

Given all of the above challenges, faculty in STEM who teach undergraduates could benefit greatly from practical guidance regarding techniques for improving learning among diverse undergraduate student populations. The scholarly literature and an increasing number of websites now provide this kind of assistance (see, e.g., Project Kaleidoscope <http://www.pkal.org> or the National Institute for Science Education <http://wcer.wisc.edu/nise>). However, many faculty never were introduced to this knowledge base during their graduate or postdoctoral years and have not acquired this perspective. These instructors may struggle through teaching assignments, often redeveloping techniques and approaches that others already have tested and disseminated.

3

Aligning the Cultures of Research and Teaching in Higher Education

In calculating academic rewards, it has been painfully difficult to evaluate the quality of research as separated from its mass. Nevertheless, departments and deans find that for passing judgment on peers, research productivity is a much more manageable criterion than teaching effectiveness. Faculty gossip, student evaluations, and alumni testimonials have all been notoriously weak reeds, and reliable self-evaluation is all but impossible.... At this point promotion and tenure committees still find teaching effectiveness difficult to measure. Publication is at least a perceptible tool; the relative ease of its use has reinforced the reliance on it for tenure and promotion decisions. Evaluating good teaching will always be difficult, but effective integration of research and teaching should be observable, as should the development of interdisciplinary approaches to learning. Departments and deans must be pressed to give significant rewards for evidence of integrated teaching and research and for the imagination and effort required by interdisciplinary courses and programs. When publication is evaluated, attention should be paid to the pedagogical quality of the work as well as to its contribution to scholarship.

Boyer Commission on Educating Undergraduates in the Research University (1998, p. 41)

Both within and outside higher education, the perception (and too often the reality) is that at many colleges and universities, research productivity is valued more than teaching effectiveness (e.g., Bleak et al., 2000; Boyer Commission on Educating Undergraduates in the Research University, 1998; Gray et al., 1996; Rice et al., 2000). At other kinds of institutions, such as community colleges and some liberal arts institutions and comprehensive universities, teaching is considered paramount, and the evaluation of teaching and learning has received greater attention. Even in some of these schools, however, the increased availability of public and private funds for research has shifted this priority such that some faculty may question whether effective teaching is valued as highly in their institutions as it has been in the past.

This gap can be attributed both to the ways in which research is sponsored and to the importance ascribed to scholarship that emphasizes discovery of new knowledge, application of that knowledge through technology transfer, or impact on regional economic growth. There also is a perceived difference in objectivity and credibility between the evaluation of research productivity and that of teaching effectiveness.

In the world of research, peers who work in closely related areas are the rigorous evaluators of the quality of a research scholar's work. Serving as anonymous reviewers for granting agencies and professional journals, these referees are the main source of formal critical feedback to researchers. Less formally, researchers are assessed, and assess themselves, when they take advantage of their many opportunities to share ideas and learn from colleagues in their own or other institutions. Home institutions bask in the reflected glory of their most distinguished research faculty. In turn, institutions often provide them with perquisites such as endowed positions; additional research support; laboratory space; higher salaries; and few or no other responsibilities, including teaching and advising of undergraduate students. On the other hand, researchers who fail to produce or who become unproductive may lose institutional support, are given diminished space in which to work, are assigned fewer student assistants, or are denied tenure or promotion.

In contrast to the well-established norms for scientific research, many colleges and universities rely heavily on faculty initiative to nurture and sustain improvement of teaching and learning. Although criteria for assessing performance in the research arena are well established relative to those for assessing performance in teaching, the committee agrees with Boyer's (1990) contention that teaching in higher education has many parallels with the research enterprise. The products of sound teaching are effective student learning[1] and academic achievement. The major challenge for colleges and universities is to establish as an institutional priority and policy the need for both *individual* and *collective* (i.e., departmental) responsibility and accountability for improving student learning. As this report demonstrates, criteria and methodologies for assessing teaching effectiveness and productivity in ways that are comparable with the measurement of productivity in scholarship are becoming increasingly available (e.g., Gray et al., 1996; Licata and Morreale, 1997, 2002; National Institute of Science Education, 2001b). Many of these criteria and methods are examined in Part II of this report.

While we now know a great deal more about practices that can contribute to effective teaching and learning (see,

e.g., Annex Box 1-1, Chapter 1), criteria and methods for assessing undergraduate teaching performance in accordance with that emerging knowledge have not yet seen widespread use. Instead, the measure of a teacher's effort often is reduced to the numbers of courses or laboratory sections he or she teaches, the numbers of students taught, or grade distributions. These are not measures of outcomes and results. End-of-course student evaluations are common, but even they usually lead to a numeric ranking, which often confuses evaluation of the teacher and the course. Because many factors, such as the size of the course, its grade distributions, or whether it is being taken as an elective or distribution requirement can influence responses on such evaluations (see Chapter 4), rankings are rarely directly comparable among courses or instructors.

The committee maintains that the goals and perception of excellence in research and teaching at the undergraduate level can and must become more closely aligned. Five key areas in which steps can be taken to this end are (1) balancing the preparation provided for careers in research and teaching; (2) increasing support for effective teaching on the part of professional organizations; (3) developing and implementing improved means for evaluating undergraduate teaching and learning; (4)

---

[1]There are numerous definitions of what constitutes effective student learning. For purposes of this report, the committee has adopted the definition from the NRC report *How People Learn: Brain, Mind, Experience, and School: Expanded Edition* (National Research Council [NRC], 2000c, p. 16): "To develop competence in an area of inquiry, students must (a) have a deep foundation of factual knowledge, (b) understand facts and ideas in the context of a conceptual framework, and (c) organize knowledge in ways that facilitate retrieval and application."

according greater stature to the intellectual challenge of the scholarship of learning and teaching for those faculty in the sciences, technology, engineering, and mathematics (STEM) who wish to pursue such objectives; and (5) recognizing and rewarding those faculty who pursue such scholarship.

BALANCING PREPARATION FOR CAREERS IN RESEARCH AND TEACHING

Faculty advisors mentor most graduate students in science and technology in U.S. universities in their selection of coursework, choice of research topics, and research progress. During this period, students are encouraged to participate in professional meetings and conferences where they can present their findings, receive suggestions on their work, and learn about new developments in their field. The expectation that as researchers, they will interact with and learn from colleagues around the country and the world is ingrained from the start. Also conveyed to students during the graduate school and postdoctoral years is the expectation that other members of the research community will contribute time and intellectual effort to assist them in their research efforts by, for example, reviewing manuscripts and grant applications

[T]here are many kinds of good teaching, in many kinds of teaching situations, at many different levels. Attempts to reduce it to a formula are doomed to failure. There will always be teachers who will break all our rules and yet be profoundly successful. In other words, it is the good teacher, not teaching in the abstract, that counts.

Goheen (1969, p. 80)

or serving on the dissertation committees of colleagues' advisees.

In the postgraduate years, when young researchers assume faculty positions, they are expected to establish an independent line of inquiry quickly and to make significant progress, generally within 6 years. The pressure to produce creditable results at many universities and a growing number of smaller colleges is extreme (e.g., Rice et al., 2000), but young researchers in the natural sciences and engineering generally can count on a considerable support structure provided by their home institutions, departments, and more senior colleagues. Such support can include generous start-up funds, reduced expectations for teaching and committee work during the pretenure years, and nominations for awards and for invitations to professional meetings.

In contrast to the more formalized preparation for research, many new faculty who are expected to teach undergraduates in the sciences and engineering have little training in or exposure to the craft of teaching and virtually no experience with the emerging culture of teaching and learning communities. Depending on the needs of their graduate institution and its sources of funding, new faculty members may have taught an undergraduate laboratory, recitation, or course when they were graduate students. They also may have assisted a course instructor by grading examinations, laboratory reports, and other papers. While many faculty mentors do offer graduate teaching assistants helpful formative feedback on their teaching (especially in their roles as laboratory instructors), the broader paradigms of teaching and learning, such as appropriate content, effective pedagogy, and the ways students learn (e.g., NRC, 1997a, 1999b) often are not discussed in depth (Gaff et al., 2000; Golde and Dore, 2001; Reis, 1997). In addition, the pressures to pursue research actively make it difficult for many graduate teaching assistants to become acquainted with the extensive body of educational research that could guide them as they assume independent faculty positions (e.g., NRC 2000b, 2001, 2002a).

Moreover, because the focus of graduate education is productivity in independent research, graduate students may view negatively the time they spend teaching, or at least assume that their faculty advisors regard this time as reducing research productivity. The comments from one graduate student cited by Nyguist et al. (1991, p. 2) are telling:

> I think any research advisor in their right mind would kill me for [seeking additional teaching assistant opportunities]. It's certainly not something I would do. It'd be ludicrously unfair to a professor—to the professor that you are working for—to seek out another teaching assistantship. You are literally robbing them of thousands of dollars of effective research. It would almost be stealing from your employer to do that. The professor depends on the graduate students because the graduate students do all of the work in the lab. Not a whole lot of people tend to volunteer [their graduate assistants as teaching assistants] because it would mean sacrificing their own careers.

Thus, implicit messages about the importance of preparing to become an effective teacher are often conveyed to graduate students and postdoctoral fellows even before they vie for positions in academe. These messages continue beyond graduate school. Job announcements may precisely specify research qualifications and areas of expertise while referring only obliquely to qualifications for teaching. During interviews, candidates for positions usually are required to present in colloquia or other venues details on their current interests, achievements, and future plans for research, but may not be asked to demonstrate either teaching prowess or knowledge of critical teaching and learning issues in STEM education. Orientation for new faculty, if it exists at all, is often completed within a few days prior to the beginning of the academic year. During orientation or earlier, new faculty may learn of the existence of a teaching and learning center on campus, which can provide access to resources that would be useful for development and refinement of their teaching skills. Even when such centers exist,[2] however, faculty may or may not be encouraged to use their services.

Indeed, many faculty in the STEM disciplines who teach undergraduates are unfamiliar with the burgeoning research on education and human learning. This lack of knowledge and awareness leaves them ill equipped to

mentor the next generation of faculty in new pedagogies or in the use of techniques for effectively assessing student learning. For many faculty, their most successful instructional methods are usually self-taught—a reflection at least in part of the ways they themselves were taught—and consistent with personal styles and areas of expertise. Such methods are not necessarily transferable to student assistants or less-senior colleagues. Moreover, teaching as modeled by faculty advisors has been based primarily on the lecture, to the point that the unstated assumption of graduate or postdoctoral students could very well be that this is the only "real" form of teaching. While lectures may be an effective method when used by certain faculty in certain settings, a mix of pedagogies is likely to be more successful, particularly for the broader spectrum of students that now characterizes the nation's undergraduate population (Cooper and Robinson, 1998; McKeachie, 1999; McNeal and D'Avanzo, 1997; Shipman, 2001; Springer et al., 1998; Wyckoff, 2001).

Senior colleagues could serve as sources of teaching support, advice, and feedback for new faculty, but those new faculty may be reluctant to initiate such a relationship for several reasons. One is the tradition of academic freedom, in which classrooms are viewed as private domains where faculty members have

_____

[2]Teaching and learning centers on many campuses are providing leadership in addressing these issues. A list of these centers around the world can be found at <http://www.ku.edu/~cte/resources/websites.html>.

the freedom to conduct their courses as they deem appropriate. Less-experienced faculty also may be reluctant to share their ideas and concerns about teaching and learning because they fear exposing their pedagogical naiveté or missteps to those who may later evaluate their suitability for tenure and promotion. Such reluctance to seek feedback and advice may be especially pronounced should a new faculty member be experimenting with alternative approaches to teaching and learning that may appear suspect to faculty colleagues. In turn, senior faculty may be reluctant to sit in on the courses of less experienced colleagues because they lack the time to do so or believe their presence could interfere with those colleagues' abilities to conduct the classes as they see fit.

Research universities are recognizing this problem and increasingly are developing programs to help graduate and postdoctoral students in the art and craft of teaching. The availability of such programs in the natural sciences, however, currently lags behind that in other disciplines (Golde and Dore, 2001).

INCREASING SUPPORT FOR EFFECTIVE TEACHING BY PROFESSIONAL ORGANIZATIONS

Dozens of professional societies and umbrella or multidisciplinary organizations are devoted to the support and improvement of research. Far fewer organizations exist whose primary focus is the improvement of teaching and learning in STEM, especially for undergraduate students. Most of these organizations have the potential to influence positively their members' recognition that teaching can be a scholarly endeavor parallel to research in the discipline.

In the past 10 years, however, disciplinary societies and organizations have shown increased interest in finding ways to assist their membership in improving undergraduate teaching and learning. For more than a decade, for example, the research-based American Mathematical Society and the Society for Industrial and Applied Mathematics have worked closely with mathematics education organizations, such as the Mathematical Association of America, the National Council of Teachers of Mathematics, and the American Mathematics Association of Two Year Colleges. Together they have examined mathematics curricula and standards for learning for grades K–14. Likewise, the American Chemical Society offers extensive resources for undergraduate chemistry education and has produced a textbook and supporting materials for students not planning to major in chemistry.[3] And the American Physical Society sponsors regular meetings of department chairs where issues surrounding undergraduate physics education are discussed.[4]

Other professional societies also are beginning to examine their role in supporting the improvement of undergraduate education. In 1996, for example, the American Geophysical Union produced the report *Shaping the Future of Undergraduate Earth Science Education*, which advocates an "earth systems" approach to teaching and learning (Ireton et al., 1996). In 1999, the American Institute for Biological Sciences sponsored a summit of presidents from its 63 member organizations to consider comprehensive approaches to improving undergraduate education in the life sciences.[5] In November 1999, Sigma Xi convened a three-day conference on

improving undergraduate education in the sciences and mathematics that preceded its annual meeting.[6] In 2001, the American Institute of Physics published a compendium of papers from a symposium it had sponsored on the role of physics departments in preparing K–12 teachers (Buck et al., 2000).[7]

Foundations also have assigned greater importance to learning outcomes. The Carnegie Foundation for the Advancement of Teaching recently released a new "Millennial Edition" classification system for American higher education institutions, which places greater emphasis on teaching and service after a decades-long focus on research productivity and the number of doctoral degrees awarded (Basinger, 2000; McCormick, 2001).[8] The Council for the Advancement and Support of Education, in collaboration with the Carnegie Foundation for the Advancement of Teaching,[9] gives faculty from higher education institutions national recognition for excellence

---

[3]Additional information about this program is available at <http://www.acs.org/portal/Chemistry?PID=acsdisplay.html&DOC=education/curriculum/context.html>.

[4]See, for example, Undergraduate Education in Physics: Responding to Changing Expectations <http://www.aps.org/educ/conf97/01.Chairs.homepage.html>.

[5]Additional information is available at <http://alidoro.catchword.com/vl=85083249/cl=13/nw=1/rpsv/catchword/aibs/00063568/v50n3/s13/p277l>.

---

[6]Additional information about this convocation is available at <http://www.sigmaxi.org/forum/1999Forum/forum99.htm>.

[7]Additional information about this symposium is available at <http://www.sigmaxi.org/forum/1999Forum/forum99.htm>.

[8]This new classification system is available at <http://www.carnegiefoundation.org/Classification/index.htm>.

[9]Additional information is available at <http://www.carnegiefoundation.org/>.

in undergraduate teaching.[10] The American Association for Higher Education (AAHE) sponsors an Assessment Forum, designed to promote "…effective approaches to assessment that involve faculty, benefit students, and improve the quality of teaching and learning. It helps campuses, programs, and individuals to plan, implement, and share the results of their assessment efforts by publishing, networking, and sponsoring an annual national conference" (e.g., Cambridge, 1997; Suskie, 2000).[11] AAHE also has published a directory of some 300 assessment books and articles, journals, newsletters, audiocassettes, organizations, conferences, and electronic resources such as listservs and websites (Gardiner et al., 1997). Another important source of exemplary success stories is Project Kaleidoscope's *Programs That Work*. Project Kaleidoscope has collected a large body of information from a wide variety of postsecondary institutions about innovative practices for the improvement of teaching, curriculum, and institutionalization of reform.[12]

Public and private funding organizations have begun to stress the role of assessment in improving undergraduate teaching and learning. For example, the National Science Foundation (NSF) recently instituted an initiative for Assessment of Student Achievement in Undergraduate Education. This program supports the development and dissemination of assessment practices, materials, and metrics designed to improve the effectiveness of undergraduate courses, curricula, programs of study, and academic institutions in promoting student learning in STEM.[13] The Pew Charitable Trust has supported several efforts to make public what undergraduates are learning at the nation's colleges and universities.[14] The Howard Hughes Medical Institute, which has contributed more than $475 million toward improving undergraduate and K–12 education in the sciences since 1988, has begun to compile and will share on a website information about the various kinds of assessments being used by its grantees to demon-

---

[10]Additional information about this prize is available at <http://www.case.org/awards>.

[11]Additional information about this forum and its related activities is available at <http://www.aahe.org/assessment/>.

[12]Additional information about the Project Kaleidoscope program, including specific case studies and publications that are available in print and on the organization's website, are available at <http://www.pkal.org>.

---

[13]Additional information about this NSF initiative is available at <http://www.ehr.nsf.gov/ehr/DUE/programs/asa/>.

[14]Additional information is available at <http://www.pewtrusts.com/ideas/index.cfm?issue =22>.

strate increases in student learning and greater teaching effectiveness.[15]

Some professional accrediting organizations and disciplinary societies also are becoming involved with efforts to improve undergraduate education within their disciplines. Beginning in 2001, engineering programs will be subject to new criteria for accreditation established by the Accreditation Board for Engineering and Technology (ABET).[16] These outcome-based standards include a call for engineering programs to demonstrate that their graduates have the necessary knowledge and skills to succeed in the profession. To help member institutions prepare to meet these new expectations, ABET began holding conferences on Outcomes Assessment for Program Improvement and now sponsors annual national conferences on this issue.[17] Similarly, in 1991 the American Psychological Association (APA) drafted a set of voluntary, outcome-based standards

for undergraduate education in this discipline that can be applied to all students who enroll in psychology courses.[18] A task force established by APA's Board of Scientific Affairs has developed a set of guidelines for "undergraduate psychology competencies" (APA, 2002).

The committee applauds the efforts of professional and disciplinary organizations in helping members recognize their roles and responsibilities for improving undergraduate education and in offering sessions about how to do so. However, these groups could contribute significantly to efforts aimed at improving teaching and learning if they were also to convene serious discussions addressing the broader issues and conflicts that serve as barriers to those efforts, such as allocation of faculty time, expectations for professional advancement, and recognition and rewards.

---

[15]Additional information about the organization's increasing emphasis on examining and disseminating new ideas about assessment is available at <http://www.hhmi.org/grants/undergraduate/assessment/>.

[16]Additional information is available at <http://www.abet.org/accreditation.html>.

[17]Additional information about the ABET conferences is available at <http://www.abet.org/annual_meeting_cover.html>.

---

[18]APA's *Principles for Quality Undergraduate Psychology Programs* is available at <http://www.apa.org/ed/stmary.html>.

DEVELOPING AND IMPLEMENTING IMPROVED MEANS FOR EVALUATING EFFECTIVE TEACHING AND LEARNING

Finally, if teaching and learning are to improve, a broader array of equitable and acceptable ways must be found to evaluate faculty teaching on the basis of evidence of student learning. The issues involved here go far beyond the individual faculty member; they also reach deeply into academic depart-ments and institutions. Evidence for effective teaching will need to be coupled with greater recognition and rewards for teaching by peers, academic departments, and institutions of higher education (Bleak et al., 2000; Boyer, 1990; Glassick et al., 1997; Joint Policy Board on Mathematics, 1994). Part II of this report provides more specific guidance on criteria and methods for developing effective evaluations for both individual faculty members and academic departments.

4
Evaluating Teaching in Science, Technology, Engineering, and Mathematics: Principles and Research Findings

Every department, college, and university is unique, and thus no one model for evaluating teaching effectiveness that is based on learning outcomes will be appropriate for all institutions. Nonetheless, if effective methodologies for evaluating teaching and student learning are to be implemented, administrators and senior faculty must become more aware of emerging research on effective practices. Knowledge of this work is particularly important at the departmental level, where the evaluation of individual faculty members counts most. This chapter reviews what is known about how research findings can shape best practices in evaluating undergraduate teaching in science, technology, engineering, and mathematics (STEM). Chapter 5 builds on this research to highlight ways in which expectations and guidelines for evaluating teaching can be made clear to both faculty and administrators.

GENERAL PRINCIPLES AND OVERALL FINDINGS

The research literature suggests that for purposes of any formative or summative evaluation,[1] assessment that is based on a single teaching activity (e.g., classroom presentation) or depends on information from a single source (e.g., student evaluation forms) is less reliable, useful, and valid than an assessment of an instructor's strengths and weaknesses that is based on multiple sources (Centra, 1993). Comprehensive assessments of teaching are

---

[1]Informal assessments of a faculty member's work that are used primarily to provide feedback and reinforcement to a colleague for purposes of ongoing professional development and improvement are characterized as *formative evaluations*. In contrast, evaluations that are used for purposes of rendering formal personnel decisions and that are based on a variety of data are often called *summative evaluations* (Scriven, 1993; review by Licata and Moreale, 1997).

more accurate, particularly when based on the views of current and former students, colleagues, and the instructor or department being reviewed. The process of evaluating teaching has been found to work best when all faculty members in a given department (or, in smaller colleges, from across the institution) play a strong role in developing policies and procedures. This is the case because evaluation criteria must be clear, well known and understood, scheduled regularly, and acceptable to all who will be involved with rendering or receiving evaluation (Alverno College Faculty, 1994; Gardiner et al., 1997; Loacker, 2001; Wergin, 1994; Wergin and Swingen, 2000).[2]

Evidence that can be most helpful in formatively evaluating an individual faculty member's teaching efficacy and providing opportunities for further professional development includes the following points:

---

[2]Alverno College has sponsored a comprehensive research program on assessment of student learning and means of tying that assessment to ongoing improvement of both teaching by individuals and departmental approaches to education. For additional information, see Alverno College Faculty (1994). A more recent monograph edited by Loacker (2001) describes Alverno's program, with a focus on how students experience self-assessment and learn from it to improve their performance. Then from the perspective of various disciplines, individual faculty explain how self-assessment works in their courses.

Input from Students and Peers

- Evidence of learning from student portfolios containing samples of their writing on essays, examinations, and presentations at student research conferences or regional or national meetings. Additional direct and indirect classroom techniques that demonstrate student learning are discussed in Chapter 5.

- Informed opinions of other members of the faculty member's department, particularly when those opinions are based on direct observation of the candidate's teaching scholarship or practice. The ability to offer such input comes from the reviewer's observing a *series* of the candidate's classes, attending the candidate's public lectures or presentations at professional association meetings, serving on curricular committees with the candidate, or team teaching with the candidate. Opinions of faculty colleagues also can be based on their observations of student performance in courses that build upon those taught by the faculty member being evaluated.

- Input by faculty from "user" departments for service courses and from related disciplines for interdisciplinary courses. Such information can be very helpful in determining whether students are learning subject matter in ways that will enable them to transfer that learning to other disciplines or learning situations.[3]

- Input from undergraduate and graduate teaching assistants, based on their participation in a range of courses and laboratories taught by the faculty member being evaluated, as well as post hoc input some time after they have had the opportunity to work with and learn from the candidate. This input can be solicited from graduating seniors and alumni selected randomly from a faculty member's class lists or in accordance with the candidate's recommendations.

- Input from undergraduate and graduate students who have worked with the faculty member as teaching or research assistants or as collaborators on original research. Input from these students can be useful both at the time they are working with the faculty member and sometime after that relationship has ended.

- A summary of the professional attainments of undergraduate students who engaged in research under the tutelage of the faculty member being evaluated.

---

[3]Accountability to other departments should include evaluation of individual faculty members and discussion of departmental program content. A department's accountability for its service to other disciplines is considered in Chapter 8. Academic deans can provide leadership in fostering interdepartmental communication.

Review of Departmental and Institutional Records

- The number and levels of courses taught and the number of students enrolled in each course or section taught by the instructor over time. This information can provide evaluators with insight and perspective regarding the number of preparations required; the amount of time needed for advising students; and, in some cases, the commitment of time necessary to correct examinations, term papers, and reports.

- The number of undergraduate students advised, mentored, or supervised by the faculty member. This information can be accompanied by opinions about the quality of the advice or mentoring received.

- The number of undergraduate students the faculty member has guided in original or applied research, the quality of their research as measured through presentations and publications, and their professional attainments while under the faculty member's supervision and later in their careers.

- The number of graduate students mentored in their preparation as teaching assistants or future faculty members and their effectiveness in teaching.

Review of the Faculty Member's Teaching Portfolio and Other Documentation

- Evidence of the faculty member's adaptation of instructional techniques for courses, laboratories, or field activities so as to demonstrably improve student learning by achieving course objectives.[4]

- Evidence of the faculty member's participation in efforts to strengthen departmental or institutional curriculum, to reform undergraduate education, or to improve teaching in the discipline or across disciplinary boundaries.

- The faculty member's self-assessment of his or her own teaching strengths and areas for improvement.

- The faculty member's participation in seeking external support for activities that further the teaching mission.

SPECIFIC SOURCES OF DATA FOR EVALUATING TEACHING QUALITY AND EFFECTIVENESS

This section reviews evidence on the effectiveness of various kinds of input into procedures for evaluating teaching quality and effectiveness. The committee acknowledges and emphasizes that each source of data for evaluating the teaching of individual faculty members has both advantages and disadvantages. Multiple inputs to any evaluation process can help overcome the shortcomings of any single source.

Undergraduate Student Evaluations

The use of student evaluations in higher education is contentious. Faculty often complain that student evaluations are predicated on such variables as what emotions students are experiencing when they complete the questionnaire, what they perceive as the faculty member's ability to "entertain," and whether they were required to enroll in the course (Centra, 1993). Faculty also challenge whether the questions on student evaluation instruments encourage students to reflect longer-term instructional success in their responses.

Despite these misgivings, extensive research[5] has established the efficacy of student evaluations *when they are used*

---

[4]Under its Course, Curriculum, and Laboratory Improvement program, the National Science Foundation (NSF) now supports faculty members who adopt and adapt successful models for courses and pedagogy in their own teaching. Additional information about this program is available at <http://www.ehr.nsf.gov/ehr/due/programs/ccli/>.

[5]The U.S. Department of Education's Educational Resources Information Center system cites more than 2,000 articles on research that focus on student evaluations. Additional information is available at <http://ericae.net/scripts/ft/ftcongen.asp?wh1=STUDENT+ EVALUATION>.

as one of an array of techniques for evaluating student learning. Students can, at a minimum, provide opinions on such dimensions of teaching as the effectiveness of the instructor's pedagogy, his or her proficiency and fairness in assessing learning, and how well he or she advises students on issues relating to course or career planning. Students also can assess their own learning relative to goals stated in the course syllabus, thereby providing some evidence of whether they have learned what the instructor intended. Self-reports of learning have been shown to be reasonably reliable as general indicators of student achievement (Pike, 1995).

The following discussion focuses on three critical issues associated with fair and effective use of student evaluation: reliability, validity, and possible sources of bias. A more complete review of the various types of instruments used for student evaluation and specific issues related to their use is provided in Appendix A. The application of these instruments in practice is discussed in Chapter 5.

Reliability

Reliability has several meanings in testing. Here, the term refers to interrater reliability. The issue is whether different people or processes involved in evaluating responses, as is often the case with performance or portfolio assessments, are likely to render reasonably similar judgments (American Educational Research Association [AERA], American Psychological Association [APA], and National Council on Measurement in Education [NCME], 1999).

The reliability of student evaluations has been a subject of study for more than 60 years. Remmers (1934) reports on reliability studies of student evaluations that he conducted at Purdue University in the 1930s. He investigated the extent of agreement among ratings that students within a classroom gave to their teacher and concluded that excellent intraclass reliability typically resulted when 25 or more students were involved. More recently, Centra (1973, 1998) and Marsh (1987) found similar intraclass reliabilities even with as few as 15 students in a class.

For tenure, promotion, and other summative decisions, both the numbers of students rating a course and the number of courses rated should be considered to achieve a reliable mean from a good sample of students. For example, Gilmore et al. (1978) find that at least five courses with at least 15 students rating each are needed if the ratings are to be used in administrative decisions involving an individual faculty member.[6] To achieve the reliability for summative evaluations advocated by Gilmore et al., a newly hired tenure-track faculty member would need to be evaluated each term for each course taught during each of his or her pretenure years.

On the other hand, the need for such constant levels of student evaluation could have the negative effect of stifling creativity and risk taking by the instructor in trying new teaching or assessment techniques. Indeed, on some campuses, academic administrators are waiving the requirement for counting student evaluations as part of faculty members' dossiers (although such evaluations may be collected from students) when those faculty agree to introduce alternative approaches to teaching their courses and assessing student learning (Project Kaleidoscope, personal communication).

How reliable are student evaluations when faculty members teach different types of courses, such as large, lower division lecture classes and small graduate research courses? According to the results of one study (Murray et al., 1990), instructors who received high ratings in one type of course did not necessarily receive similar ratings in other types of courses they taught. These differences may or may not be directly associated with variations in teaching effectiveness in different courses. For example, the same instructor may receive better evaluations for a course that students elect to take than for a course that fulfills a general education requirement.

Research employing coefficient alpha analyses[7] to establish the reliability (relative agreement) of items within factors or scale scores has revealed students' ratings of faculty over short periods of time (test–retest within a semester) to be stable. These results suggest that student evaluations are unlikely to be subject to day-to-day changes in the moods of either students or teachers (Marsh, 1987).

Validity

Validity is the degree to which evidence and theory support interpretations of test scores. The process of validation involves accumulating evi-

---

[6]Gilmore et al. (1978) observe that if fewer than 15 students per class provide the ratings, a greater number of courses need to be rated—preferably 10.

[7]Coefficient alpha analysis is a form of factor analysis, used to verify the major dimensions (factors) and the items within that dimension in an instrument. Coefficient alpha determines the extent to which the items within a factor or scale are intercorrelated and thus measure a similar characteristic.

dence to provide a sound scientific basis for proposed score interpretations (AERA, APA, and NCME, 1999).

The key questions related to validity of student evaluations are how well results from student evaluations correlate with other measures of teaching effectiveness and student learning, and whether students learn more from effective than ineffective teachers. To explore the relationship between learning and student evaluations, Cohen (1981) examined multisection courses that administered common final examinations. Mean values of teaching effectiveness from student evaluations in each section were then correlated with the class's mean performance on the final examination. A meta-analysis of 41 such studies reporting on 68 separate multisection courses suggested that student evaluations are a valid indicator of teacher effectiveness (Cohen, 1981). Correlations between student grades and student ratings of instructors' skills in course organization and communication were higher than those between student grades and student ratings of faculty–student interaction.

One limitation of Cohen's study is that multisection courses are typically lower division courses. Therefore, the question arises of whether similar correlations exist for upper level courses, where higher level learning outcomes

are generally critical. Two recent studies have shed light on this question by using students' ratings of their own learning as a proxy measure of examination achievement scores. In both studies, analyses of large datasets revealed a highly statistically significant relationship between a student's self-rated learning and his or her rating of teacher effectiveness in the course (Cashin and Downey, 1999; Centra and Gaubatz, 2000b).

Other validity studies have compared students' evaluations of their instructors with those prepared by trained observers for the same instructors. In one study, the trained observers noted that teachers who had received high ratings from students differed in several ways from those who had received lower ratings. Highly rated teachers were more likely to repeat difficult ideas several times and on different occasions, provide additional examples when necessary, speak clearly and expressively, and be sensitive to students' needs (Murray, 1983). In short, student evaluations appear to be determined by the instructor's actual classroom behavior rather than by other indicators, such as a pleasing personality (see Ambady and Rosenthal, 1993).

Although all of the studies cited above address short-term validity (end-of-course measures), critics have argued that students may not appreciate demanding teachers who have high expectations until years later, when they are able to reflect maturely on their classroom experiences. However, research into this question has indicated that there is good long-term stability—1 to 5 years later—in student and alumni ratings of the same teachers (Centra, 1974; Drucker and Remmers, 1951; Overall and Marsh, 1980).

Bias

A circumstance that unduly influences a teacher's rating but has nothing to do with actual teaching or learning effectiveness is considered to be a *biasing* variable. Possible biasing effects may derive from the course, the student, or the teacher's personal characteristics (e.g., dress or appearance). For example, instructors who teach small classes may receive higher ratings than those who teach large classes (Centra and Creech, 1976; Feldman, 1984). However, it is also likely that small classes produce better learning and instruction (because teachers can more easily address individual questions, involve students more actively, provide one-on-one feedback, and so forth). Strictly speaking, small classes may not be a biasing variable in student evaluations, yet it is probably unfair to compare the ratings of someone who teaches only small classes with those of someone who

routinely teaches classes of 50 or more students, or those of someone who teaches large lecture courses with hundreds of students.

It is important to be aware of possible biases and to understand accordingly how to interpret evaluations fairly. Studies that have examined these effects have been largely correlational and thus do not necessarily demonstrate definite cause-and-effect relationships. Increasingly, multivariate analyses have been used that control for extraneous variables. These analyses have helped clarify the data, as follows.

Studies of course characteristics that might bias the results of student evaluations have looked at class size, discipline or subject area being taught, type of course (i.e., required versus elective), and level of difficulty of the course. With regard to the more favorable ratings accorded teachers of small classes noted above (Centra and Creech, 1976; Feldman, 1984), the difference in ratings based on class size accounted for only about 25 percent of the standard deviation, not enough to be statistically meaningful. The same studies found that the instructor's methods for teaching the course were more important, with active-learning classes receiving more favorable ratings than lecture classes.

In comparisons of student ratings in different disciplines, classes in mathematics and the natural sciences were found to be more likely to receive lower ratings than classes in other disciplines (Cashin, 1990; Feldman, 1978). The differences were not apparent for all dimensions, however—the organization of courses and the fairness of tests and assignments were two areas in which students rated the disciplines similarly. Lower ratings for natural science and mathematics classes in such dimensions as faculty–student interaction, course difficulty and pace, and presentation format (lecture versus discussion) suggested that these courses were less student-oriented, more difficult, faster-paced, and more likely to include lecture presentations. What this appears to indicate is that students did not like these aspects of the courses and may have learned less (Centra, 1993).

Student ratings can be influenced by many other variables that may interact with or counteract the influence of discipline or course format. For example, studies have shown that students tend to give slightly higher ratings to courses in their major field or to courses they chose to take, as opposed to those they were required to take. The likely reason is that students (and possibly teachers as well) are generally less interested in required courses. These often include introductory or survey courses that meet distribution requirements in a college's general education

sequence, but that students may perceive as having little to do with their immediate academic interests or future needs.

Contrary to what one might otherwise expect, studies have found that instructors who received higher ratings did not assign less work or "water down" their courses (Marsh, 1987; Marsh and Roche, 1993; Marsh and Roche, 2000). Natural science courses not only were generally rated less highly, but also were judged to be more difficult. In this particular case, students within those disciplines who gave teachers high ratings also noted that those teachers assigned more work.

The student characteristics most frequently studied for their effects in biasing evaluations of teaching include grade point average, expected grade in the course, academic ability, and age. According to most studies (e.g., Marsh and Roche, 2000; McKeachie, 1979, 1999), none of these characteristics consistently affects student ratings. Despite this finding, some instructors still firmly believe that students give higher ratings to teachers from whom they expect to receive high grades.

Instructor characteristics that could possibly influence ratings are gender, race, and the students' perception that the faculty member is especially "entertaining" during instruction (Abrami et al., 1982). Several studies have analyzed the effect of gender—of both the evaluating student and the teacher—on student evaluations. Most of these studies indicate there is no significant difference in ratings given to male and female instructors by students of the same or the opposite sex (Centra and Gaubatz, 2000a; Feldman, 1993). In certain areas of the natural sciences and engineering in which women faculty members are a distinct minority, female teachers have been found to receive higher ratings than their male counterparts from both male and female students. Female teachers also were more likely than male teachers to use discussion rather than lecturing as a primary method for teaching, which may help account for the higher ratings they received (Centra and Gaubatz, 2000a).

The question of whether teachers who are highly entertaining or expressive receive higher ratings from students has been examined in a series of "educational-seduction" studies (Abrami et al., 1982; Naftulin et al., 1973). In one study, researchers employed a professional actor to deliver a highly entertaining but inaccurate lecture. The actor received high ratings in this single lecture, particularly on his delivery of content. A reasonable conclusion from these studies is that by teaching more enthusiastically, teachers will receive higher ratings (Centra, 1993).

Graduating Seniors and Alumni

Evaluations of an instructor's teaching by graduating seniors and alumni can be useful in providing information about the effectiveness of both individual teachers and the department's overall curriculum. Current students can comment on day-to-day aspects of teaching effectiveness, such as the instructor's ability to organize and communicate ideas. Graduating seniors and alumni can make judgments from a broader, more mature perspective, reflecting and reporting on the longer-term value and retention of what they have learned from individual instructors and from departmental programs. They may be particularly effective contributors to evaluations based on exit interviews (Light, 2001). There are, however, drawbacks to surveying seniors and alumni, including difficulties in locating graduates and deciding which students to survey (e.g., the percentage of students included in an evaluation process based on random surveys versus those recommended by the faculty member being evaluated), and the hazy memory alumni may have about particular instructors (Centra, 1993).

Teaching Assistants

Teaching assistants are in a unique position to provide information about the teaching skills of the faculty members with whom they work. They also can offer useful insight and perspective on the collection of courses and curricula offered by their academic department (Lambert and Tice, 1992; National Research Council [NRC], 1995b, 1997b, 2000b). Because teaching assistants routinely observe classes and work with students throughout the term, they can comment on course organization, the effectiveness of an instructor's presentations and interactions with students, the fairness of examinations, and the like. Teaching assistants also can assess how well the instructor guides, supervises, and contributes to the development and enhancement of his or her own pedagogical skills. As continuing graduate students, however, teaching assistants may be vulnerable to pressures that make it difficult to provide candid evaluations. Thus when they are asked to evaluate their instructors, special precautions, such as ensuring confidentiality, must be taken.

Faculty Colleagues

Compared with the extensive research on the utility[8] of student evalua-

tions of teaching, few studies exist concerning the efficacy of peer review, and those available tend to be limited in scope. Research has demonstrated that *extended* direct observation of teaching by peers can be a highly effective means of evaluating the teaching of an individual instructor (e.g., American Association for Higher Education [AAHE], 1995; Hutchings, 1996). However, colleges and universities do not use classroom observation widely in the assessment of teaching.

A common but erroneous assumption is that peer evaluations of teaching, including evaluations by department chairs, are best conducted through classroom observation (Seldin, 1998). Even when peer evaluation does involve extensive classroom observation, problems can occur. For example, some research has shown that when an instructor's evaluation is based solely on classroom observation, the raters exhibit low levels of concurrence in their ratings (Centra, 1975). This may be because many faculty and administrators have had little experience in conducting such reviews in ways that are fair and equitable to those being reviewed. Another reason may be that such observation is not part of the culture of teaching and learning within a department. It may be possible to train faculty in observation analysis, providing them with the skills, criteria, and

---

[8]*Utility* denotes the extent to which using a test to make or inform certain decisions is appropriate, economical, or otherwise feasible. The criterion of *fairness* is beginning to replace *utility* in the scholarly literature on measurement.

standards needed for consistent ratings of a colleague's classroom performance. However, such efforts are time-consuming and require more serious dedication to the task than is usually given to teaching evaluations in higher education.

Some studies have shown that faculty believe they are better able to judge the research productivity of their colleagues than their teaching effectiveness. Kremer (1990) found that evaluations of research were more reliable than evaluations of teaching or service. In that study, as is generally the case, faculty had access to more information about their colleagues' research than about their teaching or service. According to other studies, when faculty members have an extensive factual basis for their evaluations of teaching, there is higher reliability in their ratings. For example, Root (1987) studied what happened when six elected faculty members independently rated individual dossiers of other faculty. The dossiers included course outlines, syllabi, teaching materials, student evaluations, and documentation of curriculum development. The faculty members being evaluated also submitted information about their scholarly and service activities. Using cases that illustrated high and low ratings, the six-member committee reviewed and discussed criteria for evaluation before making their

ratings. The reliabilities of the evaluations (based on average intercorrelations) were very high (above 0.90) for each of the three performance areas. In fact, Root concluded that even a three-member committee working in similar fashion would be able to provide sufficiently reliable evaluations and in a very short period of time—no more than an hour or two. This study supports the use of colleague evaluations for summative decisions providing that the committee has previously discussed evaluative criteria and expected standards of performance, and has a number of different sources of data on which to base its evaluations.

This is a particularly critical point because at present, although tenure and promotion committees at the college or university level always include faculty representatives, such faculty usually do not have the authority or the time needed to make their own independent evaluation of a candidate's performance in teaching, research, or service. Instead they must rely almost entirely on other sources, such as written or oral evaluations from colleagues in the candidate's discipline or student evaluations.

When conducted properly, review and evaluation by one's colleagues can be an effective means of improving teaching at the college level, providing feedback for ongoing professional development in teaching, and enabling more informed personnel decisions (AAHE, 1993; Chism, 1999; French-Lazovik, 1981; Hutchings, 1995, 1996; Keig and Waggoner, 1994). AAHE recently undertook an extensive, multiyear initiative to examine ways of maximizing the effectiveness of peer review of teaching. A website describes the results and products of this initiative in detail.[9] The ideas reviewed below reflect the findings of the AAHE initiative and other sources as cited.

Evaluation of Course Materials

Departments can obtain valuable information about course offerings from individual instructors by asking faculty to review and offer constructive criticism of each other's course materials and approaches to teaching and learning. Faculty who teach comparable courses or different sections of the same course or who are particularly knowledgeable about the subject matter can conduct reviews of selected course materials. They can analyze those materials with regard to such matters as the accuracy of information, approaches to encouraging and assessing student learning, and the consistency of expectations among instructors who teach

---

[9]Information about AAHE's peer review of teaching initiative is available at <http://www.aahe.org/teaching/Peer_Review.htm>.

different sections of the same course (Bernstein and Quinlan, 1996; Edgerton et al., 1991; Hutchings, 1995, 1996).

Instructional Contributions

In addition to classroom observation, faculty colleagues can examine and comment on an instructor's teaching-related activities. These kinds of evaluations might include examining syllabi, distributed materials, or the content of tests and how well the tests align with course goals. They might also address the faculty member's involvement with curriculum development, supervision of student research, contributions to the professional development of colleagues and teaching assistants, publication of articles on teaching in disciplinary journals, authorship of textbooks, development of distance-learning or web-based materials, and related activities (Centra, 1993).

Use of Students for Classroom Observation

As noted above, peer observation can be an effective evaluation technique if the observers are trained in the process. Understandably, observation of colleagues remains a highly sensitive issue for some faculty members. In some cases, the presence of the observer may even affect the instructional dynamics of the course. For this reason, and also on the grounds of fairness and balance, the best use of peer observation may be as a voluntary and informal procedure that enables faculty members to gain insight on the strengths and weaknesses of their teaching skills, rather than as a basis for personnel decisions. In this spirit, some institutions also are experimenting with the use of student consultants—students not enrolled in a particular course—to assist faculty who have requested input on their teaching but are reluctant to ask colleagues (e.g., Emerson et al., 2000).[10] At a few institutions, classroom teachers from local secondary schools have volunteered or are paid to provide such input.

Self-Evaluation by Faculty

Reports on Teaching Activities and Teaching Portfolios

Most institutions require faculty to describe their teaching, student advising, scholarship, and service activities each year and in greater detail for promotion or tenure and other personnel decisions. In response, faculty

---

[10]For example, Worcester Polytechnic Institute and Brigham Young University are using such student consultants to provide instructors with "off-the-record" or private midcourse feedback on such factors as what they gained from a particular class and how others in the class responded to the material. For additional information, see Greene (2000). See also <http://www.wpi.edu/Academics/CEDTA> and <http://www.byu.edu/fc/pages/fchomepg.html>.

members traditionally have provided a list of basic information about their teaching. These lists might include details about instructional goals and objectives, conduct and supervision of laboratory instruction, teaching methods, syllabi and other course materials, websites, student supervision and advising, and efforts at self-improvement.

In recent years, however, increasing numbers of faculty have elected to develop, or departments and institutions have required the submission of, teaching portfolios to be used for purposes of both formative and summative evaluation (e.g., Anderson, 1993; Bernstein and Quinlan, 1996; Centra, 1994; Edgerton et al., 1991; Hutchings, 1998; Seldin, 1991). Teaching portfolios have the advantage of providing continuing documentation of teaching and advising; that is, teachers can accumulate evidence of their effectiveness as it appears. Teachers' personal reflections on their teaching and evidence of student learning that is supported, perhaps, by their own classroom research are key components of a portfolio. Self-analysis for formative evaluation of teaching effectiveness—as opposed to quantified self-evaluation for summative evaluation—gives faculty the opportunity to present their own best case for their success in achieving their teaching goals (Centra, 1979; Hutchings, 1998).

Teaching portfolios pose opportunities and challenges to both those who are asked to create them and those who must review them. For example, because they are more qualitative in nature than other sources of information, teaching portfolios are likely to be more difficult to evaluate objectively. When they are used for summative purposes, it may be difficult for committees on promotion and tenure to compare the contents of one faculty member's portfolio with those of another's. Recognizing this challenge, AAHE is now sponsoring a multiyear initiative to examine the most effective ways of developing and utilizing information in teaching portfolios for teacher evaluation and ongoing professional development.[11] In addition, AAHE recently acquired and posted on the World Wide Web "The Portfolio Clearinghouse," a database of some 30 portfolio projects from a variety of types of colleges and universities around the world. This database provides information about portfolios as a means of demonstrating student learning, effective teaching, and institutional self-assessment.[12] Another recent product of AAHE's ongoing project on teaching portfolios is a series of papers (Cambridge, 2001) that provides guidance to faculty members, departments, and institutions wishing to maintain electronic portfolios.

Self-Review

To supplement descriptive information, faculty who engage in self-review reflect on their accomplishments, strengths, and weaknesses as instructors. Research has shown that self-evaluation can be helpful in summative personnel decisions by providing context for the interpretation of data from other sources. For example, a faculty member may have a particularly difficult class or may be teaching a course for the first time. Or she or he may be experimenting with new teaching methods that may result in both improved student learning and retention and lower student ratings (Hutchings, 1998).

The committee found that much of the research on self-evaluation has focused on instructors rating their teaching performance rather than simply describing or reflecting on it. One analysis indicated that self-evaluations did not correlate with evaluations by current students, colleagues, or administrators, although the latter three groups agreed in high measure with one another (Feldman, 1989). At the same

_____

[11]Additional information is available at <http://www.aahe.org/teaching/portfolio_projects.htm>.

[12]This database is available at <http://www.aahe.org/teaching/portfolio_db.htm>.

time, it was found that while teachers tended to rate themselves higher than their students did, they identified the same relative strengths and weaknesses as did other evaluators (Centra, 1973, Feldman, 1989). Therefore, self-evaluations may be most useful in improving instruction, although corroborating evidence from other sources may be necessary to underscore needed changes. For summative purposes, however, most of the faculty queried in one survey agreed with the findings of research: self-evaluations lack validity and objectivity (Marsh, 1982). Although quantifiable self-evaluations should thus probably not be used in summative evaluations, teaching portfolios can be useful in improving instruction if they are considered in conjunction with independent evaluations from students, colleagues, or teaching improvement specialists.

Institutional Data and Records

Grade Distributions, Course Retention, and Subsequent Enrollment Figures

Historical records of grade distributions and enrollments within a department may provide supplemental information about a faculty member's teaching when compared with data collected from colleagues who have taught similar courses or are teaching different sections of the same course. However, this kind of evidence should be interpreted very cautiously since many factors other than teaching effectiveness may account for the findings. For example, recent changes in an institution's policy on dropping courses may influence which students decide to leave or remain in a course and when they elect to do so, independently of the instructor's teaching effectiveness. If, however, records show that a larger-than-normal fraction of the students in a professor's course regularly drop out and repeat the class at a later time, the attrition may be relevant to the quality of the instructor's teaching. Similarly, questions might be raised about the quality of an instructor's teaching effectiveness (especially in lower division courses) if a higher-than-normal fraction of students who have declared an interest in majoring in the subject area fails to enroll in higher level courses within the department (e.g., Seymour and Hewitt, 1997).

In contrast, an unusual grade distribution may reflect some anomaly in a particular class and should be considered in that light. For example, while the motives or competence of an instructor who consistently awards high grades might be questioned, it is entirely possible that this individual has engaged his or her students in regular formative evaluations, which has helped them overcome academic problems and learn more than might otherwise be expected. These students' performance on standardized quizzes or examinations might therefore exceed that of students being taught by other instructors, so that a skewed, high grade distribution would be entirely warranted. Similarly, if a large proportion of students from a faculty member's introductory class later enroll in the instructor's upper division advanced elective course, one might reasonably assume that this instructor has captured students' interest in the subject matter.

Quality and Performance of Undergraduate Research Students

Faculty members who have supervised independent undergraduate research will have had the opportunity to build a record of attracting high-quality students. Strong indicators of how effective their mentoring has been include the disseminated scholarly products or subsequent academic and professional accomplishments of their former students in research as well as in teaching. Again, it must be acknowledged that many factors affect students' decisions to enroll in a particular academic program, and many factors affect their subsequent achievements as well. However, evidence, if any, that links a particular faculty member to students' selection of supervisors and their future scholarly productivity and professional aspirations and accomplishments can be considered useful as supplemental evidence of teaching effectiveness.

PART II

Applying What Is Known: Strategies for Evaluating Teaching Effectiveness

5

Evaluation Methodologies

Part I of this report describes recent research on ways to rethink and restructure teaching and learning, coupled with new approaches to evaluation and professional development for faculty. Those findings have the potential to reshape undergraduate education in science, technology, engineering, and mathematics (STEM) for a much larger number of undergraduates. However, developing strategies for implementing and sustaining such changes requires the commitment of all members of a college or university community.

In a teaching and learning community, the most effective evaluation is that which encourages and rewards effective teaching practices on the basis of student learning outcomes (Doherty et al., 2002; Shapiro and Levine, 1999). Assessment of student learning at its best enables students to identify their own strengths and weaknesses and to determine the kinds of information they

need to correct their learning deficiencies and misconceptions. When such evaluation is properly employed, students learn that they can engage in self-assessment and continuous improvement of performance throughout their lives.

Accordingly, this chapter offers practical guidance to postsecondary faculty and administrators on ways to institute a system of both evaluation and professional development that can contribute to significant gains in teaching effectiveness for faculty who teach undergraduates. The chapter describes how input from students (undergraduates and graduate teaching assistants), colleagues, and faculty self-evaluation can be used for evaluating individual instructors. It also describes the advantages and disadvantages of these various approaches.

As stated in Chapter 1, ongoing formative assessment of student learning can have powerful benefits both in improving learning and in helping faculty improve their teaching on the basis of the feedback they receive from a variety of sources. The information gathered during such assessments also can serve as a basis for more formal, summative evaluations that have an impact on important personnel decisions.

The technique of outcomes assessment as a means of measuring student learning and the use of that information to improve teaching are considered first. Additional strategies and methods for formative evaluation follow. The chapter concludes with a series of suggestions for improving summative evaluation of faculty. The committee emphasizes that the approaches described in this chapter are but a sampling of the techniques that appear in the research literature on improving the evaluation of teaching and student learning. They are

---

Assessment Is More Than Grades

To many, the word "assessment" simply means the process by which we assign students grades. Assessment is much more than this, however. Assessment is a mechanism for providing instructors with data for improving their teaching methods and for guiding and motivating students to be actively involved in their own learning. As such, assessment provides important feedback to both instructors and students.

Assessment Is Feedback for Both Instructors and Students

Assessment gives us essential information about what our students are learning and about the extent to which we are meeting our teaching goals. But the true power of assessment comes in also using it to give feedback to our students. Improving the quality of learning in our courses involves not just determining to what extent students have mastered course content at the end of the course; improving the quality of learning also involves determining to what extent students are mastering content throughout the course.

SOURCE: Excerpted from National Institute for Science Education (2001b).

---

included here on the basis of the committee's analysis of the research literature and the expertise of individual committee members, and with the expectation that each institution will adapt or modify these approaches according to its individual needs.

IMPROVING TEACHING BY EXAMINING STUDENT LEARNING: OUTCOME ASSESSMENT

One approach to improving student learning is outcome assessment—the process of providing credible evidence that an instructor's objectives have been obtained. Outcome assessment enables faculty to determine what students know and can do as a result of instruction in a course module, an entire course, or a sequence of courses. This information can be used to indicate to students how successfully they have mastered the course content they are expected to assimilate. It can also be used to provide faculty and academic departments with guidance for improving instruction, course content, and curricular structure. Moreover, faculty and institutions can use secondary analysis of individual outcome assessments to demonstrate to prospective students, parents, college administrators, employers, accreditation bodies,

and legislators that a program of study produces competent graduates (Banta, 2000).

Outcome Assessment Activities

Faculty members, both individually and as colleagues examining their department's education programs, have found the following activities helpful when undertaking outcome assessment:

- Developing expected student learning outcomes for an individual course of study, including laboratory skills.
- Determining the point in a student's education (e.g., courses, laboratories, and internships) at which he/she should develop the specified knowledge and skills.
- Incorporating the specified learning outcomes in statements of objectives for the appropriate courses and experiences.
- Selecting or developing appropriate assessment strategies to test student learning of the specified knowledge and skills.
- Using the results from assessment to provide formative feedback to individual students and to improve curriculum and instruction.
- Adjusting expected learning outcomes if appropriate and assessing learning again. Such a process can lead to continual improvement of curriculum and instruction.

Faculty in STEM are challenged in their teaching by a set of circumstances that most faculty in other disciplines do not encounter, such as designing laboratory and field components of courses, incorporating modern technology into courses, or supervising students involved with original research (see Chapter 2 for additional detail). However, faculty in these disciplines also have an array of assessment methodologies from which to choose that address particular learning outcomes (e.g., see Doherty et al., 2002). Student responses in each of the following formats can first be studied for the information they provide about individual student learning and performance, and then compared across students and classes for clues about the strengths and weaknesses of curriculum and instruction:

- Classroom quizzes and exams
- Projects
- Poster presentations of library or laboratory research
- Cooperative experiences
- Portfolios (collections of work)
- Standardized tests both within and across disciplines
- Student journals
- Questionnaires
- Interviews
- Focus groups

Scoring of Outcome Assessments: Primary Trait Analysis

Increasingly, primary trait analysis (Lloyd-Jones, 1977) is being used as a scoring mechanism in outcome assessment (Walvoord and Anderson, 1998). Primary trait analysis is a technique whereby faculty members consider an assignment or test and decide what traits or characteristics of student performance are most important in the exercise. They then develop a scoring rubric (Freedman, 1994) for these traits and use it to score each student's performance.

For example, Emert and Parish (1996) developed multiple-choice and short-answer tests for undergraduate students enrolled in courses in algebra, discrete mathematics, and statistics. Students were asked to submit supporting work to provide additional insight into their thought processes and the extent to which they had developed an understanding of mathematical concepts. Emert and Parish developed the following scoring rubric to assess performance on each item their students provided:

Score	Criterion
3	Conceptual understanding apparent; consistent notation, with only an occasional error; logical formulation; complete

or near-complete solution/response

2   Conceptual understanding only adequate; careless mathematical errors present (for example, algebra, arithmetic); some logical steps lacking; incomplete solution/response

1   Conceptual understanding not adequate; procedural errors; logical or relational steps missing; poor or no response to the question posed

0   Does not attempt problem, or conceptual understanding totally lacking

By studying the aggregate scores for each item, Emert and Parish and their colleagues discovered that students missed most items because they lacked the conceptual understanding to address the problem appropriately (as opposed to making careless errors). By inspecting the items missed by large numbers of students, faculty discovered which concepts needed to be addressed through instruction again, perhaps in alternative ways. Understanding such misconceptions by students can provide instructors with valuable insights into how they might adjust their teaching techniques or emphases to address these kinds of problems (see, e.g., National Research Council [NRC], 1997a, 1999b).

Benefits of Outcome Assessment

It can be difficult and time-consuming for faculty to redesign course objectives to focus on student learning outcomes, to agree with colleagues on comprehensive learning outcomes for the entire curriculum, and to select or develop appropriate assessment tools. It can be equally or more difficult for faculty to adopt a routine of systematically collecting and studying assessment data and then making improvements based on that feedback. However, some examples of positive, multidimensional change have been documented from departments that have taken assessment seriously. These departments update curricula continuously. They develop new courses and phase out others as needs change. And they can document improvement in student learning (Wergin, 1995; Wergin and Swingen, 2000).

Other changes that have been prompted by outcome assessment include faculty employing more active learning strategies that enable students to practice the concepts they are learning in class. Alumni and employers are being asked to comment on curriculum and instruction and even to serve as evaluators of teaching and learning. For example, at Virginia Polytechnic Institute and State University, the Department of Civil Engineering created an alumni advisory board and asked its members to debrief a group of juniors and seniors regarding the department's curriculum. The students discussed such issues as overcrowding due to space limitations. In response, the soil mechanics laboratory was expanded through privately sponsored renovation. In addition, students' concerns about opportunities to learn to use the latest software led to the development of a new computer laboratory. And a perceived need for improved communication skills encouraged faculty to develop new writing-intensive courses and introduce them into the civil engineering curriculum (Banta et al., 1996).

Outcome assessment can be difficult to implement because it requires that faculty reorient their course and curriculum objectives to focus on what students learn rather than what faculty teach. Nonetheless, the committee has concluded that outcome assessment can be an important approach to emphasizing and focusing on what and how students learn.

OTHER STRATEGIES AND METHODS FOR FORMATIVE EVALUATION

Formative Evaluation by Undergraduate Students

Research has shown that the best way to improve teaching is to provide indi-vidual faculty members, particularly in their first years of teaching, with *ongoing* individualized formative feedback from students and colleagues (Brinko, 1993; Cambridge, 1996; Centra, 1993; Hutchings, 1996). Instructors are best served by informal evaluation activities that take place throughout a course, especially when coupled with consultations with learning experts.[1] Such informal activities can help instructors identify what is working and what needs to be improved while the course is still in progress.

For example, helpful and regular feedback from students allows midcourse corrections in such areas as organization, methods of teaching, and the introduction or modification of activities designed to enhance learning. Many institutions have already recognized the benefits of such midcourse corrections and offer faculty guidance and appropriate forms for conducting various levels of student surveys (see Appendix B). The National Institute for Science Education (NISE) provides a "Student Assessment of Learning Gains" website where faculty can use and modify questionnaires designed to

---

[1]In contrast, Marsh and Roche (1993) report that feedback gathered at the end of a course had significantly greater long-term impact on the improvement of teaching than midcourse evaluations.

offer both formative and summative feedback from their students about how various elements of their courses are helping the students learn. This innovative website also allows students to complete the survey form on line and provides instructors with a statistical analysis of the students' responses.[2]

The results of studies on formative evaluations of student learning indicate that the techniques described below require modest effort, are easy to carry out, and consume very little class time. In addition, faculty can obtain regular feedback from their students through the use of course listservs, electronic mail, or a website for student feedback connected to a course's website.

Repeated Measurements of Student Learning and Teaching Effectiveness

The typical end-of-course student evaluation form is an indirect assessment tool that can help an instructor understand what worked to assist learning in a course and what did not. Instructors may feel that students' scores on final examinations in their courses provide a valid measure of student learning and that this measure

can also be used to assess their effectiveness as a teacher summatively. However, many factors other than the instructor's teaching competence can affect examination results, including prior knowledge; students' preconceptions; and their ability, interest, and skills in the subject area (Centra, 1993).

Another factor is student effort. Even the most effective teachers can do only so much to motivate students. Although most college teachers try to motivate students to learn, in the end students must take responsibility for their own learning and academic achievement. For the past three years, the Carnegie Foundation for the Advancement of Teaching and Pew Forum on Undergraduate Learning (2002) have published annually the *National Survey of Student Engagement: The College Student Report*. Each of these reports is compiled from responses to a questionnaire whose respondents consist of thousands of first-year and senior undergraduates at 4-year colleges and universities.[3] The students are asked about the extent to which they participate in classroom and campus activities shown by research studies to be important to learning. Questions from the

_____

[2]Additional information and links to the survey forms are available at <http://www.wcer.wisc.edu/salgains/instructor/>.

[3]The list of institutions that participated in this project is available at <http://www.indiana.edu/~nsse/>.

2001 survey instrument are provided in Appendix B.[4] This instrument and its parent, the College Student Experiences Questionnaire (Indiana University, 2000), can provide important information about the quality of effort students are committing to their work.

If a teaching evaluation form is distributed only at the end of a course, it cannot help the instructor make useful modifications for students who are currently enrolled. A better way to assess student learning and teaching effectiveness is to test students at the beginning and then again at the end of a course and inspect the "gain scores." An instructor's willingness and ability to use gain scores to improve a course may be considered favorably during a summative evaluation of teaching. At the same time, gain scores are easily misinterpreted and manipulated and may not be statistically reliable (both pre- and post-tests are characterized by unreliability that is compounded when the two are used together). Therefore, they should not be used exclusively to examine student learning for purposes of summative evaluation.

Another indirect measure of student learning that some faculty have found particularly useful is a questionnaire that lists the learning outcomes for a course or series of courses. Students may be asked to indicate how much the course or the entire curriculum increased their knowledge and skills in the specified areas.

For maximum usefulness, teachers may want to add their own course-related items to student evaluation forms, as well as encourage written or oral communication from students, including computer-assisted feedback. Evaluations of laboratory, field, and extra clinical or discussion sections require special questions, as do evaluations of student advising (NISE, 2001a).

Direct Questioning of Students

The easiest way to find out whether students understand what is being said is to ask them directly. But unless instructors have developed sufficient rapport and mutual respect among the students in their class, they should avoid questions or situations that could make it awkward for students to respond ("Who is lost?") or are so generic as to lead to nonresponses ("Are there any questions?"). Instead, instructors should pose questions that encourage more specific responses, (e.g., "How many of you are understanding what we are talking about?"). Various forms of information technology, such as in-class response keypads, can facilitate asking such questions, allowing students to

_____
[4]The survey instruments for both 2000 and 2001 are also available at <http://www.indiana.edu/~nsse/>.

answer without fearing that they will be singled out or ridiculed by their peers if they indicate their lack of understanding.

Even better, instructors can ask students to paraphrase briefly the key points or essence of a discussion or lecture. At the end of a class session, students can be asked individually or in pairs to write a brief summary of the main ideas presented and submit it to the instructor (anonymously). If this method is used, students should clearly understand that the written summary is not a quiz and will not be graded.

Minute Papers and Just-in-Time Teaching

At the end of a class, instructors can ask students to write for a minute or two on one of the following kinds of questions: "What is the most significant thing you've learned today?" "What points are still not clear?" or "What question is uppermost in your mind at the end of today's class?" Responses can help instructors evaluate how well students are learning the material. Student responses to the second and third questions also can help instructors select and structure topics for the next class meeting. Large numbers of such short papers can be read quickly, and a review of unclear concepts can take place at the next class meeting (Angelo and Cross, 1993; Schwartz, 1983).

A similar approach, developed by the physics education community, is "just-in-time" teaching (Dougherty, 1999). Students are asked to respond to one or two short questions posed by the instructor the day before a subject is to be taught. They submit their responses via e-mail or to a website. These responses give the instructor a good idea of what the students do and do not understand about the concepts to be considered. The instructor can then adjust the amount of time spent on explaining the concepts, working through problems, or providing examples that will help the students learn and understand the concepts.

Student Teams

Another documented approach involves asking a team of students to work throughout the term on continuous course evaluation (Baugher, 1992; Greene, 2000; Wright et al., 1998). The team members are encouraged to administer questionnaires and interview their peers about how the instructor is or is not promoting learning.

For larger classes, a liaison committee of two to four students can be established that meets periodically with the instructor to discuss difficulties or dissatisfactions. Membership on the committee can be rotated from a list of volunteers as long as the entire class knows who the liaisons are at any given time. Alternatively, students who are not enrolled in a course can be hired to attend the class and offer ongoing feedback to the instructor (e.g., Greene, 2000).

Students' Course Notes

With students' permission, instructors can ask to borrow a set of notes. This technique allows teachers to see what students consider to be the main points presented and whether there is misinformation or confusion about various topics. Alternatively, to ensure student anonymity, students can be asked to photocopy selected portions of their notes and submit them to the instructor without identifying information (Davis, 1993).

Chain Notes

In small classes, it may be possible to pass around a piece of paper midway through a session and ask students to jot down the main point of what is being discussed at that moment. The instructor then has a listing of what students consider to be the key concepts discussed in that class period, which can be used (Angelo and Cross, 1993).

Student Study Groups

Students can be encouraged to form small study groups and to send representatives to discuss any difficulties or questions with the instructor. Study groups provide students with opportunities to learn from one another, and a group may find it easier to seek assistance from the instructor. In turn, having group representatives rather than individual students approach the instructor can reduce the amount of time required to answer repetitive questions, especially in larger classes.

Informal Conversations

Instructors can seek feedback through informal conversations with students during office hours, before or after class, or through e-mail. They can ask students about what has been working well or what is problematic. Instructors should not pose these questions to students in ways or at times that might force them to answer quickly. Questions should be directed to those students the teacher thinks would be most likely to respond candidly. Whenever this kind of feedback is solicited, instructors should keep in mind that such evidence is anecdotal and may not be representative of the entire class. However, informal responses from individual students can serve as the basis for index card questions to the entire class (discussed next). Asking such questions based on informal conversations with students can also reinforce the message that the instructor is listening to students and takes input from them seriously.

Index Cards

Several times during the term, an instructor can pass out index cards to students and ask them to respond to two questions, one on the front of the card, the other on the back. General questions can be posed, such as "What are your overall impressions of the course?" "What's good about the course?" "Do you have any suggestions for changing the course?" or "Are there any problems?" Alternatively, the instructor can ask more specific questions about aspects of the course, such as "Are the problem sets too difficult?" or "Is the laboratory section well connected to other aspects of the course?" Providing prompts (such as "I would like you to do more . . . " or "I would like you to do less . . . ") and asking students to complete the sentence is another useful technique (Davis, 1993).

Outside Evaluators

Midway through the term, an instructor can invite an instructional improvement specialist from the campus-wide or discipline-based teaching and learning center or a departmental colleague to conduct an oral evaluation with his or her students. At the beginning of the class, the teacher introduces the guest evaluator and then leaves the room for 20 minutes. During that time, the evaluator asks students to cluster into groups of five or six and take 10 minutes to (1) select a spokesperson who will write down the group's comments, (2) name something in the course they find very helpful or worthwhile, (3) name something they would like to see changed, and (4) suggest how the course could be improved. After the groups have completed their work, the evaluator asks the spokesperson from each group to report. The evaluator summarizes the points of consensus for the entire class and also clarifies points of disagreement. The evaluator then provides an oral or written summary for the instructor (Clark and Redmond, 1982).

Small Group Instruction Diagnosis[5]

This technique (also known by its abbreviation, SGID) originated at the University of Washington and is now promoted by teaching and learning centers on a variety of types of cam-

---

[5]The description of small group instruction diagnosis presented here is based on information taken from the websites of several campus centers for teaching and learning. A more detailed description of this approach, along with links to other websites and resources on the subject, is available from a website at Miracosta Community College, <http://www.miracosta.cc. ca.us/home/gfloren/sgid.htm>. *Small Group Instructional Diagnosis*, an online journal from the National Teaching and Learning Forum that publishes research on the uses of the method, is available at <http://www.ntlf.com/html/pi/9705/ sgid.htm>.

puses. The goal of SGID is to align expectations for improving teaching and learning. Consultants are employed to gather information directly from students and instructors. The technique provides feedback to instructors, including suggestions for strengthening their courses, and generally increases communication between students and instructors. The consultative process takes anywhere from 15 to 60 minutes and is most effective when conducted near midsemester so the faculty member will have sufficient time to amend the course.

Classroom interviews involve the consultant interviewing students, in the instructor's absence, to identify course strengths and areas for change. The consultant summarizes this information and meets with the instructor to discuss students' perceptions and pedagogical options. Research at the University of Washington on the use of class interviews indicates that students appreciate the opportunity to provide feedback to their instructor before the end of the quarter.

Response to Students' Concerns

It is important that the issues posed in a midsemester evaluation be ones to which the instructor will be able to respond during the term. Otherwise, students may develop false expectations about the remainder of the course.

Instructors should emphasize to students that they would like to receive candid, constructive responses that will help them improve the course.

It also is important for the instructor to respond quickly and candidly to students' comments and concerns. Davis (1993) discusses strategies for responding to student feedback. She sorts student suggestions for improvement into three categories: (1) improvements that can be instituted immediately during the current semester (e.g., the turnaround time on grading homework assignments); (2) those that must wait until the next time the course is offered (e.g., the textbook or readings assigned); and (3) those that the instructor either cannot or, for pedagogical or curricular reasons, will not change (e.g., the number of tests, specific content).

At the class meeting after an evaluation exercise, the instructor should thank students for their comments and clarify any confusion or misunderstandings noted in those comments about the instructor's goals or the students' expectations. The instructor should then indicate which suggestions would be implemented this term, those that must wait until the course is next offered, and those on which action cannot or will not be taken. In the third case, it would be helpful to explain briefly the reasons for this decision.

Formative Evaluation by Graduate Teaching Assistants

Teaching assistants can be an invaluable source of feedback for faculty members about successes and problems that are occurring in classes, discussion sections, and teaching laboratories. Such feedback can be especially illuminating if teaching assistants are encouraged to attend class sessions regularly and to meet with the faculty member in charge of the course and with each other. Ways in which teaching assistants can provide appropriate feedback to individual faculty and to their academic department include the following:

- Encouraging teaching assistants to provide information throughout the term about the difficulties students may be having in the courses with which the teaching assistants are involved. Through conversations with and direct observation of students in the course, teaching assistants can tell an instructor what aspects of the course readings, assignments, and presentations are causing problems for students. Such information is more likely to be offered if instructors make it clear that identifying students' difficulties is a normal and expected part of a teaching assistant's responsibilities. Some faculty ask teaching assistants to give them brief weekly reports on the one or two things that cause students the most difficulty.

- Asking teaching assistants to review examinations and quizzes before they are given to students. Having participated in the course, teaching assistants can identify ambiguous or unclear exam items before the tests are administered. After midterms or quizzes have been graded, teaching assistants can provide detailed information about patterns of error or misunderstanding. Collecting this kind of information from a number of teaching assistants from different courses, from sections within a course, and over an extended period of time can also enable departments to determine which concepts need to be reinforced in several courses or which misconceptions persist as students advance through the curriculum.

- Soliciting from teaching assistants constructive suggestions on aspects of a course or the department's programs, such as websites, laboratory offerings, and similarities and differences in approaches to teaching and assessing student learning in different sections of the same course.

Formative Evaluation by Faculty Colleagues

Traditionally, faculty members have willingly and candidly judged their colleagues' scholarly work through a variety of means (see Chapter 3) but have hesitated when asked to judge their colleagues' teaching effectiveness. Yet many senior faculty have the background and perspective needed to provide judgments about such matters as the candidate's knowledge of the subject, course content, appropriateness of course objectives and instructional materials, examination skills, testing proficiency, and breadth and depth of student learning. Under the right circumstances, these judgments can be used to assist in summative evaluations of faculty (see also Chapter 4). Similar judgments from colleagues also can be useful in formative evaluations for professional development of faculty.

At small institutions or in very small departments, a lack of resources or limited numbers of faculty may make faculty input more difficult to obtain than in larger institutions or departments. In addition, friendships or rivalries that arise within any department may be amplified in smaller departments. In such cases, balanced and objective evaluations of teaching colleagues may be achieved only by including in the evaluation process additional faculty from outside the academic unit of the person being evaluated. Even when these issues do not surface, engaging faculty from outside the department, particularly those who are knowledgeable about effective pedagogies for promoting student learning, should enable review

of such critical aspects of teaching as course organization, teaching methods, and the instructor's choice of appropriate assessment practices.

Observation

Instructors who are being evaluated can ask a mentor, colleague, or instructional improvement specialist at the campus or discipline-based teaching and learning center to visit their classes and provide feedback on their teaching. Prior to each visit, instructors can discuss with observers the specific classroom issues or techniques on which the observers should focus (e.g., student–teacher interaction, the nature of questions posed, use of class time, and other issues important to the instructor).

Faculty also can ask colleagues, particularly those known to be excellent teachers, for permission to visit their courses. Visitors can note the specific techniques used by the colleague in leading discussions, conducting teaching laboratories, and so on. If time permits after class, the observing and observed faculty members can discuss their respective teaching philosophies, goals, instructional methods, out-of-class preparation, and similar matters. It is usually most helpful for a faculty member to attend a series of classes (say, all classes dealing with a specific topic or issue) to obtain a broad perspective on the range of pedagogical approaches used by the colleague in his or her teaching.

Role of Colleagues in "Formal" Formative Evaluation

Informal discussions and efforts to improve instruction among faculty members take place daily, but some departments and institutions employ more systematic and formal efforts to assist in the improvement of teaching through formative evaluation. In addition to the evaluation questionnaires reprinted in Appendix C, the following approaches to formative evaluation can be especially useful for the purposes of faculty professional development.

Faculty mentoring faculty. Increasingly, departments are assigning senior faculty as mentors to untenured faculty. Boice (1992) found that it was not necessary for successful mentors to be from the same department. Whether from within or outside of the faculty member's department, the ideal faculty mentor appears to play four major roles: friend, source of information, and career and intellectual guide (NRC, 1997b; Sands et al., 1991).

At a variety of higher education institutions, Katz and Henry (1988) developed a strategy of transdisciplinary mentoring based on faculty working together to understand both how

students learn and how to improve their teaching. Referred to as the Master Faculty Program, this initiative involves faculty working together in pairs or in triads. Faculty members observe each other's classes and interview each other's students several times during the semester. Interviewers' questions emphasize student learning in the course (for example, topics that may be difficult or reactions to specific class sessions). With these observations in hand, the faculty participating in the program meet periodically to discuss candidly, and confidentially, how each participant has or has not fostered student learning. Chandler (1991) has documented the generally positive results of this type of program involving some 300 faculty at 21 different colleges and universities.

Formative evaluation by faculty colleagues from other institutions. Faculty at higher education institutions across the country and around the world can provide formative evaluation to colleagues via the Internet. They can comment on the content of a faculty member's websites for courses, old examination questions, assignments, and student responses to questions posed by the faculty member. This kind of input from colleagues at other institutions could be included as part of a teaching portfolio or dossier for summative evaluation, but also has great potential for ongoing formative feedback.

Projects of the American Association for Higher Education. The American Association for Higher Education (AAHE) has promoted collaboration in assessing and improving teaching through a variety of projects. One such project, conducted in the mid-1990s, involved 12 universities and stressed peer review as a means of formative evaluation. In this project, participants monitored their progress in improving student learning. AAHE's (1993) *Making Teaching Community Property: A Menu for Peer Collaboration and Peer Review* provides many other examples of peer review efforts that contribute to formative evaluation and improved professional development in teaching for faculty.

More recently, AAHE, the Carnegie Foundation for the Advancement of Teaching, and the Carnegie Academy for the Scholarship of Teaching and Learning jointly developed a program for peer collaboration based on ideas and criteria advanced by Boyer (1990) and Glassick and colleagues (1997). The goals of the program are to support the development of a scholarship of teaching and learning that will foster significant, long-lasting learning for all students. The program also seeks to enhance the practice and profession of

teaching and bring to the scholarship of teaching the same kinds of recognition and reward afforded for other forms of scholarly work (Hutchings, 2000).[6] Examples of the criteria being advanced for evaluating a faculty member's scholarship in teaching are presented in Box 5-1, excerpted from Glassick et al. (1997, p. 36). Centra (2001) has extended these criteria to allow for evaluation of the scholarship of teaching and learning as practiced by academic departments and institutions (see Box 5-2).

Self-Evaluation

Self-reports and self-reflections on an instructor's teaching and promotion of student learning can be important sources of information for evaluating a teacher's effectiveness (Hutchings, 1998). These self-reports, which may be part of a required annual report or a teaching portfolio, are more useful and appropriate for formative or professional development purposes than for summative personnel decisions. Faculty who have not previously performed self-evaluation may require assistance from teaching and learning centers.

As a summary of a professor's major teaching accomplishments and

---

[6]Additional information about this program is available at <http://www.carnegiefoundation.org/CASTL/index.htm>.

Box 5-1. Evaluating the Scholarship of Teaching

Clear Goals: Does the scholar state the basic purposes of his or her work clearly? Does the scholar define objectives that are realistic and achievable? Does the scholar identify important questions in the field?

Adequate Preparation: Does the scholar show an understanding of existing scholarship in the field? Does the scholar bring the necessary skills to his or her work? Does the scholar bring together the resources necessary to move the project forward?

Appropriate Methods: Does the scholar use methods appropriate to the goals? Does the scholar apply effectively the methods selected? Does the scholar modify procedures in response to changing circumstances?

Significant Results: Does the scholar achieve the goals? Does the scholar's work add consequentially to the field? Does the scholar's work open additional areas for further exploration?

Effective Presentation: Does the scholar use a suitable style and effective organization to present his or her work? Does the scholar use appropriate forums for communicating work to its intended audiences? Does the scholar present his or her message with clarity and integrity?

Reflective Critique: Does the scholar critically evaluate his or her own work? Does the scholar bring an appropriate breadth of evidence to his or her critique? Does the scholar use evaluation to improve the quality of future work?

SOURCE: Glassick et al. (1997, p. 36).

---

strengths (Shore et al., 1986), the teaching portfolio may include the following kinds of evidence of teaching effectiveness:

- Development of new courses
- Products of good teaching (for example, student workbooks or logs, student pre- and post-examination results, graded student essays)
- Material developed by the individual (course and curriculum development materials, syllabi, descriptions of

how various materials were used in teaching, innovations the instructor has attempted and an evaluation of their success, videotapes of teaching)

- Material or assessments from others (student work and evaluations, input from colleagues or alumni)
- Descriptions of how the individual has remained current in the field, such as using knowledge gained from attending professional conferences (Edgerton et al., 1991; Shore et al., 1986)

Box 5-2. Framework and Examples of Practices/Policies for Evaluating the Scholarship of Teaching

Dimensions of the Scholarship of Teaching

Making Teaching Public	Focusing on Teaching Practices and Learning Outcomes	Having Content and Pedagogical Knowledge

Departments That Practice the Scholarship of Teaching

• Have a system of peer review of teaching. • Discuss teaching and subject content topics at department meetings. • Encourage members to prepare teaching portfolios. • Have a mentoring system for teaching. • Encourage classroom visits and discussions of teaching. • Support attendance at conferences and workshops on teaching.	• Administer major field-level exams or other assessments. • Encourage team teaching or interdisciplinary courses. • Encourage teaching innovations. • Encourage research on teaching and learning. • Seek student perceptions on teaching practices, learning practices, and learning outcomes.	• Sponsor seminars or workshops on teaching in the discipline. • Encourage diverse approaches to teaching. • Reward staff who publish or give conference papers on teaching.

Institutions That Practice the Scholarship of Teaching

- Encourage student evaluations of teaching.
- Support a mentoring program for teachers.
- Sponsor seminars, workshops, or conferences on teaching and learning.
- Require/ encourage faculty to prepare teaching portfolios or detailed reports on teaching.
- Periodically review teaching.
- Publish results of learning outcome and teaching environment surveys.
- Weigh teaching performance heavily in hiring and promotion decisions.
- Encourage a peer review program.

- Have active programs or centers to support teaching and learning.
- Have training program for teaching assistants.
- Provide grants to support research on teaching and learning.
- Have a plan for assessing student-learning outcomes.
- Survey students and graduates on learning experiences.
- Use evidence of student learning in hiring and promotion decisions.
- Reward the use and development of effective teaching practices.

- Reward teachers/ departments that promote the use of means by which discipline knowledge can be related to students.
- Have staff development programs that emphasize diverse teaching practices.

SOURCE: Centra (2001, pp. 8–9).

- External support obtained for such purposes as improving teaching or purchasing instrumentation for teaching laboratories

Videotaping

Videotaping is a useful strategy that enables instructors to see what they do well and what needs to be improved. In consultation with an expert from the campus's teaching and learning center, instructors can determine whether they exhibit such classroom behaviors as dominating a discussion, allowing students enough time to think through questions, or encouraging all students to participate in discussions. Faculty who have been videotaped find the experience extremely helpful, especially if they discuss the analysis with someone having expertise in classroom behavior. Videotaping is best used for formative evaluation.

Before-and-After Self-Assessment

Faculty members can use before-and-after self-assessment to determine whether course outcomes meet their expectations. Before a course begins, the instructor writes brief comments about the types of students for whom the course is intended. Given that audience, the instructor lists the most important course and learning goals and the teaching strategies she or he will design to achieve them. Once the semester has been completed, the instructor prepares a similar brief description of the types of students who actually enrolled, the instructional methods that were used, and how the students' achievement of major goals was measured. The evaluation should address (1) goals the instructor believes were met and evidence of student learning and academic achievement, (2) goals that were not realized, (3) the nature of and possible reasons for discrepancies between the instructor's original intentions and actual outcomes, and (4) how the instructor might modify the course in the future to achieve more of the intended goals. These self-assessments can become part of a teaching portfolio that can later be used for more summative types of evaluation.

Another form of before-and-after assessment may help instructors who are interested in examining their teaching behaviors and effectiveness rather than course outcomes. For this technique, instructors use the end-of-course evaluation form, but complete the questionnaire before their course begins (predicting how they think they will do) and again at the end of the semester (how they believe they did). They also may wish to fill out a questionnaire at the end of the term based on what they expect, on average, their students will say about their teaching. In most cases, such self-evaluations are likely to be more positive than student ratings (Centra, 1973; Feldman, 1989). In looking at the results, instructors may wish to focus on any deficiencies noted in the self-evaluation or on discrepancies between their own evaluations and those of their students.

SUMMATIVE EVALUATION OF TEACHING

Evaluations from Undergraduate Students

Questionnaires are most commonly used for summative student evaluations of teaching. The questionnaires can be machine-scored and fall into two categories: those developed locally by campus teaching and learning centers by consulting the literature or adapting forms used elsewhere, and those developed by other institutions or organizations and made available for a fee.

Questionnaires vary somewhat in the characteristics of teachers and courses covered, as well as in the quality and usefulness of the scores generated for the instructor. Typically, student evaluation instruments have attempted to identify strengths and weaknesses of instructors in the following areas:

- organization or planning;
- teacher–student interactions;
- clarity and communication skills;
- workload assigned and perceived difficulty of a course;
- quality and fairness of grading, assignments, and examinations;
- students' ratings of their own learning and progress; and
- students' ratings of their level of effort, attendance, and participation in the course, completion of assignments, and motivation.

Questionnaires used for student evaluations sometimes address aspects of a faculty member's teaching style that may or may not contribute to student learning. For example, they may ask whether the faculty member makes eye contact with students during discussions, how many questions the instructor poses during class (as compared with the nature of the questions), or how often students may be assigned to work in groups rather than work alone. Such questions are appropriate only if they are explicitly intended to provide formative feedback for the instructor, but should not be used for summative purposes. Each instructor has a unique personality, persona, and approach to teaching. The primary concern when developing or analyzing questions on student questionnaires for purposes of summative evaluation should be whether the students are actually learning at the desired level and in ways that are consistent with the course goals (Rosenthal, 1976).

Global ratings of the course overall or the teacher's instructional effectiveness also are common to most student questionnaires. For courses in science and engineering, special questions about the efficacy of laboratories, fieldwork, and research experiences also can be included as part of the standardized form or posed in a separate questionnaire. For example, the University of Washington provides separate evaluation forms for laboratories, as well as for clinics and seminars (e.g., University of Washington Education Office of Educational Assessment[7]). Appendix B provides more specific information about and several examples of student questionnaires for evaluating undergraduate teaching. See also Davis (1988) for compilation of questions that can be used on an end-of-course questionnaire.

It is important to note that questionnaires usually do not permit students to assess such characteristics as an instructor's level of knowledge of subject matter. Students cannot and should not evaluate instructors in this regard. Instead, faculty peers and colleagues should assess these characteristics of an instructor's teaching. Additional detail about the use of student evaluations for summative purposes is provided in Appendix A.

Summative Evaluation by Graduate Teaching Assistants

If a department wishes to involve teaching assistants in performing summative evaluations of faculty or improving a department's educational offerings and approaches to teaching and learning, both the teaching assistants and faculty must feel confident that the procedures for gathering information will preserve the assistants' anonymity. Teaching assistants need to know before participating how the information will be used and who will see the data.

When evaluations from teaching assistants are to be used for personnel decisions, the department might consider asking for written assessments. Alternatively, a system might be established whereby teaching assistants would be interviewed informally by a member of the evaluation committee and their comments recorded and submitted collectively. In either case, teaching assistants should be asked to indicate the basis for their assessment. Such information might include the number of courses they have taught with the instructor, descriptions of their training and supervisory activities, the nature and amount of their contact with undergraduate students, whether they

---

[7]Additional information is available at <http://www.washington.edu/oea/>.

were allowed to obtain informal student opinions about the course, and the extent to which they observed each major aspect of the course (e.g., lecture, laboratory).

Teacher assistants can be asked for the following kinds of information:

- An overall judgment of the effectiveness of the faculty member's teaching.
- An analysis of the particular strengths and weaknesses of the teaching as reflected in the design, preparation, and conduct of the course. If the department wants specific comments on particular aspects of teaching, the instructions to the teaching assistants should emphasize the need for supporting evidence.
- The extent to which working with the instructor contributed to the teaching assistant's own professional development in teaching.
- The appropriateness of the instructor's assignments and expectations of the teaching assistants.

For each question posed, the teaching assistants should be encouraged to supply specific examples. If their responses are summarized for personnel decisions, the summary must indicate the number of teaching assistants who worked with the faculty member and the number from whom information was obtained.

Summative Evaluation by Faculty Colleagues

The following approaches might help some institutions obtain more systematic and complete information on teaching performance for purposes of summative evaluation. When these approaches could also be useful for formative evaluation, this is noted.

Ad Hoc Committees on Teaching Effectiveness

The department might appoint an ad hoc committee on teaching to evaluate each faculty member who is being considered for tenure or promotion. At smaller institutions, where final decisions for promotion and tenure may rest with an institution-wide committee rather than individual departmental committees, a similar panel separate from the committee on tenure and promotion could be established regularly to review the institution's policies with regard to the process and use of summative evaluations for teaching.

The only responsibility of such ad hoc committees would be to evaluate teaching performance. The committee could consist of senior faculty members, one or two junior faculty members, and one or more graduate or senior-level undergraduate students. One or more of these ad hoc committee members should be from outside the candidate's department.

The materials to be considered by the committee could include a variety of teaching-related materials, all of which would be supplied by the candidate: course syllabi and examinations, teaching and learning aids, and evidence of the impact of the candidate's teaching on students' learning and intellectual growth. The faculty member also could be asked to submit documentation for the following: currency of course content, participation in the design of courses, contributions to curriculum and instruction, supervision of student research, advising duties, preparation of teaching assistants (if appropriate), and individual and collaborative efforts to improve teaching effectiveness.

Candidates should also prepare and submit a self-assessment of their teaching effectiveness. The self-assessment could address questions such as the following: What are the goals of your teaching? Why were these goals selected? How did you know whether students were gaining competence and learning the material? How well did the courses meet your learning goals for your students, and how do you know? What problems, if any, did you encounter in attempting to meet these goals? How did you conduct the course and challenge and engage students? How did your methods take into account the levels and abilities of students? How satisfied were you with the course?

What were the strong and weak points of your teaching? What would you change or do differently the next time you teach the course? What did you find most interesting and most frustrating about the course?

The candidate's department chair also could provide the committee with student evaluations from courses taught previously, names and addresses of student advisees, dissertation advisees, enrollees in past and current courses, and the candidate's cumulative teaching portfolio if one has been prepared. The candidate should see the list of materials submitted to the committee and be given the opportunity to supplement it.

Through brief interviews, telephone calls, letters, or brief survey questionnaires issued to the candidate's current and former students from a variety of courses, the committee could compile a picture of students' views of the teacher that would supplement the written evaluation reports from past courses. In addition, each committee member could observe and evaluate at least two of the candidate's classes.

Studies of such ad hoc committees revealed that members met several times to discuss their individual findings, used a rating form, and prepared a report, which was then submitted to a departmental tenure and promotion committee (see Centra, 1993, pp. 129–131 for details). Given the highly positive reliability coefficients reported by Root (1987) for colleague evaluations when the colleagues are properly prepared, one can conclude that the assessments of a faculty member's teaching effectiveness thus provided are reliable.

Colleagues' Evaluation Questionnaires

Several questionnaires have been designed to elicit colleagues' evaluation of a candidate's teaching effectiveness for summative evaluation purposes, although they may also be used for formative evaluation. Two forms developed at Syracuse University and the University of Texas at Austin provide scaled-response items and open-ended questions that faculty colleagues and department chairs can use to guide their analysis of a candidate's chosen instructional materials, as well as teaching behaviors they observe during classroom visits. These forms, printed in their entirety in Appendix C, cover questions grouped under the following five characteristics of good teaching:

- organization of subject matter and course,
- effective communication,
- knowledge of and enthusiasm for subject matter and teaching,
- fairness in examinations and grading, and
- flexibility in approaches to teaching.

A form designed by French-Lazovik (1981) is also provided in Appendix C. This form offers five broad questions with which faculty peers can evaluate such dimensions as the quality of materials used in teaching. The form also lists which portfolio materials should be reviewed and suggests a focus for colleagues when examining these materials. Other institutions have developed more extensive guides to help candidates prepare for peer evaluation and to assist faculty colleagues in conducting such evaluations effectively (e.g., the University of Texas's *Preparing for Peer Evaluation*;[8] see also the many resources available through the websites of college and university teaching and learning centers throughout the United States and in other countries).[9]

While the kinds of forms included in Appendix C have proven helpful to faculty in identifying what materials and characteristics of a candidate's teaching to assess, the reliability and validity of their evaluations depend on the use of

---

[8]Additional information is available at <http://www.utexas.edu/academic/cte/PeerObserve.html>.

[9]A list of websites for teaching and learning centers of colleges and universities in Asia, Australia and New Zealand, Europe, and North America is available at <http://eagle.cc.ukans.edu/~cte/resources/websites.html>.

appropriate procedures. For example, as noted above, Root's (1987) study indicated that a minimum of three departmental colleague evaluators should use the form. They should discuss the evaluation criteria before reviewing materials and making classroom visits. Evaluators also should be provided with examples of evaluations from other candidates, both internal and external, that illustrate high and low ratings.

EFFECTIVE IMPLEMENTATION OF EVALUATION METHODOLOGIES

Before revising and implementing policies and procedures for evaluating teaching, especially for summative evaluation, stakeholders should proceed in ways that will confer maximum credibility on the results of their efforts. Depending on the institution in question, administrators, the academic senate or committee on tenure and promotion, and faculty must accept that the results of evaluation efforts will be helpful both in personnel decisions and in improving the teaching effectiveness of faculty. Policies and procedures that could assist in the process include the following:

• Closely involving the institution's faculty in selecting evaluation methods,

drafting the policies and procedures to be implemented at the departmental and institutional levels, and determining the procedures to be used for analyzing and reviewing the results of summative evaluations of teaching.

• Recognizing and addressing as part of the system of evaluation the full range of teaching styles and activities, both in and out of class. Effective evaluation systems should be able to assess a broad range of teaching styles and approaches.

• Making evaluation forms and supporting documents freely available to faculty so they understand what information will be considered legitimate and relevant in the evaluation of their teaching performance.

• Establishing uniform procedures for collecting and using information from students. For example, institution-wide procedures should be defined that protect the anonymity of respondents and ensure that instructors do not see end-of-semester student evaluations until after they have submitted their grade reports.

• Establishing a uniform and equitable system for the analysis and review of evaluation data, including appropriate response rates for end-of-course student questionnaires.

• Making clear which letters and surveys will be kept confidential; which can be seen by the faculty under review;

and which information, if any, will be shared with students for purposes of selecting future courses.

In addition, the following procedures could make any evaluation process more equitable and more easily accepted.

Regular Meetings Between New Faculty Members and the Department Chair

The department chair should meet with each new faculty member and make clear the department's and the institution's general expectations and policies regarding teaching. Norms of grading for assigned courses should be described. The chair also should encourage the new faculty member to consult with other department colleagues who teach the same or related courses to develop policies and procedures for establishing desired learning outcomes, pedagogical approaches, and methods for assessing learning (see, e.g., Annex Box 1-2 in Chapter 1). New faculty members should be encouraged from the beginning of their employment to contribute actively to such discussions. The chair also should encourage and assist new faculty members to work with faculty colleagues both within and outside the department on improving their teaching, and possibly assign a senior mentor to assist them.

Formative Discussions Between the Department Chair and Individual Faculty Members

Optimally, department chairs should meet at least annually with each member of the department to discuss teaching accomplishments and issues. Such meetings are especially critical for any faculty member whose teaching evaluations are substantially below the department's expectations or those of other departmental colleagues. These meetings should occur well before summative decisions are to be made so that candidates have ample opportunities to develop a plan for improving their teaching. Additional meetings at regular intervals should be scheduled to assess progress in addressing concerns.

Sharing of Faculty-Generated Teaching Portfolios

The department's academic personnel files could include a teaching portfolio for each faculty member. Faculty members could place in the portfolio copies of their course materials (including learning objectives and expected outcomes), syllabi, reading lists, assignments, examinations, and instructional materials. A website also could be established for this purpose. Depending on institutional policy, student evaluation forms or summaries of students' course evaluations also could be included in the portfolio. It should be assumed that a faculty member would continue to have access to all materials in his or her portfolio, unless letters solicited or submitted in confidence were protected under rules of the university.

Feedback from Graduating Seniors and Alumni

As part of the department's regular academic program review, graduating seniors and alumni could be surveyed. Relevant survey information about an individual instructor's teaching effectiveness would be placed in his or her teaching portfolio. Instructors should be made aware that such information will be included in their portfolios and be allowed to provide written comments or responses, where permissible.

Departmental Panel on Teaching Effectiveness and Expectations

In addition to an ad hoc department committee to monitor candidates' progress in teaching, as discussed above, the department as a whole could establish a faculty panel that would summarize the department's policies and procedures regarding expectations for teaching effectiveness, the methods and criteria used to judge that effectiveness, and the role of evaluation in academic personnel decisions. The panel would remind faculty of the resources available to them through the

institution for improving their teaching. Members of such a panel might include a former recipient of the campus teaching award, a respected senior faculty member who teaches introductory and lower division courses, and a newly tenured associate professor.

Oversight Committee to Monitor Departmental Curriculum and Instruction

The department chair could establish a permanent faculty committee to monitor the quality and effectiveness of instruction by all members of the department. This committee would also oversee all evaluations of curriculum, teaching, and student learning and, where appropriate, nominate faculty for the campus's or college's teaching awards.

Legal Considerations

All stakeholders who are involved with the evaluation of teaching must act in accordance with institutional policies that have been designed to ensure legally equitable and fair treatment of all involved parties. Such policies might require, for example, that:

• The faculty be involved in the design of an evaluation system, as well as in evaluations of colleagues.
• The institution complies with all procedures specified in contracts or

handbooks, as both are legal documents.

• The evidence that is used for personnel decisions be job-related and nondiscriminatory.

• The faculty members be allowed to respond to individual evaluation reports or to clarify information in their dossiers or portfolios.

• The procedures used in internal review of decisions be clearly elucidated and made available to all faculty.

6

Evaluation of Individual Faculty: Criteria and Benchmarks

This report thus far has synthesized the findings of research on evaluating effective teaching, and has offered specific recommendations to leaders in the higher education community for changing the climate and culture on their campuses such that the evaluation of teaching will be valued, respected, and incorporated in the fabric of the institution. The report also has emphasized that any system of teaching evaluation should serve as a critical basis for improving student learning.

The previous chapter provides a framework that departments and institutions can apply to evaluate the teaching of individual faculty. It emphasizes the need for ongoing formative evaluation that offers faculty members ample opportunities, resources, and support systems for improving their teaching prior to any summative evaluations that

might be rendered by the department or institution. This chapter presents specific criteria that can be used when summative evaluations are undertaken. These criteria are organized according to the five characteristics of effective teaching outlined in Chapter 2. It should be emphasized that the criteria suggested below are based on the committee's identification of best practices from an examination of the scholarly literature, but they are not exhaustive. Each evaluating department or institution is encouraged to select and, if necessary, modify those criteria from the compendium presented below that best suit its specific circumstances. As emphasized in Chapter 5, those who evaluate faculty teaching should be careful to use multiple—and defensible—sources of evaluation, particularly for summative purposes.

1. KNOWLEDGE OF AND ENTHUSIASM FOR SUBJECT MATTER

Summarizing the discussion of this characteristic from Chapter 2, effective teachers:

- Understand and can help students learn and understand the general principles of their discipline (e.g., the processes and limits of the scientific method).
- Provide students with an overview of the whole domain of the discipline.
- Possess sufficient knowledge and understanding of their own and related subdisciplines that they can answer most students' questions or know how to help students find appropriate information.
- Keep their knowledge about a field of study current through an active research program or through scholarly reading and other types of professional engagement with others in their immediate and related disciplines (e.g., participation in professional meetings and workshops).
- Are genuinely interested in—and passionate about—the course materials they are teaching. Practicing scientists, mathematicians, and engineers understand and appreciate the infectious enthusiasm that accompanies original discovery, application of theory, and

design of new products and processes. Conveying that sense of excitement is equally important in helping students appreciate more fully the subject matter being taught.

The following questions might be posed for evaluation for this characteristic:

- Does the instructor exhibit an appropriate depth and breadth of knowledge?
- Is the instructor's information current and relevant?
- Does the instructor show continuous growth in the field?

Data sources and forms of evaluation for this characteristic are shown in Table 6-1.

2. SKILL, EXPERIENCE, AND CREATIVITY WITH A RANGE OF APPROPRIATE PEDAGOGIES AND TECHNOLOGIES

Summarizing the discussion of this characteristic in Chapter 2, effective teachers:

- Have knowledge of and select and use a range of strategies that offer opportunities for students with different learning styles to achieve.

TABLE 6-1 Data Sources and Forms of Evaluation for Evaluating Knowledge and Enthusiasm for Subject Matter

Source of Data	Form of Evaluation	How Evaluation Data Can Be Used (formatively, summatively, or both)	Discussed in Report Beginning on Page(s)
Students	• Student evaluations	• Both	76
	• Interviews	• Both	80
Faculty Colleagues	• Review of course materials and other products	• Both	63
	• Observation	• Both	45, 51
Instructor Under Review	• Written self-appraisal	• Both	65

• Are organized and clearly communicate to students their expectations for learning and academic achievement.

• Focus on whether students are learning what is being taught and view the learning process as a joint venture between themselves and their students.

• Give students adequate opportunity to build confidence by practicing skills.

• Ask interesting and challenging questions.

• Encourage discussion and promote active learning strategies.

• Persistently monitor students' progress toward achieving learning goals through discussions in class, out-of-class assignments, and other forms of assessment.

• Have the ability to recognize those students who are not achieving to their fullest potential and then employ the professional knowledge and skill necessary to assist them in overcoming academic difficulties.

The following questions might be posed for evaluation for this characteristic:

• Does the instructor clearly communicate the goals of the course to students?

• Is the instructor aware of alternative instructional methods or teaching strategies and able to select methods of instruction that are most effective in helping students learn (pedagogical content knowledge)?

• To what extent does the instructor set explicit goals for student learning and persist in monitoring students' progress toward achieving those goals?

TABLE 6-2 Data Sources and Forms of Evaluation for Evaluating Skill in and Experience with Appropriate Pedagogies and Technologies

Source of Data	Form of Evaluation	How Evaluation Data Can Be Used (formatively, summatively, or both)	Discussed in Report Beginning on Page(s)
Current Students	• Student ratings	• Both	139
	• Outcome assessment of learning	• Both	73
Faculty Colleagues	• Review of course materials and other evidence of teaching effectiveness	• Both	63
	• Observation	• Both	45, 51
Instructor Under Review	• Written self-appraisal	• Both	65

Data sources and forms of evaluation for this characteristic are shown in Table 6-2.

3. UNDERSTANDING OF AND SKILL IN USING APPROPRIATE TESTING PRACTICES

Summarizing the discussion of this characteristic in Chapter 2, effective teachers:

• Assess learning in ways that are consistent with the learning objectives of a course and integrate stated course objectives with long-range curricular goals.

• Know whether students are truly learning what is being taught.

• Determine accurately and fairly students' knowledge of the subject matter and the extent to which learning has occurred throughout the term (not just at the end of the course).

The following questions might be posed for evaluation for this characteristic:

• Is the instructor aware of a range of tools that can be used to assess student learning?

• Does the instructor select assessment techniques that are valid, reliable, and consistent with the goals and learning outcomes of the course?

- Are students involved in contributing to the development of the assessment tools used?

- Are assignments and tests graded carefully and fairly using criteria that are communicated to students before they begin a task?

- Do students receive prompt and accurate feedback about their performance at regular intervals throughout the term?

- Do students receive constructive suggestions on how to improve their course performance?

Data sources and forms of evaluation for this characteristic are shown in Table 6-3.

4. PROFESSIONAL INTERACTIONS WITH STUDENTS WITHIN AND BEYOND THE CLASSROOM

Summarizing the discussion of this characteristic in Chapter 2, effective instructors:

- Meet with all classes and assigned teaching laboratories, post and keep regular office hours, and hold exams as scheduled.

- Demonstrate respect for students as individuals; this includes respecting the confidentiality of information gleaned from advising or student conferences.

TABLE 6-3 Data Sources and Forms of Evaluation for Evaluating Proficiency in Assessment

Source of Data	Form of Evaluation	How Evaluation Data Can Be Used (formatively, summatively, or both)	Discussed in Report Beginning on Page(s)
Current Students	• Student ratings	• Both	91
	• Interviews with selected students	• Both	59
Faculty Colleagues	• Review of course materials and other evidence of teaching effectiveness	• Both	63
	• Observation	• Both	45, 51
Instructor Under Review	• Written self-appraisal	• Both	65
Institutional Records	• Grade distribution	• Summative	66

- Encourage the free pursuit of learning and protect students' academic freedom.

- Address sensitive subjects or issues in ways that help students deal with them maturely.

- Contribute to the ongoing intellectual development of individual students and foster confidence in their ability to learn and discover on their own.

- Act as an advisor to students who are having problems with course material and know how to work with such students in other venues besides the classroom to help them achieve. When a student clearly is not prepared to undertake the challenges of a particular course, the effective instructor may counsel that student out of the course or suggest alternative, individualized approaches for the student to learn the subject matter that is prerequisite for the course.

- Uphold and model for students the best scholarly and ethical standards (e.g., University of California Faculty Code of Conduct).[1]

The following questions might be posed for evaluation for this characteristic:

---

[1]The University of California System's *Faculty Code of Conduct Manual* is available at <http://www.ucop.edu/acadadv/acadpers/apm/>.

- Taking into account differences in the difficulty and cost of undertaking research in various disciplines, undergraduate research experiences should engage students in interesting and challenging projects that help them develop additional insight into and understanding of science, as well as the specific topic on which they are working. How active has the instructor been in directing student research projects and independent studies? What is the caliber of these student projects? To what extent has the instructor fostered independent and original thinking by students and inspired them to develop sufficient independence to pursue the subject on their own? Have students been encouraged to participate in professional meetings? Has student work led to professional publications or acknowledgments?

- Does the instructor take an active interest in advisees' individual academic and career choices? How well informed is the instructor about department and university policies and procedures that concern advisees? Does the instructor provide sufficient office time for students to obtain clarification and guidance?

- How effectively does the instructor train and supervise teaching assistants assigned to his or her courses? How does the instructor contribute to the professional development of teaching

TABLE 6-4 Data Sources and Forms of Evaluation for Evaluating Professionalism with Students Within and Beyond the Classroom

Source of Data	Form of Evaluation	How Evaluation Data Can Be Used (formatively, summatively, or both)	Discussed in Report Beginning on Page(s)
Current Students	• Student ratings • Interviews • Special surveys	• Both • Summative • Summative	91 139 93
Former Students	• Retrospective assessment	• Both	60
Teaching Assistants	• Written appraisal	• Both	60
Faculty Colleagues	• Review of instructor's contributions to curriculum design and development	• Both	63
Instructor Under Review	• Written self-appraisal	• Summative	65, 93

assistants? Does the instructor treat his or her assistants with courtesy and as professional colleagues?

Data sources and forms of evaluation for this characteristic are shown in Table 6-4.

5. INVOLVEMENT WITH AND CONTRIBUTIONS TO ONE'S PROFESSION IN ENHANCING TEACHING AND LEARNING

Much can be learned from teachers who work with colleagues both on and beyond the campus. Effective teaching needs to be seen as a scholarly pursuit that takes place in collaboration with departmental colleagues, faculty in other departments in the sciences and engineering, and even more broadly across disciplines. Such conversations enable faculty to better integrate the course materials they present in their courses with what is being taught in other courses.

Summarizing the discussion of this characteristic in Chapter 2, effective teachers:

• Work with colleagues both on and beyond campus, collaborating with departmental colleagues; faculty in other departments in the sciences, mathematics, and engineering.

- Work to better integrate the materials they present in their courses with what is being taught in other courses.

The following questions might be posed for evaluation for this characteristic:

- During the term, has the instructor specifically elicited feedback from students, colleagues, or instructional experts (e.g., from the campus teaching and learning center) about the quality of his or her teaching?
- To what extent does the instructor meet his or her teaching obligations and responsibilities?

- Has the instructor made noteworthy contributions to the design and development of the department's curriculum? Has the instructor produced valuable instructional materials or publications related to teaching effectiveness or classroom activities? Has the instructor been involved in efforts to improve education or teaching within the discipline or across disciplines? Has the instructor participated in seeking external support for instrumentation or education research projects?

Data sources and forms of evaluation for this characteristic are shown in Table 6-5.

TABLE 6-5 Data Sources and Forms of Evaluation for Evaluating Professional Involvement and Contributions

Source of Data	Form of Evaluation	How Evaluation Data Can Be Used (formatively, summatively, or both)	Discussed in Report Beginning on Page(s)
Current Students	• Student ratings • Formative procedures	• Both • Formative	91 61
Instructor Under Review	• Written self-appraisal • Grant applications • Publications	• Both	65 46 48
Colleagues from Within and Outside the Institution	• Written reviews of work	• Both	79

7

Evaluation of Departmental Undergraduate Programs

The discussion in this report thus far has focused primarily on attributes of effective teaching by individual faculty members. The central theme has been that evidence of high-quality student learning should be the major criterion for measuring a faculty member's teaching effectiveness. The report has also emphasized the importance of using multiple indicators and different kinds of evaluators (e.g., students, alumni, graduate assistants, colleagues), as well as increasing reliance on ongoing formative evaluation, to provide a more holistic view of an individual's teaching effectiveness.

The committee believes that similar expectations can and should apply to academic departments and colleges. Departments should regularly evaluate their current undergraduate programs and their commitment to fostering an environment that recognizes and rein-

forces effective teaching practices and student learning. This position is consistent with the National Science Foundation's report *Shaping the Future* (NSF, 1996, pp. 63–64), which recommends that college and university governing boards and academic administrators:

- Accept responsibility for the learning of all students and make that clear not only by what the institution says but also by putting in place mechanisms to discharge that responsibility at the institutional and departmental levels.

- Hold accountable and develop reward systems for departments and programs, not just individuals, so that the entire group feels responsible for effective STEM (science, technology, engineering, and mathematics) learning for all students.

- Provide resources to ensure that faculty, particularly new faculty, have the opportunity to both learn how to and have the time to design effective instruction, use technology appropriately, foster inquiry-based and collaborative learning, and assess learning achieved.

- Make sure that the faculty reward system, in practice as well as in theory, supports faculty who effectively help students learning in hospitable environments that recognize individual students' differences and that provide reasonable opportunities to address those differences.

Academic departments serve many roles, including general education of nonmajors, professional preparation of majors, contributions to interdisciplinary or honors programs, and professional preparation of teachers and health professionals. Departments can encourage and support their members to work collectively to integrate courses and curricula and improve teaching and learning. They also can redirect their physical and financial resources to encourage continual improvement in teaching and learning. In summary, academic departments can become both the primary units for catalyzing change in undergraduate education and true learning communities (American Association for Higher Education

[AAHE], 1993; Wergin, 1994; Wergin and Swingen, 2000; Wyckoff, 2001).

Because the organization and roles of academic departments vary so widely within and among institutions, and especially among disciplines (Diamond and Adams, 1995, 2000), the task of performing any kind of systematic evaluation of these entities would appear to be nearly insurmountable. However, a number of reports have suggested how members of academic departments might assume collective responsibility for developing a coherent set of courses, programs, and other educational experiences that can enable all participating students to maximize their opportunities to learn (e.g., Shulman, 1993; Wergin, 1994; Wergin and Swingen, 2000). In addition, some disciplines have developed guidelines for evaluating undergraduate programs (e.g., for chemistry, American Chemical Society, 1992; for earth sciences, Ireton et al., 1996; for engineering, Accreditation Board for Engineering and Technology, 1998; for mathematics, Mathematical Association of America, 2000). However, many of these guidelines focus primarily on defining what is expected of students who will major in those subjects. Little attention has been paid to defining a quality education for other students who enroll in courses primarily to fulfill graduation requirements for future teachers (see McNeal and D'Avanzo, 1997).

There is growing consensus on the characteristics of effective undergraduate programs in STEM but too little effort has been expended to date on determining how measures of quality might be made more consonant and consistent with national efforts to improve undergraduate STEM education (e.g., Boyer Commission, 1998; National Research Council [NRC], 1995a, 1996a, 1999a; NSF, 1996, 1998; Rothman and Narum, 1999) or to align such programs more closely with national standards and benchmarks in these disciplines for grades K–12 (American Association for the Advancement of Science [AAAS], 1993; International Technology Education Association [ITEA], 2000; National Council of Teachers of Mathematics [NCTM], 1989, 2000; NRC, 1996b).

Members of academic departments, in conjunction with the principal academic and executive officers on their campuses, need to examine critically the criteria they currently use to evaluate the efficacy of their approaches to undergraduate education. The first step in accomplishing this task is for each department to adopt a mission statement on improving teaching and student learning. Other issues on which departmental members might focus include classroom teaching, academic advising for students, and the roles of teaching laboratories and independent research opportunities in enhancing student learning. Faculty and administrators also need to reach consensus on the underlying assumptions, guidelines, and metrics they will use to improve undergraduate programs.

Many of the issues surrounding the evaluation of teaching for individual faculty also apply to the collective performance of academic departments. The principles set forth in this report for evaluating the teaching effectiveness of individuals can easily be reshaped to apply to academic departments. This chapter lays a foundation for such discussions.

Unlike the rest of the report, this chapter offers no findings or recommendations. Instead, it articulates a series of questions that members of departments might ask themselves and each other as they examine their unit's role in fostering the improvement of undergraduate education. These questions are organized in accordance with the major responsibilities of departments in the STEM disciplines.

EVALUATING A DEPARTMENT'S ABILITY TO ENHANCE TEACHING AND LEARNING IN CLASSROOMS AND OTHER VENUES

Engaging student interest in the department's curricular offerings:

• Does the department encourage faculty members to discuss how to employ the most effective teaching techniques and educational experiences for students with various educational backgrounds and aspirations? Are the department's programs designed to engage and excite students about the discipline specifically and about STEM generally?

• Does the department evaluate the effectiveness of courses for nonmajors and for preparation of students pursuing other science or engineering majors, especially for prospective elementary and secondary teachers?

Applying research on human cognition and learning:

• Does the department encourage faculty to base instructional techniques on modern research on human cognition and learning (e.g., NRC, 1997a, 2000e)?

• Does the department sponsor seminars, workshops, or other activities to help faculty members become familiar with this research and its implications for improving teaching and learning?

Employing effective pedagogy:

• Has the department examined ways in which teaching effectiveness and student learning can be enhanced in large classes, especially large sections of introductory courses?

• Has the department established protocols for evaluating teaching based on the kinds of criteria described in this report? Have members of the department been trained to undertake evaluative procedures such as peer review of teaching (e.g., Bernstein and Quinlan, 1996; Huber, 1999)?

• Has the department developed expectations regarding the teaching expertise of new hires?

• Does the department support faculty who become engaged in active scholarship on teaching and learning? Have guidelines been established for evaluating such work for personnel decisions? Does the department encourage and support graduate students to pursue future faculty programs designed to introduce them to issues and scholarship in teaching and learning?

Assessing student learning:

• Does the department encourage faculty to discuss ways of optimizing the assessment of student learning and provide sufficient time and resources to support such efforts?

• Are student learning outcomes considered a primary criterion when assessing the success of the department's curriculum and programs?

Emphasis on improving teaching and learning in introductory and lower division courses:

• Have members of the department agreed on the role and mission of introductory courses for both majors and nonmajors?

• Does the department encourage faculty members to work together in structuring the subject matter of and approaches to teaching introductory courses?

• Do introductory courses meet the educational needs of those who will become the next generation of students in STEM, future teachers, and nonmajors in the discipline?

Incorporating advances in the discipline and related subject areas:

• Do the department's introductory and advanced courses and other educa-tional programs incorporate cutting-edge topics and skills of the discipline and present them to students in ways that are pedagogically appropriate?

• Does the department encourage colleagues to focus some of the coursework at both the introductory and upper levels on real-world applica-tions and on connections between STEM and other disciplines?

• Do members of the department seek ways to provide students who will never again have formal exposure to the sciences, mathematics, or engineering with the intellectual skills and back-ground needed to appreciate and en-gage in lifelong learning in these disci-plines?

• Does the department offer encour-agement and funding to purchase, maintain, and integrate into undergradu-ate courses cutting-edge tools and technologies (e.g., information technol-ogy, real-time data acquisition and processing, remote sensing) so that students can better appreciate and experience how advances in the disci-pline are achieved?

• Given the increasing proliferation of always-available databases, real-time data acquisition through remote sensing and instrumentation, and similar ad-vances, is the department finding ways to extend the teaching and learning of STEM beyond traditional classroom and laboratory settings?

• Does the department encourage faculty members to integrate the curriculum of lower and upper division courses?

Providing academic advising and career planning:

• Does the department view academic and career advising as central to its mission?

• Does the department encourage faculty members to become more effective academic and career advisors and provide the necessary resources and time for the purpose?

• Does the department encourage undergraduate students to undertake real-world work and academic experiences through summer and academic-year internships?

• Does the department bring people to campus for presentations to students about career options and opportunities?

EVALUATING DEPARTMENTAL EFFORTS TO IMPROVE TEACHING LABORATORIES AND OTHER UNDERGRADUATE RESEARCH EXPERIENCES

Emphasizing the role and importance of teaching laboratories:

• Have members of the department collectively established criteria for assessing the role and nature of teaching laboratories in the department's curriculum? For example, is there general agreement on whether laboratory exercises should parallel coursework, provide students with learning experiences not directly related to work in classrooms, or some combination of the two?

• Does the department encourage faculty to develop inquiry-based laboratory exercises that encourage students to develop their own hypotheses, design original experiments, and analyze data?

• Have members of the department discussed the criteria for assessing students' work in laboratories?

• Is the department familiar with the use of virtual laboratories and the current status of research comparing real and simulated approaches to laboratory teaching and learning?

Encouraging students to engage in independent research:

• Does the department encourage faculty to oversee and support students who wish to engage in independent, original research either on campus or off site (e.g., cooperative arrangements with other universities, private and government research establishments, or industry)? Does the department take advantage of undergraduate research as a way for its graduate students to grow professionally by helping to supervise such work?

- Are venues available for providing academic credit or financial compensation to students and teaching credits, time, equipment, and rewards to faculty who undertake such supervisory responsibilities?

- Has the department discussed what the role of undergraduate research should be in relation to advancing its mission of teaching, research, and service?

- Has the department considered how it might offer opportunities to engage in short- or long-term research experiences to both current and prospective teachers (especially those who will teach in the primary grades) and students who will not major in STEM?

EVALUATING INTERDEPARTMENTAL COOPERATION IN IMPROVING UNDERGRADUATE SCIENCE, TECHNOLOGY, ENGINEERING, AND MATHEMATICS EDUCATION

- Has the department established dialogues with other departments about the suitability and usefulness of its introductory courses as prerequisite or corequisite requirements for other STEM disciplines?

- Is the department's curriculum structured in ways that offer gateways for students from other departments, including those who will not major in the sciences, to continue studies within the discipline?

- Has the department worked with other STEM departments to discuss ways in which the presentation of topics common to courses in several disciplines (e.g., energy) might be better coordinated and the connections between disciplines emphasized (see NRC, 1999a, p. 36)?

- Has the department worked recently with other STEM departments and the institution's college of education to improve the preparation and continuing professional development of K–12 teachers in STEM (especially those students who plan to teach in the primary and middle grades)?

- Given the recent national emphasis on partnerships between higher education and local schools, has the department discussed with other STEM departments and local schools ways to establish such partnership programs and to recognize and reward faculty colleagues who undertake such efforts?

- Has the department worked with counterparts in local community colleges and 4-year institutions to establish policies and agreements that allow students to move more seamlessly between institutions?

8

Recommendations

In formulating its recommendations, the committee was struck by the diversity of educational institutions in the United States, the types and numbers of students they serve, and the educational traditions they represent. Two-year community colleges, small liberal arts colleges, and public and private research universities offer different educational experiences and represent different scholarly environments. Average class size, age or preparation of students, the frequently conflicting demands of teaching and research, and the degree of collective (as opposed to individual) faculty commitment to teaching can vary greatly among institutions. A problem in one setting may not be an issue in another.

The recommendations presented below are based on the four fundamental premises stated in Chapter 1 (and reiterated in Box 8-1). All of them are

A major transformation is coming in the American professoriate, if for no other reason than we are on the verge of a generational changing of the guard. Our senior faculty, appointed in large numbers during higher education's expansionist period circa 1957–1974, have begun to make choices about their retirement and later-life careers. And the next generation of faculty is already beginning to succeed them.... Leaders among the faculty and administration now in our colleges and universities have a time-limited window of opportunity to influence this transformation, and in so doing to contribute to setting future course of higher learning.

SOURCE: Rice et al. (2000, p. 1).

Box 8-1. Four Fundamental Premises

- Effective postsecondary teaching in science, technology, engineering, and mathematics (STEM) should be available to *all* students, regardless of their major.
- The design of curricula and the evaluation of teaching and learning should be collective responsibilities of faculty in individual departments or, where appropriate, performed through other interdepartmental arrangements.
- Scholarly activities that focus on improving teaching and learning should be recognized as bona fide endeavors that are equivalent to other scholarly pursuits. Scholarship devoted to improving teaching effectiveness and learning should be accorded the same administrative and collegial support that is available for efforts to improve other research and service endeavors.
- Faculty who are expected to work with undergraduates should be given support and mentoring in teaching throughout their careers; hiring practices should provide a first opportunity to signal institutions' teaching values and expectations of faculty.

To be useful, teaching evaluation has to become a feedback process. Given the aging of faculty and the public demand for better teaching, we need to consider ways of using comprehensive evaluation systems to provide faculty with feedback or information about their performance that includes recommendations for future improvement.

SOURCE: Ory (2000, p. 13).

based on the premise that evidence of student learning should be an important criterion for evaluating teaching. In turn, evaluation of teaching that is predicated on learning outcomes has implications for how teaching is honored and supported by educational institutions.

The kind of evaluation being recommended here requires the collection of different kinds of evidence that can be used to determine whether faculty and departments are indeed promoting student learning. Thus, if tenure review committees of senior faculty rely exclusively on outside letters evaluating research and teaching accomplishments, if they have had no personal involvement with methods of evaluating teaching or understanding how students learn, and if their teaching experience has been bounded only by the lecture hall, the messages they send about the importance of formative evaluation of teaching will be crystal clear and will not contribute to more effective teaching.

Another major difficulty in implementing more effective evaluation of teaching is that these activities take time from other commitments. Unless there are incentives to undertake evaluation of teaching in ways that truly enhance student learning, little change is likely to occur. As discussed in Chapter 4, Root (1987) has shown that, with appropriate training and motivation, improved evaluation can be accomplished with a manageable investment of time by the instructor's colleagues.

In addition to the priorities they set through their leadership, deans and presidents have some budgetary authority that can be used to improve teaching and its evaluation. For example, the number of faculty teaching positions in a department is generally influenced by several factors: numbers of students taught, institutional budgetary constraints, and decisions to have faculty in particular areas of expertise. In research universities and growing numbers of other types of institutions, the last criterion can be the most important, driven by external forces at work in the discipline as perceived and advocated by the resident faculty. Sometimes departments are asked to develop plans for new appointments that are based on these disciplinary issues. Less often, departments are also challenged by administrations to prepare overarching instructional plans that embrace the needs of both majors and nonmajors.

Departments that take the time to examine their educational goals and the effectiveness of their curricula should be more deserving of institutional support than those that maintain the status quo. But there is a broader purpose to this exercise than departmental self-interest in slot allocation. Faculties that explore their goals for student learning and reach consensus on how best to accomplish those goals will have created the basis for a culture and community of teaching and learning that now characterizes the research domain.

Investments of time and funds undoubtedly will be required initially for such efforts. The costs of these investments will vary greatly, depending on the kinds and levels of commitment and resources a department or institution has already expended to improve its system of evaluating teaching effectiveness. For all of the reasons highlighted in this report, however, the committee is convinced that such investment is essential to improving teaching, learning, and curriculum, and will provide ample rewards through improved efficacy of teaching and student learning.

Faculty acceptance and ownership of any process for evaluating teaching effectiveness is central to the success of that process on any campus. This report focuses on helping faculty understand the roles that various kinds of teaching evaluation can play in making them more effective instructors. Chapters 5 and 6 provide specific advice and recommendations for improving teaching through appropriate evaluation procedures. Chapter 6 also provides specific cross-references to other parts of the report where faculty can find discussion of evidence that supports the efficacy of various approaches to collecting and analyzing data used for formative and summative evaluation of teaching. Therefore, this chapter does not contain a separate set of recommendations for faculty. Instead, the recommendations listed below are directed primarily to policy makers, administrators, and leaders of organizations associated with higher education. It is they who must become deeply involved with promoting and supporting the kinds of evaluations of teaching that can lead to improved student learning. They also must establish opportunities for faculty to engage in ongoing professional and leadership development directed at the improvement of teaching and learning as a scholarly endeavor, and reward them for doing so in ways that are commensurate with those associated with other forms of scholarship.

1. Overall Recommendations

(1.1) Teaching effectiveness should be judged by the quality and extent of student learning. Many different teaching styles and methods are likely to be effective.

Although many factors are involved in judging effective teaching, evidence of student learning should be foremost among them. Reaching institution-wide consensus on this principle is a critical step that will require consideration of such questions as what different kinds of students (STEM majors, preprofessionals, and nonmajors) should be learning in each discipline and how that learning can best be fostered. Definitions of effective teaching in STEM courses in the institution should take into account what is known about student learning and academic achievement (e.g., Coppola and Jacobs, 2002; Huber and Morreale; 2002).

(1.2) Scholarly activities that focus on improving teaching and learning should be recognized and rewarded as a bona fide scholarly endeavor and accorded the types of institutional supports aimed at improving scholarship generally.

Scholarship that is devoted to improving teaching effectiveness and learning should be accorded the same administrative and collegial support that is available for other research and service endeavors. Faculty who wish to pursue scholarly work by improving teaching or engaging in educational research should be expected to conform to standards of quality similar to those for other types of scholarship (see Box 5-1 in Chapter 5). They also should be rewarded in ways that are comparable to those associated with other forms of scholarship during personnel decisions on such matters as tenure, promotion, and merit increases in salary.

(1.3) Valid summative assessments of teaching should not rely only on student evaluations, but should include peer reviews and teaching portfolios used for promotion, tenure, and post-tenure review.[1] Such assessments should be designed to provide fair and objective information to aid faculty in the improvement of their teaching. Building consensus among faculty, providing necessary resources, and relying on the best available research on teaching, learning, and measurement are critical for this approach to evaluation.

As discussed in Chapters 4 and 5, teaching portfolios, including a careful self-evaluation by the person being evaluated, can be an important tool for documenting a faculty member's accomplishments in facilitating student learning and academic achievement. Such portfolios can be used for performing summative evaluation, but equally important, for maintaining a record of personal accomplishments and teaching issues that can serve as the basis for ongoing professional development.

Regardless of whether formalized teaching portfolios are required for evaluation of teaching, faculty should collect a broad array of evidence of teaching effectiveness that can be used for both formative and summative evaluations. This evidence could include, but not be limited to, the following:

- Covering content at a level appropriate to course goals (particularly for a course in a vertical sequence).

---

[1]Other organizations, such as the American Association for Higher Education (AAHE), are currently engaged in efforts to explore issues associated with post-tenure review of faculty, including the effectiveness of their teaching. Therefore, the committee did not consider this issue in detail and offers no specific recommendations about policies for post-tenure review of faculty. Additional information about the program at AAHE and its recent publications on this issue (e.g., Licata and Morreale, 1997, 2002) is available at <http://www.aahe.org/Bulletin/aprilf1.htm>. Links to numerous other resources and policy statements on post-tenure review at individual colleges and universities are available at <http://www.google.com/search?hl=en&ie=UTF-8&oe=UTF-8&q=post-tenure+review>.

- Promoting classroom continuity by minimizing absences and providing high-quality substitutes when an absence is necessary.
- Providing time for consultation with students for informal and friendly advising.
- Being open to critiques of one's own teaching.
- Actively fostering infrastructure improvements that enhance undergraduate learning.
- Participating in departmental, college-level, or university-wide discussions of curriculum and improvement of teaching and learning.
- Supervising undergraduate research and encouraging active participation of undergraduates as contributing coauthors of published works.
- Being willing to promote participation of undergraduates in professional meetings.
- Exposing undergraduates to professional settings (e.g., industry internships, government laboratories, or study abroad).
- Being aware of and adopting innovative pedagogical approaches, including thoughtful teaching and assessment methods.
- Participating in the design of valuable laboratory experiences.
- Helping to develop innovative designs for upper division and honors courses and for lower division

multidisciplinary offerings for nonmajors.
- Participating in effective mentoring and evaluation of departmental and other colleagues.
- Supporting other colleagues' efforts to improve their teaching.

In addition, STEM departments could consider hiring faculty who have specific expertise in learning within their disciplines. These hires would know the salient resources and could share them with their departmental colleagues. Departmental cultures should encourage and provide venues for such sharing of expertise in learning, thereby fostering new teaching and learning communities (Coppola and Jacobs, 2002; Shapiro and Levine, 1999). Faculty also might be evaluated for the extent to which they help their department integrate curriculum and attend more closely to the academic needs of a broader array of students.

(1.4) Individual faculty—beginners as well as more experienced teachers—and their departments should be rewarded for consistent improvement of learning by both major and nonmajor students. All teaching-related activities—such as grading, reporting of grades, curriculum development, training of teaching assistants, and related

committee work—should be included in evaluation systems adopted for faculty rewards.

Departments should encourage their faculty to improve teaching and learning through active participation in ongoing professional development programs. Departmental faculty need to initiate and coordinate changes in departmental curricula. Chief academic and executive officers should extend significant honors to both faculty members and departments that demonstrate excellence in the practice and scholarship of teaching, as defined by members of the campus teaching and learning community and the criteria presented in this report (e.g., Svinicki and Menges, 1996).

(1.5) Faculty should accept the obligation to improve their teaching skills as part of their personal commitment to professional excellence. Departments and institutions of higher education should reinforce the importance of such professional development for faculty through the establishment and support of campus resources (e.g., centers for teaching and learning) and through personnel policies that recognize and reward such efforts.

At the same time, institutions should recognize that disciplines approach teaching differently and that such differences should be reflected in evaluation procedures.

Activities that demonstrate a faculty member's commitment to improving teaching skills might include participating in programs at the institution's teaching and learning center. They might also include organizing or participating in departmental or all-campus presentations or seminars on teaching and learning, or engaging in formative evaluations of colleagues. These efforts both by individual faculty and academic departments to improve teaching and learning should be publicly rewarded. Moreover, dissemination of information on campus-wide successes in evaluating teaching and learning can inform evaluation practices in other disciplines.

When evaluating teaching, it is critical to recognize the different emphases and approaches among disciplines. For example, departments that stress laboratory-based teaching and learning as integral components of their curriculum will have different approaches to teaching than departments in which laboratory and field work are not typically part of the curriculum.

2. Recommendations for Presidents, Overseeing Boards, and Academic Officers

Scientists, mathematicians, and engineers who are accomplished in research often enjoy national and even international reputations, whereas those who excel in teaching are rarely known beyond the boundaries of their own campuses. If institutions are to make a concerted effort to enhance the importance of undergraduate teaching and student learning within and across these disciplines, they will need to find ways of recognizing and enhancing the status of faculty who make distinctive contributions to this critical endeavor. Faculty cannot be fully successful if they alone undertake the measures required to improve teaching and learning; faculty, as well as departments, need direct encouragement and support from the highest levels of leadership on campus.

(2.1) Quality teaching and effective learning should be highly ranked institutional priorities. All faculty and departmental evaluations and accreditation reviews should include rigorous assessment of teaching effectiveness. University leaders should clearly assert high expectations for quality teaching to newly hired and current faculty.

Candidates for faculty positions who are expected to teach undergraduates should demonstrate knowledge of and enthusiasm for teaching. Position announcements and the interview process should make explicit the institution's emphasis on and expectation for high-quality teaching (e.g., by expecting candidates to teach a class or to discuss their approaches to teaching and improving student learning). In addition, all instructors, including senior faculty, should be given opportunities for ongoing professional development in teaching and recognized and rewarded for taking advantage of those opportunities. Support also should be provided for long-term, ongoing research projects that enable effective teaching and learning practices on campus to be analyzed and applied to additional courses and programs.

(2.2) Campus-wide or disciplinary-focused centers for teaching and learning should be tasked with providing faculty with opportunities for ongoing professional development that include understanding how people learn, how to improve current instruction though student feedback (formative evaluation), and how educational research can be translated into improved teaching practice. Such centers should

provide equipment and facilities required for innovative teaching.

Centers for excellence in teaching and learning should be provided with sufficient resources to enable them to work with a broad array of departments and individual faculty. The centers' assistance might include giving faculty and administrators access to new information about advances in the cognitive sciences. Centers might direct faculty to ongoing research and innovative practices and offer specific guidance for improving teaching and student learning. They also might be charged specifically with helping faculty use formative evaluation to assess the effectiveness of teaching and learning.

(2.3) At least one senior university-level administrator should be assigned responsibility for encouraging departmental faculty to adopt effective means (as proven by research) to improve instruction.

This individual would oversee and coordinate efforts on campus to establish and sustain the kinds of teaching and learning communities described in this report and elsewhere (e.g., Shapiro and Levine, 1999; the Campus Program initiative established by the American Association for Higher Education [AAHE] and the Carnegie Foundation for the Advancement of Teaching[2]). He or she would report directly to the provost or, where appropriate, to the president or chancellor.

(2.4) Faculty who have excelled in teaching should be publicly recognized and rewarded. Endowments should be established to recognize the serious contributions of faculty who have made a sustained contribution to quality teaching.

Such recognition might include permanent increases in salary, promotions, and monetary awards in amounts comparable to those given to faculty being recognized for other kinds of scholarly accomplishments. Monetary awards might allow recipients to purchase teaching equipment to support their teaching efforts or hire student workers or others to assist with the development of new laboratory or field exercises. Recipients might also use such awards to attend professional conferences or visit with colleagues on other campuses to share information and ideas for improving teaching and

---

[2]Additional information is available at <http://www.aahe.org/teaching/Teaching_Initiative_Home.htm>.

learning. In addition, funds could be made available to establish on campus a series of convocations at which awardees would be invited to speak about their teaching and approaches to enhancing student learning. Excellence in education would be determined through a comprehensive evaluation of faculty members' teaching based on the kinds of evidence described in Chapter 4 of this report.

(2.5) Faculty should be encouraged to develop curricula that transcend disciplinary boundaries, through a combination of incentives (including funding), expectations of accountability, and development of standards for disciplinary and interdisciplinary teaching.

(2.6) Willingness to emphasize student learning and to make allocations of departmental resources in support of teaching should be an essential requirement in appointing deans, department chairs, and similar administrative positions.

(2.7) Graduate school deans should require that departments that employ graduate students in fulfilling their teaching mission should show evidence that their faculties are effectively mentoring graduate teaching assistants and advising them about their duties to undergraduate students.[3]

3. Recommendations for Deans, Department Chairs, and Peer Evaluators

(3.1) Departments should periodically review a departmental mission statement that includes appropriate emphasis on teaching and student learning. These reviews should address not only the major curriculum, but also service offerings, such as courses designed for nonmajors and prospective teachers.

(3.2) Individual faculty members should be expected to contribute to

---

[3]For additional information and strategies for implementing this recommendation, see National Research Council (NRC), 1999a, pp.53–59. Other major initiatives to expose graduate students to the challenges they will face as faculty members include Preparing Future Faculty, a joint effort by the Association of American Colleges and Universities, the Council of Graduate Schools, and the National Science Foundation. Additional information about Preparing Future Faculty is available at <http://www.preparing-faculty.org/>. Tomorrow's Professor Listserv, a website maintained by the Stanford University Learning Laboratory, provides continuing updates and new insights to future and recently hired faculty members following the publication of *Tomorrow's Professor: Preparing for Academic Careers in Science and Engineering* (Reis, 1997). The list serv/website is available at <http://sll.stanford. edu/projects/tomprof/newtomprof/ index.shtml>.

a balanced program of undergraduate teaching. Participation of established faculty in lower division, introductory, and general education courses should be encouraged. Faculty who are most familiar with new developments in the discipline can provide leadership in departmental curricular review and revision. Not all faculty must contribute equally to instruction at every level, but it is a departmental responsibility to ensure that the instructional needs of all students are met by caring, responsible faculty.

(3.3) Departments should contribute to campus-wide awareness of the premium placed on improved teaching. They should build consensus among their own faculty on the suitability of the institution's procedures for summative evaluation of teaching, recognizing that the way practitioners of a specific discipline approach learning will affect the ways that teaching should be evaluated.

(3.4) In addition to numerical data from end-of-course student evaluations and on participation in specific courses, effective peer reviews of teaching should provide a subjective assessment of a faculty member's commitment to quality teaching. Generally, this should include evaluation of a faculty member's knowledge and enthusiasm for the subject matter; familiarity with a range of appropriate pedagogical methods; skills in using appropriate tests and laboratory experiences; quality of advising and other professional interactions with students within and beyond the classroom; and active scholarly commitment to enhancing top-quality teaching and learning.

(3.5) Department heads, in submitting personnel recommendations, should provide separate ratings on teaching, research, and service, each with supporting evidence, as key components of their overall rating and recommendation.

(3.6) Normal departmental professional development activity should include informing faculty about research findings that can improve student learning.

(3.7) As appropriate for achieving departmental goals, departments should provide funds to faculty to enhance teaching skills and knowledge and encourage them to undertake or rely upon educational research that links teaching strategies causally to student learning. Additional funds should be made available to departments that adopt this strategy.

Faculty should be able to apply for these funds to participate in education workshops, to present papers on their teaching at professional meetings, or to work with consultants or colleagues on improving teaching and student learning. When a university has provided such support, evaluations of teaching should include evidence that the knowledge and innovations gained from such activities have been incorporated in some way into the faculty member's teaching. How well departments meet or exceed these goals might be gauged using the evidence and evaluation instruments described in Chapter 7 of this report. Members of departments should be free to use the additional funds as they deem appropriate. Departments awarded such merit funds should be publicly recognized.

(3.8) Departments should recognize that in the course of their careers, some faculty may shift the balance of their departmental obligations to place a greater emphasis on instruction or educational leadership. These shifts should be supported, consistent with a departmental mission, so long as active

engagement with innovative teaching is being addressed.

Such work may be particularly important in teaching undergraduates. Thus, the institution should support faculty who wish to change the focus of their career (e.g., Huber, 2001). However, institutions should also expect these faculty to provide evidence of new or continued scholarly productivity and improvements in teaching (in accordance, for example, with the standards listed in Box 5-1 in Chapter 5). Such evidence should be evaluated using protocols similar to those for other types of scholarship.

4. Recommendations for Granting and Accrediting Agencies, Research Sponsors, and Professional Societies

(4.1) Funding agencies should support programs to enable an integrated network of national and campus-based centers for teaching and learning. An important goal of such a network is to conduct and disseminate research on approaches that enhance teaching and learning in STEM. The network can also provide information on the use of formative and summative assessment for improving teaching and learning. To the extent possible, these investments should not be

made at the expense of sponsored research.

These centers would focus on higher education issues in STEM, and especially on research on how college-level students learn these subjects most effectively. Teaching and learning centers also might be supported in their efforts to disseminate resources beyond their campuses, particularly through electronic means.[4]

(4.2) Funding agencies and research sponsors should undertake self-examination by convening expert panels to examine whether agency policies might inadvertently compromise a faculty member's commitment to quality undergraduate teaching.

(4.3) Accreditation agencies and boards should revise policies to emphasize quality undergraduate learning as a primary criterion for program accreditation.

(4.4) Professional societies should offer opportunities to discuss undergraduate education issues during annual and regional meetings. These events might include sessions on teaching techniques and suggestions for overcoming disciplinary and institutional barriers to improved teaching.

(4.5) Professional societies should encourage publication of peer-reviewed articles in their general or specialized journals on evolving educational issues in STEM.

---

[4]The National Science Foundation recently initiated a program that addresses this recommendation. Its Centers for Learning and Teaching program is designed to "...provide a rich environment that melds research, teacher professional development, and education practice." Additional information about this initiative is available at <http://www.nsf.gov/cgi-bin/getpub?nsf00148>.

References

Abd-El-Khalick, F., Bell, R.L., and Lederman, N.G. (1998). The nature of science and instructional practice: Making the unnatural natural. *Science Education 82*(4): 417–437.

Abrami, P.C., Leventhal, L., and Perry, R.P. (1982). Educational seduction. *Review of Educational Research* 52, 446–464.

Allen, D.E., and Duch, B. (1998). *Thinking towards solutions: Problem-based learning activities for general biology*. Philadelphia, PA: Saunders College.

Allen, D., Groh, S.E., and Allen, D.E. (Eds.). (2001). *The power of problem-based learning: A practical "how-to" for teaching undergraduate courses in any discipline*. Sterling, VA: Stylus.

Alverno College Faculty. (1994). *Student assessment-as-learning at Alverno College* (3rd Ed.). Milwaukee, WI: Alverno College.

Ambady, N., and Rosenthal, R. (1993). Half a minute: Predicting teacher evaluations from thin slices of nonverbal behavior and physical attractiveness. *Journal of Personality and Social Psychology 64*(3), 431–441.

American Association for the Advancement of Science. (1989). *Science for all Americans*. Washington, DC: Author.

American Association for the Advancement of Science. (1990). *The liberal art of science*. Washington, DC: Author.

American Association for the Advancement of Science. (1993). *Benchmarks for science literacy*. New York: Oxford University Press.

American Association for Higher Education. (1993). *Making teaching community property: A menu for peer collaboration and peer review*. Washington, DC: Author.

American Association for Higher Education. (1995). *From idea to prototype: The peer review of teaching—A project workbook*. Washington, DC: Author.

American Association for Higher Education. (1996). *Teaching, learning and technology (TLT) roundtable workbook*. Washington, DC: Author.

American Educational Research Association, American Psychological Association, and National Council on Measurement in Education. (1999). *Standards for educational and psychological measurement*. Washington, DC: American Educational Research Association.

American Psychological Association. (2002). *National guidelines and suggested learning outcomes for the undergraduate psychology major* (draft). Washington, DC: Author.

Anderson, E., (Ed.). (1993). *Campus use of the teaching portfolio: Twenty-five profiles*. Washington, DC: American Association for Higher Education.

Anderson, L.W., Krathwohl, D.R., and Bloom, B.S. (Eds.). (2001). *A taxonomy for learning, teaching, and assessing: A revision of Bloom's taxonomy of educational objectives, 2001*. Boston: Allyn and Bacon.

Angelo, T.A. (1995, November). Assessing (and defining) assessment. *AAHE Bulletin 48*(2).

Angelo, T.A. (1999). The campus as a learning community: Seven promising shifts and seven powerful levers. In B.A. Pescosolido, and R. Aminzade (Eds), *The social worlds of higher education: Handbook for teaching in a new century* (pp. 110–116). Thousand Oaks, CA: Pine Forge Press.

Angelo, T.A., and Cross, K.P. (1993). *Classroom assessment techniques: A handbook for college teachers* (2nd ed.). San Francisco: Jossey-Bass.

Armstrong, L. (2000). Distance learning: An academic leader's perspective on a disruptive product. *Change 32*(6), 20–27.

Astin, A.W., Banta, T.W., Cross, K.P., El-Khawas, E., Ewell, P.T., Hutchings, P., Marchese, T.J., McClenney, M., Mentkowski, M., Miller, M.A., Moran, E.T., and Wright, B.D. (1996). *Assessment forum: 9 principles of good practice for assessing student learning.* Washington, DC: American Association for Higher Education. See <http://www.aahe.org/principl.htm>.

Baker, P. (1999). Creating learning communities: The unfinished agenda. In B.A. Pescosolido, and R. Aminzade (Eds), *The social worlds of higher education: Handbook for teaching in a new century* (pp. 95–109). Thousand Oaks, CA: Pine Forge Press.

Banta, T.W. (2000). That second look. *Assessment Update 10*(4), 3–14.

Banta, T.W., Lund, J.P., Black, K.E., and Oblander, F. W. (1996). *Assessment in practice: Putting principles to work on college campuses.* San Francisco: Jossey-Bass.

Barr, R.B., and Tagg, J. (1999). From teaching to learning: A new paradigm for undergraduate education. In B.A. Pescosolido, and R. Aminzade (Eds.), *The social worlds of higher education: Handbook for teaching in a new century* (pp. 565–581). Thousand Oaks, CA: Pine Forge Press.

Basinger, J. (2000, August 7). Carnegie issues broad changes in system of classifying colleges. *Chronicle of Higher Education.* See <http://chronicle.com/daily/2000/08/2000080701n.htm>.

Baugher, K. (1992). *LEARN: The student quality team manual.* Nashville, TN: LEARN.

Bernstein, D.J. (1996, Spring). A departmental system for balancing the development and evaluation of college teaching: A commentary on Cavanaugh. *Innovative Higher Education 20*(4), 241–248.

Bernstein, D.J., and Quinlan, K.M. (Eds.). (1996, Spring). The peer review of teaching [Special issue]. *Innovative Higher Education 20*(4).

Bleak, J., Neiman, H., Sternman, C., and Trower, C. (2000). *Faculty recruitment study: Statistical analysis report, August 2000.* Cambridge, MA: Harvard Graduate School of Education.

Bloom, B.S. (Ed.). (1956). *Taxonomy of educational objectives: The classification of educational goals. Handbook I: Cognitive domain.* New York: Longmans, Green.

Boice, R. (1992). *The new faculty member.* San Francisco: Jossey-Bass.

Borgman, C.L., Bates, M.J., Cloonan, M.V., Efthimiadis, E.N., Gilliland-Swetland, A.J., Kafai, Y.B., Leazer, G.H., and Maddox, A.B. (1996). Social aspects of digital libraries. In *Proceedings of the University of California Los Angeles-National Science Foundation Social Aspects of Digital Libraries Workshop*, February 15–17, 1996. See <http://is.geis.ucla.edu/research/dl/index.html>.

Boyer, E.L. (1990). *Scholarship reconsidered: Priorities of the professoriate.* Princeton, NJ: Carnegie Foundation for the Advancement of Teaching.

Boyer Commission on Educating Undergraduates in the Research University. (1998). *Reinventing undergraduate education: A blueprint for America's research universities.* Menlo Park, CA: Carnegie Foundation for the Advancement of Teaching. See <http://notes.cc.sunysb.edu/Pres/boyer.nsf>.

Brand, M. (2000). Changing faculty roles in research universities: Using the pathways strategy. *Change 32*(6), 42–45.

Braskamp, L., and Ory, J. (1994). *Assessing faculty work: Enhancing individual and institutional performance.* San Francisco: Jossey-Bass.

Brinko, K.T. (1993). The practice of giving feedback to improve teaching: What is effective? *Journal of Higher Education 64*(5), 574–593.

Brookfield, S.D. (1995). *Becoming a critically reflective teacher.* San Francisco: Jossey-Bass.

Buck, G.A., Hehn, J.G., and Leslie-Pelecky, D.L. (Eds.). (2000). *The role of physics departments in preparing k–12 teachers.* College Park, MD: American Institute of Physics.

Cambridge, B.L. (1996, Spring). The paradigm shifts: Examining quality of teaching through assessment of student learning. *Innovative Higher Education 20*(4), 287–298.

Cambridge, B.L. (Ed.). (1997). *Assessing impact: Evidence and action*. Washington, DC: American Association of Higher Education.

Cambridge, B.L. (1999, December). The scholarship of teaching and learning: Questions and answers from the field. *AAHE Bulletin*. See <http://www.aahe.org/Bulletin/dec99f2.htm>.

Cambridge, B.L. (Ed.). (2001). *Electronic portfolios: Emerging practices in student, faculty, and institutional learning*. Washington, DC: American Association for Higher Education.

Capelli, P. (Ed.). (1997). *Change at work: Trends that are transforming the business of business*. Washington, DC: National Policy Association.

Carnegie Foundation for the Advancement of Teaching and Pew Forum on Undergraduate Learning. (2002). *National survey of student engagement: The college student report*. Menlo Park, CA: Author. See <http://www.indiana.edu/~nsse/1>.

Cashin, W.E. (1990). Students do rate different academic fields differently. In M. Theall, and J. Franklin (Eds.), *Student ratings of instruction: Issues for improving practice*. San Francisco: Jossey-Bass.

Cashin, W.E., and Downey, R.G. (1999). *Using global student rating items for summative evaluation: Convergence with an overall instructor evaluation criteria*. Paper presented at American Educational Research Association, April, Washington, DC.

Centra, J.A. (1973). *Item reliabilities, the factor structure, comparison with alumni ratings*. (Student Instructional Report, No. 3). Princeton, NJ: Educational Testing Service.

Centra, J.A. (1974). The relationship between student and alumni ratings of teachers. *Educational and Psychological Measurement 34*(2), 321–326.

Centra, J.A. (1975). Colleagues as raters of classroom instruction. *Journal of Higher Education 46*, 327–337.

Centra, J.A. (1979). *Determining faculty effectiveness*. San Francisco: Jossey-Bass.

Centra, J.A. (1987). *Faculty evaluation: Past practices, future directions*. Manhattan, KS: Kansas State University, Center for Faculty Evaluation and Development.

Centra, J.A. (1993). *Reflective faculty evaluation: Enhancing teaching and determining faculty effectiveness*. San Francisco: Jossey-Bass.

Centra, J.A. (1994). The use of the teaching portfolio and student evaluations for summative evaluation. *Journal of Higher Education 65*(5), 555–570.

Centra, J.A. (1998). *The development of the student instructional report II, Higher Education Assessment Program*. Princeton, NJ: Educational Testing Service.

Centra, J.A. (2001). *A model for assessing the scholarship of teaching*. Presentation at the 9th Annual American Association of Higher Education Conference on Faculty Roles and Rewards, February, Tampa, FL.

Centra, J.A., and Creech, F.R. (1976). *The relationship between student, teacher, and course characteristics and student ratings of teacher effectiveness*. (Report No. PR-76-1). Princeton, NJ: Educational Testing Service.

Centra, J.A., and Gaubatz, N.B. (2000a). Is there gender bias in student evaluations of teaching? *Journal of Higher Education 70*(1), 17–33.

Centra, J.A., and Gaubatz, N.B. (2000b). *Student perceptions of learning and instructional effectiveness in college courses, Higher Education Assessment Program*. (Report No. 9). Princeton, NJ: Educational Testing Service.

Chandler, S. (1991). *Issues in evaluating multi-institutional models*. Paper presented at the American Educational Research Association Symposium, Chicago.

Chickering, A.W., and Gamson, Z.F. (1987). Seven principles for good practice in undergraduate education. *AAHE Bulletin 39*, 3–7.

Chism, N.V.N. (1999). *Peer review of teaching: A sourcebook*. Boston: Anker.

Clark, J., and Redmond, M. (1982). *Small group instructional diagnosis*. (ERIC Ed. 217954). Seattle: University of Washington, Department of Biology Education.

Cochran, K.F. (1997). Pedagogical content knowledge: Teachers' integration of subject matter, pedagogy, students, and learning environments. *Research Matters–to the Science Teacher, #9702*.

Cohen, P.A. (1981). Student ratings of instruction and student achievement: A meta-analysis of multisection validity studies. *Review of Educational Research 51*, 281–309.

Collis, B., and Moonen, J. (2001). *Flexible learning in a digital world: Experiences and expectations.* London, UK: Kogan Page.

Cooper, J., and Robinson, P. (1998). *Small-group instruction: An annotated bibliography of science, mathematics, engineering and technology resources in higher education* (Occasional Paper #6). Madison: University of Wisconsin–Madison, National Institute for Science Education.

Coppola, B.P., and Smith, D.H. (1996). A case for ethics. *Journal of Chemical Education 73,* 33–34.

Coppola, B.P., Ege, S.N., and Lawton, R.G. (1997). The University of Michigan undergraduate chemistry curriculum 2— Instructional strategies and assessment. *Journal of Chemical Education 74,* 84–94.

Coppola. B.P., and Jacobs, D. (2002). Is the scholarship of teaching and learning new to chemistry? In M.T. Huber, and S. Morreale (Eds.), *Disciplinary styles in the scholarship of teaching and learning: Exploring common ground.* Washington, DC: American Association for Higher Education and the Carnegie Foundation for the Advancement of Teaching.

Cornell University. (1993). *Teaching evaluation handbook.* Ithaca, NY: Cornell University, Office of Instructional Support.

Cross, K.P., and Steadman, M.H. (1996). *Classroom research: Implementing the scholarship of teaching.* San Francisco: Jossey-Bass.

Daffinrud, S.M., and Herrera, O.L. (2000). *Evaluation methods and findings: The Field-Tested Learning Assessment Guide (FLAG) final report.* Madison, WI: University of Wisconsin, LEAD Center.

Darling-Hammond, L. (Ed.). (1997). *Doing what matters most: Investing in quality teaching.* New York: National Commission on Teaching and America's Future.

Davis, B.G. (1988). *Sourcebook for evaluating teaching.* Berkeley: University of California at Berkeley, Office of Educational Development.

Davis, B.G. (1993). *Tools for teaching.* San Francisco: Jossey-Bass.

Diamond, R.M., and Adams, B.E. (Eds.). (1995). *The disciplines speak: Rewarding the scholarly, professional, and creative work of faculty.* Washington, DC: American Association for Higher Education.

Diamond, R.M., and Adams, B.E. (Eds.). (2000). *The disciplines speak II: More statements on rewarding the scholarly, professional, and creative work of faculty.* Washington, DC: American Association for Higher Education.

Diamond, R.M., and Gray, P.J. (1998). *1997 National Study of Teaching Assistants.* Syracuse, NY: Syracuse University Center for Instructional Development.

Doherty, A., Riordan, T., and Roth, J. (Eds.). (2002). *Student learning: A central focus for institutions of higher education.* (A report and collection of institutional practices of the Student Learning Initiative.) Milwaukee, WI: Alverno College Institute.

Dougherty, A. (1999). *Just-in-time, teaching using Web feedback to guide learning and teaching.* See <http://ww2.lafayette.edu/~doughera/talks/ets9912/>.

Doyle, M.P. (Ed.). (2000). *Academic excellence: The role of research in the physical sciences at undergraduate institutions.* Tucson, AZ: Research Corporation.

Drucker, A.J., and Remmers, H.H. (1951). Do alumni and students differ in their attitudes toward instructors? *Journal of Educational Psychology 42*(3), 129–143.

Ebert-May, D., Brewer, C.A., and Allred, S. (1997). Innovation in large lectures: Teaching for active learning through inquiry. *BioScience 47*(9), 601–607.

Edgerton, R., Hutchings, P., and Quinlan, K. (1991). *The teaching portfolio: Capturing the scholarship in teaching.* Washington, DC: The American Association for Higher Education.

Ehrmann, S.C. (2000, November/December). *On the necessity of grassroots evaluation of educational technology: Recommendations for higher education.* See <http://horizon.unc.edu/TS/assessment/2000-11.asp>.

Ehrmann, S.C. (In press). Technology and educational revolution: Ending the cycle of failure. *Liberal Education.* See draft <http://www.tltgroup.org/resources/V_Cycle_of_Failure.html>.

Emerson, J.D., Mosteller, F., and Youtz, C. (2000). Students can help improve college teaching: A review and an agenda for the statistics profession. In C. R. Rao, and G. Szekely (Eds.), *Statistics for the 21st century.* New York: Marcel Dekker.

Emert, J. W., and Parish, C. R. (1996). Assessing concept attainment in undergraduate core courses in mathematics. In T.W. Banta, J. P. Lund, K.E. Black, and F.W. Oblander (Eds.), *Assessment in practice.* San Francisco: Jossey-Bass.

Ewell, P.T. (1991). To capture the ineffable: New forms of assessment in higher education. *Review of Research in Education 17,* 75–125.

Feldman, K.A. (1978). Course characteristics and college students' ratings of their teachers and courses: What we know and what we don't. *Research in Higher Education 9,* 199–242.

Feldman, K.A. (1984). Class size and college students' evaluations of teachers and courses: A closer look. *Research in Higher Education* 21(1):45–116, September.

Feldman, K.A. (1989). Instructional effectiveness of college teachers as judged by teachers themselves, current and former students, colleagues, administrators and external (neutral) observers. *Research in Higher Education 30,* 137–189.

Feldman, K.A. (1993). College students' views of male and female college teachers: Part II–Evidence from students' evaluations of their classroom teachers. *Research in Higher Education 34*(2), 151–211.

Fisch, L. (1998). *AD REM: Spotters. The national teaching and learning forum.* Phoenix, AZ: Oryx Press.

Fosnot, C. (Ed.). (1996). *Constructivism: Theory, perspectives, and practice.* New York: Teachers College Press.

Freedman, R.L.H. (1994). *Open-ended questioning.* New York: Addison Wesley.

French-Lazovik, G. (1981). Documentary evidence in the evaluation of teaching. In J. Millman (Ed.), *Handbook of teacher evaluation* (pp. 73–89). Newbury Park, CA: Sage.

Gabel, D.L. (Ed.) (1994). *Handbook of research on science teaching and learning.* New York: Macmillan.

Gabelnick, F., MacGregor, J., Matthews, R., and Smith, B. (1990). *Learning communities: Creating connections among students, faculty, and disciplines.* San Francisco: Jossey-Bass.

Gaff, J.G., Pruitt-Logan, A.S., and Weibl, R.A. (2000). *Building the faculty we need: Colleges and universities working together.* Washington, DC: Association of American Colleges and Universities.

Gardiner, L., Anderson, C., and Cambridge, B. (Eds.). (1997). *Learning through assessment: A resource guide for higher education.* Washington, DC: American Association for Higher Education.

Gavin, R. (2000). The role of research at undergraduate institutions: Why is it necessary to defend it? In M.P. Doyle (Ed.), *Academic excellence: The role of research in the physical sciences at undergraduate institutions* (pp. 9–17). Tucson, AZ: Research Corporation.

Gilmore, G.M., Kane, M.T., and Naccarato, R.W. (1978). The generalizability of student ratings of instruction: Estimation of teacher and course components. *Journal of Educational Measurement 15*(1), 1–13.

Glassick, C.E., Huber, M.T., and Maeroff, G.I. (1997). *Scholarship assessed: Evaluation of the professoriate.* San Francisco: Jossey-Bass.

Goheen, R.F. (1969). *The human nature of a university.* Princeton, NJ: Princeton University Press.

Golde, C.M., and Dore, T.M. (2001). *At cross purposes: What the experiences of today's doctoral students reveal about doctoral education.* Philadelphia, PA: Pew Charitable Trusts.

Gray, J., Diamond, R.M., and Adam, B.E. (1996). *A national study on the relative importance of research and undergraduate teaching at colleges and universities.* Syracuse, NY: Syracuse University Center for Instructional Development.

Greene, E. (2000, June 23). Some colleges pay students to go to class—to evaluate teaching. *The Chronicle of Higher Education,* A18.

Greenspan, A. (2000). *The economic importance of improving math-science education.* Testimony to the U.S. House of Representatives Committee on Education and the Workforce, Washington, DC. See <http://www.federalreserve.gov/boarddocs/testimony/2000/20000921.htm>.

Grouws, D.A. (1992). *Handbook of research on mathematics teaching and learning.* New York: Macmillan.

Herron, J.D. (1996). *The chemistry classroom: Formulas for successful teaching.* Washington, DC: American Chemical Society.

Hestenes, D. (1987). Toward a modeling theory of physics instruction. *American Journal of Physics 55,* 440–454.

Hestenes, D., and Halloun, I. (1995). Interpreting the force concept inventory. *Physics Teacher* 33(8), 502–506.

Heterick, R., and Twigg, C. (1999). *Lectures are not cheap!* See <http://www.center.rpi.edu/LForum/LM/Sept99.html>.

Huber, M.T. (1999). *Disciplinary styles in the scholarship of teaching: Reflections on the Carnegie Academy for the Scholarship of Teaching and Learning.* Paper presented at the 7th International Improving Student Learning Symposium Improving Student Learning Through the Disciplines, Menlo Park, CA.

Huber, M.T. (2001, July/August). Balancing acts: Designing careers around the scholarship of teaching. *Change*, 21–29.

Huber, M.T., and Morreale, S. (Eds.). (2002). *Disciplinary styles in the scholarship of teaching and learning: Exploring common ground.* Washington, DC: American Association for Higher Education and the Carnegie Foundation for the Advancement of Teaching.

Hutchings, P. (Ed.). (1995). *From idea to prototype: The peer review of teaching, a project workbook.* Washington, DC: American Association for Higher Education.

Hutchings, P. (Ed.). (1996). *Making teaching community property: A menu for peer collaboration and peer review.* Washington, DC: American Association for Higher Education.

Hutchings, P. (Ed.). (1998). *The course portfolio: How faculty can examine their teaching to advance practice and improve student learning.* Washington, DC: American Association for Higher Education.

Hutchings, P. (Ed.). (2000). *Opening lines: Approaches to the scholarship of teaching and learning.* Menlo Park, CA: Carnegie Foundation for the Advancement of Teaching.

Indiana University. (2000). *The college student experiences questionnaire.* See <http://www.indiana.edu/~cseq/cseq_content.htm>.

International Technology Education Association. (2000). *Standards for technological literacy: Content for the study of technology.* Reston, VA: Author. See <http://www.iteawww.org/TAA/STLstds.htm>.

Ireton, M.F.W., Manduco, C.A., and Mogk, D.W. (1996). *Shaping the future of undergraduate earth science education: Innovation and change using an earth system approach.* Washington, DC: American Geophysical Union.

Johnson, D.W., Johnson, R.T., and Smith, K. (1998). *Active learning: Cooperation in the college classroom.* Edina, MN: Interaction Books.

Joint Policy Board for Mathematics. (1994). *Recognitions and rewards in the mathematical sciences.* Washington, DC: American Mathematical Society.

Katz, J., and Henry, M. (1988). *Turning professors into teachers: A new approach to faculty development and student learning.* New York: Macmillan.

Keig, L., and Waggoner, M.D. (1994). *Collaborative peer review: The role of faculty in improving college teaching.* (ASHE-ERIC Higher Education Report #2). Washington, DC: George Washington University.

Kellogg Commission on the Future of State and Land-Grant Universities. (1997). *Returning to our roots: The student experience.* Washington, DC: National Association of State Universities and Land-Grant Colleges.

Kennedy, D. (1997). *Academic duty.* Cambridge, MA: Harvard University Press.

King, P.M., and Kitchener, K.S. (1994). *Developing reflective judgment: Understanding and promoting intellectual growth and critical thinking in adolescents and adults.* San Francisco: Jossey-Bass.

Koon, J., and Murray, H.G. (1995). Using multiple outcomes to validate student ratings of overall teacher effectiveness. *Journal of Higher Education* 66(1), 61–81.

Kremer, J. (1990). Constant validity of multiple measures in teaching, research, and service and reliability of peer ratings. *Journal of Educational Psychology* 82, 213–218.

Lambert, L.M., and Tice, S.L. (Eds.). (1992). *Preparing graduate students to teach: A guide to programs that improve undergraduate education and develop tomorrow's faculty.* Washington, DC: American Association for Higher Education.

Landis, C.R., Ellis, A.B., Lisenky, G.C., Lorenz, J.K., Meekder, K., and Wamser, C.C. (Eds.). (2001). *Chemistry concept tests: A pathway to interactive classrooms.* Upper Saddle River, NJ: Prentice Hall.

Lederman, N.G., and O'Malley, M. (1990). Students' perceptions of tentativeness in science: Development, use, and sources of change. *Science Education 74,* 225–239.

Lederman, N.G., Schwartz, R.S., Abd-El-Khalick, F., and Bell, R.L. (In press). Preservice teachers' understanding and teaching of the nature of science: an intervention study. *Canadian Journal of Science, Mathematics, and Technology Education.*

Licata, C.M., and Morreale, J.C. (1997). *Post-tenure review: Policies, practices, precautions.* Washington, DC: American Association for Higher Education.

Licata, C.M, and Morreale, J.C. (2002). *Post-tenure faculty review and renewal: Experienced voices.* Washington, DC: American Association for Higher Education.

Liebowitz, W.R. (1999, October 22). Course evaluations proliferate on the Web—to the chagrin of many professors. *Chronicle of Higher Education,* A59.

Light, R.L. (2001). *Making the most of college: Students speak their minds.* Cambridge, MA: Harvard University Press.

Lloyd-Jones, R. (1977). Primary trait scoring. In C. Cooper, and L. Odell (Eds.), *Evaluating writing: Describing, measuring, judging.* Urbana, IL: National Council of Teachers of English.

Loacker, G. (Ed.). (2001). *Self-assessment at Alverno College by Alverno College faculty.* Milwaukee, WI: Alverno College.

Lopez, R.E., and Schultz, T. (2001). Two revolutions in k–8 science education. *Physics Today 54*(9), 45–49. See <http://www.physicstoday.org/pt/vol-54/iss-9/current.html>.

Lovitts, B., and Nelson, C. (2000). The hidden crisis in graduate education: Attrition from Ph.D. programs. *Academe 86*(6), 44–50.

Lowman, J. (1995). *Mastering the techniques of teaching.* (2nd Ed.). San Francisco: Jossey-Bass.

MacGregor, J., Cooper, J., Smith, K., and Robinson, P. (2000). *Strategies for energizing large classes: From small groups to learning communities.* (No. 81). San Francisco: Jossey-Bass.

Marsh, H.W. (1982). Validity of students' evaluations of college teaching: A multitrait-multimethod analysis. *Journal of Educational Psychology 74,* 264–279.

Marsh, H.W. (1987). Student evaluations of university teaching: Research findings, methodological issues, and directions for future research. *International Journal of Educational Research 11,* 253–388.

Marsh, H.W., and Roche, L.A. (1993). The use of student evaluations and an individually structured intervention to enhance university teaching effectiveness. *American Educational Research Journal 30*(1), 217–251.

Marsh, H.W., and Roche, L.A. (2000). Effects of grading leniency and low workload on students' evaluations of teaching: Popular myth, bias, validity or innocent bystander? *The Journal of Educational Psychology 92*(1), 202–228.

Mathematical Association of America. (2000). *Guidelines for programs and departments in undergraduate mathematical sciences.* Washington, DC: Author. See <http://www.maa.org/guidelines/guidelines.html>.

Mazur, E. (1997). *Peer instruction: A user's manual.* Upper Saddle River, NJ: Prentice Hall.

McCormick, A.C. (2001). (Ed.). *The Carnegie classification of institutions of higher education, 2000 edition.* Menlo Park, CA: Carnegie.

McKeachie, W.J. (1979, October). Student ratings of faculty: A reprise. *Academe 384–397.*

McKeachie, W.J., Pintrich, P.R., Lin, Y., Smith, D.A.F., and Sharma, R. (1990). *Teaching and learning in the college classroom: A review of the research literature.* Ann Arbor, MI: National Center for Research to Improve Post-Secondary Teaching and Learning.

McKeachie, W.J. (1999). *McKeachie's teaching tips, strategies, research, and theory for college and university teachers.* (10th Ed.). New York: Houghton-Mifflin.

McNeal, A.P., and D'Avanzo, C.D. (Eds.) (1997). *Student active science: Models of innovation in college science teaching.* Fort Worth, TX: Harcourt Brace.

Menges, R., and Svinicki, M. (Eds.). (1991). *College teaching: From theory to practice.* San Francisco: Jossey-Bass.

Millar, S.B. (Ed.). (1998). *Indicators of success in postsecondary SMET education: Shapes of the future.* (Synthesis and Proceedings of the Third Annual National Institute for Science Education Forum). Madison: University of Wisconsin-Madison, Wisconsin Center for Education Research.

Mintzes, J.J., Wandersee, J.H., and Novak, J.D. (Eds.). (2000). *Assessing science understand-*

ing: A human constructivist view. San Diego, CA: Academic Press.

Mullin, R. (2001). The undergraduate revolution: Change the system or give incrementalism another 30 years? *Change 33*(5), 54–58.

Murnane, R.J., and Levy, F. (1996). *Teaching the new basic skills: Principles for educating children to thrive in a changing economy*. New York: Free Press.

Murray, H.G. (1983). Low inference classroom teaching behaviors and student ratings of college teaching effectiveness. *Journal of Educational Psychology 71*, 856–865.

Murray, H.G., Rushton, P.J., and Paunonen, S.V. (1990). Teacher personality traits and student instructional ratings in six types of university courses. *Journal of Educational Psychology 82*, 250–261.

Murray, H.G, Gillese, E., Lennon, M., Mercer, P., and Robinson, M. (1996). *Ethical principles in university teaching*. Vancouver, BC: The Society for Teaching and Learning in Higher Education. See <http://www.umanitoba.ca/academic_support/uts/stlhe/Ethical.html>.

Naftulin, D.H., Ware, J.E., and Donnelly, F.A. (1973). The Doctor Fox lecture: A paradigm of educational seduction. *Journal of Medical Education 48*, 630–635.

Narum, J. (1995). *Structures for science: A handbook on planning facilities for undergraduate natural science communities* (Vol. III). Washington, DC: Project Kaleidoscope.

National Academy of Sciences. (1997). *Preparing for the 21st century: The education imperative*. Washington, DC: National Academy Press. See <http://www.nap.edu/catalog/9537.html>.

National Center for Education Statistics. (1999). *Teacher quality: A report on the preparation and qualification of public school teachers*. Washington, DC: U.S. Department of Education.

National Center for Public Policy and Higher Education. (2001). *Measuring up 2000: The state-by-state report card for higher education*. San Jose, CA: Author. See <http://www.highereducation.org>.

National Council of Teachers of Mathematics. (1989). *Curriculum and evaluation standards for school mathematics*. Reston, VA: Author.

National Council of Teachers of Mathematics. (2000). *Principles and standards for school mathematics*. Reston, VA: Author.

National Institute for Science Education. (2001a). *Learning through technology*. Madison, WI: Author. See <http://www.wcer.wisc.edu/nise/cl1/ilt/>.

National Institute for Science Education. (2001b). *Field-tested learning assessment guide*. Madison, WI: Author. See <http://www.wcer.wisc.edu/nise/cl1/flag/>.

National Institute for Science Education. (2001c). *Cooperative learning*. See <http://www.wcer.wisc.edu/nise/CL1/CL/>.

National Research Council. (1991). *Moving beyond myths: Revitalizing undergraduate mathematics*. Washington, DC: National Academy Press. See <http://books.nap.edu/catalog/1782.html>.

National Research Council. (1995a). *Engineering education: Designing an adaptive system*. Washington, DC: National Academy Press. See <http://books.nap.edu/catalog/4907.html>.

National Research Council. (1995b). *Reshaping the graduate education of scientists and engineers*. Washington, DC: National Academy Press. See <http://books.nap.edu/catalog/4935.html>.

National Research Council. (1996a). *National science education standards*. Washington, DC: National Academy Press. See <http://books.nap.edu/catalog/4962.html>.

National Research Council. (1996b). *From analysis to action*. Washington, DC: National Academy Press. See <http://books.nap.edu/catalog/9128.html>.

National Research Council. (1996c). *The role of scientists in the professional development of science teachers*. Washington, DC: National Academy Press. See <http://books.nap.edu/catalog/2310.html>.

National Research Council. (1997a). *Science teaching reconsidered: A handbook*. Washington, DC: National Academy Press. See <http://books.nap.edu/catalog/5287.html>.

National Research Council. (1997b). *Adviser, teacher, role model, friend: On being a mentor to students in science and engineering*. Washington, DC: National Research Council. See <http://books.nap.edu/catalog/5789.html>.

National Research Council. (1998a). *High stakes: Testing for tracking, promotion, and graduation.* Washington, DC: National Academy Press. See <http://books.nap.edu/catalog/6336.html>.

National Research Council. (1998b). *Developing a digital national library for undergraduate science, mathematics, engineering, and technology education: Report of a workshop.* Washington, DC: National Academy Press. See <http://books.nap.edu/catalog/5952.html>.

National Research Council. (1999a). *Transforming undergraduate education in science, mathematics, engineering, and technology.* Washington, DC: National Academy Press. See <http://www.nap.edu/catalog/6453.html>.

National Research Council. (1999b). *Improving student learning: A strategic plan for education research and its utilization.* Washington, DC: National Academy Press. See <http://books.nap.edu/catalog/6488.html>.

National Research Council. (1999c). *Global perspectives for local action: Using TIMSS to improve U.S. mathematics and science education.* Washington, DC: National Academy Press. See <http://books.nap.edu/catalog/9723.html>.

National Research Council. (1999d). *Myths and tradeoffs: The role of tests in undergraduate admissions.* Washington, DC: National Academy Press. See <http://books.nap.edu/catalog/9632.html>.

National Research Council. (2000a). *Building a workforce for the information economy.* Washington, DC: National Academy Press. See <http://books.nap.edu/catalog/9830.html>.

National Research Council. (2000b). *Educating teachers of science, mathematics, and technology: New practices for the new millennium.* Washington, DC: National Academy Press. See <http://books.nap.edu/catalog/9832.html>.

National Research Council. (2000c). *How people learn: Brain, mind, experience, and school: Expanded edition.* Washington, DC: National Academy Press. See <http://www.nap.edu/catalog/9853.html>.

National Research Council. (2000d). *Inquiry and the national science education standards: A guide for teaching and learning.* Washington, DC: National Academy Press. See <http://www.nap.edu/catalog/9596.html>.

National Research Council. (2000e). *LC21: A digital strategy for the Library of Congress.* Washington, DC: National Academy Press. See <http://books.nap.edu/catalog/9940.html>.

National Research Council. (2001). *Knowing what students know: The science and design of educational assessment.* Washington, DC: National Academy Press. See <http://www.nap.edu/catalog/10019.html>.

National Research Council. (2002a). *Learning and understanding: Improving advanced study of science and mathematics in U.S. high schools.* Washington, DC: National Academy Press. See <http://www.nap.edu/catalog/10129.html.

National Research Council. (2002b). *Scientific research in education.* Washington, DC: National Academy Press. See <http://www.nap.edu/catalog/10236.html>.

National Science Board. (2000). *Science and engineering indicators—2000.* Arlington, VA: Author. See <http://www.nsf.gov/search97cgi/vtopic>.

National Science Foundation. (1996). *Shaping the future: New expectations for undergraduate education in science, mathematics, engineering, and technology.* (NSF 96–139). Arlington, VA: Author. See <http://www.nsf.gov/cgi-bin/getpub?nsf96139>.

National Science Foundation. (1998). *Information technology: Its impact on undergraduate education in science, mathematics, engineering, and technology.* (NSF 98–82). Arlington, VA: Author. See <http://www.nsf.gov/cgi-bin/getpub?nsf9882>.

Neff, R.A., and Weimer, M. (Eds.). (1990). *Teaching college: Collected readings for new instructors.* Madison, WI: Magna.

Novak, J. (1998). *Learning, creating, and using knowledge: Concept maps as facilitative tools in schools and corporations.* Mahwah, NJ: Lawrence Erlbaum.

Nyquist, J.D., Abbott, R.D., Wulff, D.H., and Sprague, J. (Eds.). (1991). *Preparing the professoriate of tomorrow to teach: Selected readings in TA training.* Dubuque, IA: Kendall/Hunt.

Ory, J.C. (2000). Teaching evaluation: Past, present, and future. In K.E. Ryan (Ed.), *Evaluating teaching in higher education: A vision for the future: New directions in teaching and learning* (pp. 13–18). San Francisco, CA: Jossey-Bass.

Osterlind, S.J. (1989). *Constructing test items*. Boston: Kluwer Academic.

Overall, J.U., and Marsh, H.W. (1980). Students' evaluations of instruction: A longitudinal study of their stability. *Journal of Educational Psychology 72*, 321–325.

Palomba, C.A., and Banta, T.W. (1999). *Assessment essentials, planning, implementing, and improving assessment in higher education*. San Francisco: Jossey-Bass.

Perry, R.P., and Smart, J.C. (Eds.). (1997). *Effective teaching in higher education: Research and practice*. New York: Agathon Press.

Pescosolido, B.A., and Aminzade, R. (Eds.). (1999). *The social worlds of higher education: Handbook for teaching in a new century*. Thousand Oaks, CA: Pine Forge Press.

Pike, G.R. (1995). The relationship between self-reports of college experiences and test scores. *Journal of Research in Higher Education 36*(1), 1–21.

Project Kaleidoscope. (1991). *What works, building natural science communities: A plan for strengthening undergraduate science and mathematics* (Vol 1). Washington, DC: Author.

Project Kaleidoscope. (1994). *What works, leadership: Challenges for the future* (Vol. II). Washington, DC: Author.

Project Kaleidoscope. (1998). *Shaping the future of undergraduate science, mathematics, engineering and technology education: Proceedings and recommendations from the PKAL day of dialogue*. Washington, DC: Author. See <http://www.pkal.org/template2.cfm?2c_id=301>.

Reis, R.M (1997). *Tomorrow's professor: Preparing for academic careers in science and engineering*. Piscataway, NJ: IEEE Press.

Remmers, H.H. (1934). Reliability and halo effect on high school and college students' judgments of their teachers. *Journal of Applied Psychology 18*, 619–630.

Rice, R.E., Sorcinelli, M.D., and Austin, A.E. (2000). *Heeding new voices: Academic careers for a new generation*. Washington, DC: American Association for Higher Education.

Root, L.S. (1987). Faculty evaluation: Reliability of peer assessments of research, teaching, and service. *Research in Higher Education 26*, 71–84.

Rosenthal, R. (1976). *Experimenter effects in behavioral research*. New York: Appleton-Century-Croft.

Rothman, F.G., and Narum, J.L. (1999). *Then, now, and in the next decade: A commentary on strengthening undergraduate science, mathematics, engineering and technology education*. Washington, DC: Project Kaleidoscope. See <http://www.pkal.org/news/thennow100.html>.

Rust, E. (1998). Business cares about math and science achievement. In Business Coalition for Education Reform, *The formula for success: A business leader's guide to supporting math and science achievement* (pp. 11–14). Washington, DC: National Alliance for Business.

Sanderson, A., Phua, V.C., and Herda, D. (2000). *The American faculty poll*. Chicago: National Opinion Research Center.

Sands, R.G., Parson, L.A., and Duane, J. (1991). Faculty mentoring faculty in a public university. *Journal of Higher Education 62*, 174–193.

Schwartz, C. (1983*). ABC's of teaching with excellence: A Berkeley compendium for teaching with excellence*. See <http://teaching.berkeley.edu/compendium/>.

Scriven, M. (1981). Summative teacher evaluation. In J. Millman (Ed.), *Handbook of teacher evaluation*. Beverly Hills, CA: Sage.

Scriven, M. (1993). Hard-won lessons in program evaluation. *New Directions for Program Evaluation 58*, summer.

Seldin, P. (1991). *The teaching portfolio*. Boston: Anker.

Seldin, P. (1998, March). How colleges evaluate teaching: 1988 vs. 1998. *AAHE Bulletin 3–7*.

Seymour, E. (In press). Tracking the processes of change in U.S. undergraduate education in science, mathematics, engineering, and technology. *Science Education*.

Seymour, E., and Hewitt, N.M. (1997). *Talking about leaving: Why undergraduates leave the sciences*. Boulder, CO: Westview Press.

Shapiro, N.S., and Levine, J.H. (1999). *Creating learning communities: A practical guide to winning support, organizing for change, and implementing programs*. San Francisco, CA: Jossey-Bass.

Shipman, H.L. (2001). Hands-on science, 680 hands at a time. *Journal of College Science Teaching 30*(5), 318–321.

Shore, B.M., et al. (1986). *The teaching dossier: A guide to its preparation and use.* Montreal: Canadian Association of University Teachers.

Shulman, L. (1986). Those who understand: Knowledge growth in teaching. *Educational Researcher 15*, 4–14.

Shulman, L.S. (1993). Teaching as community property: Putting an end to pedagogical solitude. *Change 25*(6), 6–7.

Shulman, L. (1995). Faculty hiring: The pedagogical colloquium—three models. *AAHE Bulletin 47*(9), 6–9.

Siebert, E.D., and McIntosh, W.J. (Eds.). (2001). *College pathways to the science education standards.* Arlington, VA: National Science Teachers Association.

Sorcinelli, M.D. (1999). The evaluation of teaching: The 40-year debate about student, colleague, and self-evaluations. In B.A. Pescosolido, and R. Aminzade (Eds.), *The social worlds of higher education: Handbook for teaching in a new century* (pp. 195–205). Thousand Oaks, CA: Pine Forge Press.

Sorcinelli, M.D. (2000). *Principles of good practice: Supporting early career faculty. Guidance for deans, department chairs, and other academic leaders.* New Pathways II Project Forum on Faculty Roles and Rewards. Washington, DC: American Association for Higher Education. See <http://www.aahe.org/ffrr/principles_brochure.htm>.

Springer, L., Stanne, M.E., and Donovan, S.S. (1998). *Effects of small-group learning on undergraduates in science, mathematics, engineering, and technology: A meta-analysis* (Research Monograph No. 11). Madison: University of Wisconsin-Madison, National Institute for Science Education.

Suskie, L. (Ed.). (2000). *Assessment to promote deep learning.* Washington, DC: American Association for Higher Education. See <http://www.aahe.org/catalog/iteminfo.cfm?itemid=1&itemid=127&g=t>.

Suter, L., and Frechtling, J. (2000). *Guiding principles for mathematics and science education research methods: Report of a workshop.* (NSF 00-113). Arlington, VA: National Science Foundation. See <http://nsf.gov/cgi-bin/getpub?nsf00113>.

Svinicki, M., and Menges, R. (Eds.). (1996). *Honoring exemplary teaching. New directions for teaching and learning.* (No. 65). San Francisco: Jossey-Bass.

Uno, G.E. (1997). *Handbook on teaching undergraduate science classes: A survival manual.* Norman, OK: University of Oklahoma Press.

Walvoord, B.F., and Anderson, V.J. (1998). *Effective grading: A tool for learning and assessment.* San Francisco: Jossey-Bass.

Wergin, J. (1994). *The collaborative department: How five campuses are inching toward cultures of collective responsibility.* Washington, DC: American Association for Higher Education.

Wergin, J., and Swingen, J.N. (2000). *Departmental assessment: How some campuses are effectively evaluating the collective work of faculty.* Washington, DC: American Association for Higher Education.

Wiggins, G. (1998). *Educative assessment: Designing assessments to inform and improve student performance.* San Francisco: Jossey-Bass.

Wright, J.C., Millar, S.B., Kosciuk, S.A., Penberthy, D.L., Williams, P.H., and Wampold, B.E. (1998). A novel strategy for assessing the effects of curriculum reform on student competence. *Journal of Chemical Education 75*, 986–992.

Wyckoff. S. (2001). Changing the culture of undergraduate science teaching. *Journal of College Science Teaching 30*(5), 306–312.

Zimpher, N. (1998). *Ten changing demands on college teachers in the future.* Presented at Changing Demands on College Teachers: A Conference for Teaching Support Providers, April 27, Columbus, Ohio. See <http://www.acs.ohio-state.edu/education/ftad/Publications/ten-nancy.html>.

Appendix A

Selected Student
Evaluation Instruments

TYPES OF STUDENT EVALUATION INSTRUMENTS

Current Students: End-of-Course Questionnaires

Questionnaires administered at the end of the term have long been widely used to elicit students' opinions about individual courses or instructors (Seldin, 1998). Studies on the reliability and validity of these types of student ratings have been undertaken for more than 70 years (Centra, 1993). Students are in a unique position to comment on their satisfaction with a course and the impact of the instruction on their own learning. However, they are not subject matter experts, and therefore are not in a position to make judgments about the currency or accuracy of course content. In addition, research has shown that ratings by students are sometimes influenced by their level of motivation for taking the course, attitude toward the course or the instructor, and needs or contextual variables (e.g., whether the course is required). Findings from research on the use of student questionnaires suggest that when these instruments are used, the results should be compared with data from student questionnaires in similar courses.

Those who design or use data from student questionnaires must be careful to distinguish instruments that ask students to evaluate courses from those that ask them to evaluate the instruction or the instructor. Forms are often constructed to ask students to rate various aspects of a course and then to provide a rating for the professor's performance. Use of such data for evaluating teaching effectiveness becomes problematic if most of the questions asked of students focus on components of the course itself, such as the usefulness of the textbook or amount of material covered.

Current Students: Interviews

Interviewing students can provide rich, in-depth information about their responses to courses and instructors. When used appropriately, such interviews are usually either highly structured (following a specific set of questions and protocol), semistructured (with a few general items), or unstructured (e.g., "Tell me about this class"). Interviews can probe details and explore aspects of a course and the instructor's role in it in ways that written questionnaires cannot. However, interviewing sufficient numbers of students to obtain an accurate picture of the instructor's teaching and interpreting the results can require a great deal of time, rendering this approach somewhat impractical. Research also indicates that interviews are most helpful when they are used to provide feedback for improving teaching rather than for summative evaluation. Information garnered from interviews also can be more helpful to the instructor when the interviewing is done by an instructional improvement specialist, if available, or a trusted colleague (Centra, 1993).

Current Students: Measures of Learning

An extremely useful and increasingly common approach to evaluating teaching effectiveness is to measure students' knowledge or skills at the beginning of a course or unit of the course and again after some body of material has been covered in class. Instructors can then observe and quantify the amount of improvement and draw inferences about the instructor's effectiveness in helping students learn the subject matter. For measures of student learning to be considered valid and reliable, however, considerable effort is required to develop pre- and post-learning tests that actually measure the kind of learning desired. In addition, changes observed in students' learning and performance cannot be attributed solely to the effectiveness of an individual instructor. Many factors, including students' ability and motivation to learn and even their health status when taking either examination, can also influence the outcomes.

Indirect measures of student learning can be obtained through questionnaires that ask students to assess their own achievement (e.g., "How much have you learned from this course?"). Some research (e.g., Pike, 1995) has shown that students' answers to such questions are correlated with their performance on end-of-course tests.

Another useful approach is for the instructor to evaluate student learning throughout the term. Instructors can use the information obtained from these regular assessments of student learning to improve their teaching and make midcourse corrections in the approaches they are using. Faculty members can thus conduct their own classroom research, gathering measures of student learning to improve their teaching (Brookfield, 1995; National Institute for Science Education, 2001b). An instructor's use of such approaches, the range of test instruments employed (e.g., short-answer and essay questions, computer simulations, and laboratory-based problems, in addition to multiple-choice and similar kinds of questions) and the ways in which the instructor responds to indicators of student learning can be useful measures of teaching effectiveness.

Instructors also can benefit from knowing whether students who have taken their courses have mastered concepts and skills that will be needed for subsequent, higher level courses. Thus, questions about specific concepts the students will have been expected to learn can be included in pre/post-testing. Alternatively, as part of their evaluation of program effectiveness, academic departments can develop assessment instruments that can be used to examine whether students have

learned well the knowledge and skills they need to move through a vertically structured departmental curriculum.

GUIDELINES FOR THE USE OF STUDENT EVALUATIONS

Having examined the research literature and practices in several different types of institutions of higher education, the committee offers here guidelines for the use of student evaluations, particularly in making decisions about a faculty member's professional life. Centra (1993: especially 89–93) offers a detailed discussion of the issues involved; the suggestions offered below are based in part on that analysis.

Make clear to faculty and students how results of student evaluations will be used. Faculty members, administrators, and students need to understand both how the results will be used and who will have access to them.

Use student evaluation as only one piece of relevant information from several sources. Because student evaluations represent student views only, other sources of information (colleagues, self-reports, evidence of student learning) must be considered. Student evaluations are relatively easy to obtain, but that should not result in giving them undue weight. Note that when multiple sources of evaluation data are used, consensus must be reached on how each source will be weighted when making decisions about teaching effectiveness.

Use several sets of evaluation results. For personnel decisions, a pattern of evaluation results derived from different courses taught over more than one semester should be used. Using results from five or more classes is generally best. Also, the results of student evaluations should be compared with a historical record for that class or type of class, if such data are available.

Have a sufficient number of students evaluate each course. Averaging responses from a sufficient number of students minimizes the effects of a few divergent opinions. Reliability estimates (see Chapter 4 for a definition of *reliability* as used in psychometrics) are excellent for classes of 25 students or more. In classes with fewer students, it is critical to examine patterns of student responses across a number of classes. Reliability estimates for classes of 15 or more are at an acceptable level. For very large classes, a representative or random sample of students totaling 25 or more can be selected to complete the form. An effort should be made to encourage at least 60 percent of enrolled students to participate in the evaluation, and at least 15–25 questionnaires are needed for results to be considered

reliable. If the class has fewer than 10 students, it is best not to summarize the data. For sufficiently large sample sizes, means and standard deviations are used most frequently to summarize data.

Consider some course characteristics in interpretations. While any single course variable may not have a great effect, a combination (e.g., small classes, course subject area) could affect a teacher's mean rating.

Use comparative data. Comparisons among instructors within an institution or, better yet, across a large number of similar institutions can help in interpreting results by minimizing the effects of any skewed distributions.

Do not overestimate small differences. Because student evaluations typically are quantified, there may be a tendency to assign them a precision they do not possess or warrant. A 10-percentile difference between instructors generally does not represent a practical distinction.

For personnel decisions, emphasize global evaluations and estimates of learning. Overall ratings of instruction or of a course tend to correlate highly with measured student achievement— more highly than ratings dealing with different teaching styles and presentation methods. Students' estimates of their own learning also can be useful and reasonably accurate means of assessing this aspect of teaching effectiveness.

Use standardized procedures for administering forms in class. When results may be used in personnel decisions, standardized procedures are necessary to minimize possible biasing effects. These procedures include having the instructor leave the room and providing consistent information to students about how the data will be used. Departments and institutions should also develop policies to ensure uniform procedures for distributing, collecting, and analyzing standardized forms. Normally, forms are completed anonymously in class. Some schools also require that students either return their evaluation forms to an administrative office individually or give them to a student in the class who is assigned to deliver them. An ideal approach is to use special staff, such as those from the teaching and learning center, to administer and collect rating forms. Another possibility is to use department secretarial staff. Use of student volunteers is least desirable.

Student evaluations are most commonly completed at the end of the course and prior to final exams or grades. They can also be distributed at midsemester to assist in instructional improvement. Another approach is to administer the final examination early

and then require students to attend a session where they receive their graded examination and are asked to complete the evaluation form. This approach allows students to review the instructor's comments on their final examination, making the examination a more important component of the overall learning experience in the course. Having this information and perspective allows students to offer a more complete evaluation of the course. It is important to note, however, that employing this technique may well result in an instructor's receiving lower evaluations than instructors who distribute the evaluations before administering the final examination. This difference in approaches should be considered in any summative evaluation of a faculty member's teaching.

Expect those being evaluated to respond to evaluation results. Faculty should have the opportunity to discuss with their department chair or others involved in personnel decisions any circumstances they believe may have affected student evaluations of their teaching. They also should be asked to describe in writing what they were trying to accomplish in the course and how their teaching methods suited those objectives (e.g., Hutchings, 1998). Their written comments should be placed in their official dossier or wherever the student ratings are kept. It also is important to keep in mind that traditional student rating forms often do not reflect an instructor's effectiveness in less traditional teaching or testing environments.

Limit the use of rating forms. The use of student rating forms may reach a point of diminishing returns. If they are overused, neither students nor instructors will give them the level of attention required for fair evaluation of teaching or continued professional development by the faculty member in question.

Appendix B
Samples of Questionnaires
Used to Evaluate
Undergraduate Student Learning

The student questionnaires included in this appendix exemplify several approaches to assessing student learning and, in turn, using that information to improve teaching. The *College Student Report 2000* (from the Carnegie Foundation for the Advancement of Teaching and Pew Forum on Undergraduate Education, 2000) and the *Student Instructional Report II* (from the Educational Testing Service) are generic approaches to evaluating learning. Evaluation forms from several universities are presented to demonstrate the kind of information that might be sought from students and the variety of ways (e.g., end-of-semester, midsemester) and settings (e.g., classroom, laboratory) in which students can be queried.

Form	Found on Page(s)
The College Student Report 2001. From the Carnegie Foundation for the Advancement of Teaching and Pew Forum on Undergraduate Education (2002).	147–150
Student Instructional Report II. Used nationally and produced by the Educational Testing Service.	151–152

The College Student Report 2001

1 In your experience at your institution during the current school year, about how often have you done each of the following? Mark your answers in the boxes. Examples: ☒ or ▨

	Very often	Often	Some-times	Never
a. Asked questions in class or contributed to class discussions	☐	☐	☐	☐
b. Made a class presentation	☐	☐	☐	☐
c. Prepared two or more drafts of a paper or assignment before turning it in	☐	☐	☐	☐
d. Worked on a paper or project that required integrating ideas or information from various sources	☐	☐	☐	☐
e. Came to class without completing readings or assignments	☐	☐	☐	☐
f. Worked with other students on projects **during class**	☐	☐	☐	☐
g. Worked with classmates **outside of class** to prepare class assignments	☐	☐	☐	☐
h. Tutored or taught other students (paid or voluntary)	☐	☐	☐	☐
i. Participated in a community-based project as part of a regular course	☐	☐	☐	☐
j. Used an electronic medium (list-serv, chat group, Internet, etc.) to discuss or complete an assignment	☐	☐	☐	☐
k. Used e-mail to communicate with an instructor	☐	☐	☐	☐
l. Discussed grades or assignments with an instructor	☐	☐	☐	☐
m. Talked about career plans with a faculty member or advisor	☐	☐	☐	☐
n. Discussed ideas from your reading or classes with faculty members outside of class	☐	☐	☐	☐
o. Received prompt feedback from faculty on your academic performance (written or oral)	☐	☐	☐	☐
p. Worked harder than you thought you could to meet an instructor's standards or expectations	☐	☐	☐	☐
q. Worked with faculty members on activities other than coursework (committees, orientation, student life activities, etc.)	☐	☐	☐	☐

	Very often	Often	Some-times	Never
r. Discussed ideas from your readings or classes with others outside of class (students, family members, coworkers, etc.)	☐	☐	☐	☐
s. Had serious conversations with students of a different race or ethnicity than your own	☐	☐	☐	☐
t. Had serious conversations with students who differ from you in terms of their religious beliefs, political opinions, or personal values	☐	☐	☐	☐

2 During the current school year, to what extent has your coursework emphasized the following mental activities?

	Very much	Quite a bit	Some	Very little
a. **Memorizing** facts, ideas, or methods from your courses and readings so you can repeat them in pretty much the same form	☐	☐	☐	☐
b. **Analyzing** the basic elements of an idea, experience, or theory such as examining a particular case or situation in depth and considering its components	☐	☐	☐	☐
c. **Synthesizing** and organizing ideas, information, or experiences into new, more complex interpretations and relationships	☐	☐	☐	☐
d. **Making judgments** about the value of information, arguments, or methods such as examining how others gathered and interpreted data and assessing the soundness of their conclusions	☐	☐	☐	☐
e. **Applying** theories or concepts to practical problems or in new situations	☐	☐	☐	☐

3 **During the current school year, about how much reading and writing have you done?**

	None	Between 1 and 4	Between 5 and 10	Between 11 and 20	More than 20
a. Number of assigned textbooks, books, or book-length packs of course readings	☐	☐	☐	☐	☐
b. Number of books read on your own (not assigned) for personal enjoyment or academic enrichment	☐	☐	☐	☐	☐
c. Number of written papers or reports of **20 pages or more**	☐	☐	☐	☐	☐
d. Number of written papers or reports **between 5 and 19 pages**	☐	☐	☐	☐	☐
e. Number of written papers or reports of **fewer than 5 pages**	☐	☐	☐	☐	☐

4 **Mark the box that best represents the extent to which your examinations during the current school year have challenged you to do your best work.**

Very much ▼

7 ☐
6 ☐
5 ☐
4 ☐
3 ☐
2 ☐
1 ☐

▲ Very little

5 **Overall, how would you evaluate the quality of academic advising you have received at your institution?**

☐ Excellent
☐ Good
☐ Fair
☐ Poor

6 **Which of the following have you done or do you plan to do before you graduate from your institution?**

	Yes ▼	No ▼	Undecided ▼
a. Practicum, internship, field experience, co-op experience, or clinical assignment	☐	☐	☐
b. Community service or volunteer work	☐	☐	☐
c. Work on a research project with a faculty member outside of course or program requirements	☐	☐	☐
d. Foreign language coursework	☐	☐	☐
e. Study abroad	☐	☐	☐
f. Independent study or self-designed major	☐	☐	☐
g. Culminating senior experience (comprehensive exam, capstone course, thesis, project, etc.)	☐	☐	☐

7 **About how many hours do you spend in a typical 7-day week doing each of the following?**

# of hours per week

	0	1 - 5	6 - 10	11 - 15	16 - 20	21 - 25	26 - 30	More than 30
a. Preparing for class (studying, reading, writing, rehearsing, and other activities related to your academic program)	☐	☐	☐	☐	☐	☐	☐	☐
b. Working for pay on campus	☐	☐	☐	☐	☐	☐	☐	☐
c. Working for pay off campus	☐	☐	☐	☐	☐	☐	☐	☐
d. Participating in co-curricular activities (organizations, campus publications, student government, social fraternity or sorority, intercollegiate or intramural sports, etc.)	☐	☐	☐	☐	☐	☐	☐	☐
e. Relaxing and socializing (watching TV, partying, exercising, playing computer and other games, etc.)	☐	☐	☐	☐	☐	☐	☐	☐
f. Providing care for dependents living with you (parents, children, spouse, etc.)	☐	☐	☐	☐	☐	☐	☐	☐

8 To what extent has your institution experience contributed to your knowledge, skills, and personal development in the following areas?

	Very much ▼	Quite a bit ▼	Some ▼	Very little ▼
a. Acquiring a broad general education	☐	☐	☐	☐
b. Acquiring job or work-related knowledge and skills	☐	☐	☐	☐
c. Writing clearly and effectively	☐	☐	☐	☐
d. Speaking clearly and effectively	☐	☐	☐	☐
e. Thinking critically and analytically	☐	☐	☐	☐
f. Analyzing quantitative problems	☐	☐	☐	☐
g. Using computing and information technology	☐	☐	☐	☐
h. Working effectively with others	☐	☐	☐	☐
i. Voting in local, state, or national elections	☐	☐	☐	☐
j. Learning effectively on your own	☐	☐	☐	☐
k. Understanding yourself	☐	☐	☐	☐
l. Understanding people of other racial and ethnic backgrounds	☐	☐	☐	☐
m. Developing a personal code of values and ethics	☐	☐	☐	☐
n. Contributing to the welfare of your community	☐	☐	☐	☐

9 To what extent does your institution emphasize each of the following?

	Very much ▼	Quite a bit ▼	Some ▼	Very little ▼
a. Spending significant amounts of time studying and on academic work	☐	☐	☐	☐
b. Providing the support you need to help you succeed academically	☐	☐	☐	☐
c. Encouraging contact among students from different economic, social, and racial or ethnic backgrounds	☐	☐	☐	☐
d. Helping you cope with your non-academic responsibilities (work, family, etc.)	☐	☐	☐	☐
e. Providing the support you need to thrive socially	☐	☐	☐	☐

10 Mark the box that best represents the quality of your relationships with people at your institution.

Relationships with:

a. Other Students	b. Faculty Members	c. Administrative Personnel and Offices
Friendly, Supportive, Sense of Belonging ▼	Available, Helpful, Sympathetic ▼	Helpful, Considerate, Flexible ▼
7 ☐	7 ☐	7 ☐
6 ☐	6 ☐	6 ☐
5 ☐	5 ☐	5 ☐
4 ☐	4 ☐	4 ☐
3 ☐	3 ☐	3 ☐
2 ☐	2 ☐	2 ☐
1 ☐	1 ☐	1 ☐
▲	▲	▲
Unfriendly, Unsupportive, Sense of Alienation	Unavailable, Unhelpful, Unsympathetic	Unhelpful, Inconsiderate, Rigid

11 How would you evaluate your entire educational experience at this institution?

☐ Excellent
☐ Good
☐ Fair
☐ Poor

12 If you could start over again, would you go to the same institution you are now attending?

☐ Definitely yes
☐ Probably yes
☐ Probably no
☐ Definitely no

13 Write in your year of birth: [1][9][ ][ ]

14 Your sex

☐ Male   ☐ Female

15 Are you of Hispanic, Latino, or Spanish origin?

☐ Yes   ☐ No

16 What is your racial or ethnic identification?
(Mark all that apply)

☐ American Indian or other Native American
☐ Asian American or Pacific Islander
☐ Black or African American
☐ White
☐ Other: Specify [ ]

17 Are you an international student or foreign national?

☐ Yes   ☐ No

18 What is your current classification in college?

☐ Freshman/first-year   ☐ Sophomore
☐ Junior   ☐ Senior
☐ Unclassified

19 Since high school, which of the following types of schools have you attended other than the one you are attending now? *(Mark all that apply)*

☐ Vocational-technical school
☐ Community or junior college
☐ 4-year college other than this one
☐ None
☐ Other: Specify [ ]

20 Did you begin college at your current institution or elsewhere?

☐ Started here   ☐ Started elsewhere

21 Thinking about this current academic term, how would you characterize your enrollment?

☐ Full-time   ☐ Less than full-time

22 Are you a member of a social fraternity or sorority?

☐ Yes   ☐ No

23 Do you intend to teach at some pre-kindergarten through high school grade level within a year or two of completing your degree program?

☐ Yes   ☐ No   ☐ Undecided

24 Which of the following best describes where you are living now while attending college?

☐ Dormitory or other campus housing (not fraternity/sorority house)
☐ Residence (house, apartment, etc.) within **walking distance** of the institution
☐ Residence (house, apartment, etc.) within **driving distance**
☐ Fraternity or sorority house

25 Did either of your parents graduate from college?

☐ Yes, both parents   ☐ No
☐ Yes, father only   ☐ Don't know
☐ Yes, mother only

26 Which of these fields best describes your major(s) or your expected major(s)? Mark <u>only one major</u> in each column.

Primary Major	Second Major (**not** minor, concentration, etc) (if applicable)	
☐	☐	Agriculture
☐	☐	Biological/life sciences (biology, biochemistry, botany, zoology, etc.)
☐	☐	Business (accounting, business admin., marketing, management, etc.)
☐	☐	Communications (speech, journalism, television/radio, etc.)
☐	☐	Computer and information sciences
☐	☐	Education
☐	☐	Engineering
☐	☐	Ethnic, cultural studies, and area studies
☐	☐	Foreign languages and literature (French, Spanish, etc.)
☐	☐	Health-related fields (nursing, physical therapy, health technology, etc.)
☐	☐	Humanities (English, literature, philosophy, religion, etc.)
☐	☐	Liberal/general studies
☐	☐	Mathematics
☐	☐	Multi/interdisciplinary studies (international relations, ecology, environmental studies, etc.)
☐	☐	Parks, recreation, leisure studies, sports management
☐	☐	Physical sciences (physics, chemistry, astronomy, earth sciences, etc.)
☐	☐	Public administration (city management, law enforcement, etc.)
☐	☐	Social sciences (anthropology, economics, history, political science, psychology, sociology, etc.)
☐	☐	Visual and performing arts (art, music, theater, etc.)
☐	☐	Undecided
☐	☐	Other: Specify [ ]

THANKS FOR SHARING YOUR VIEWS!

After completing The Report, please put it in the enclosed postage-paid envelope and deposit it in any U.S. Postal Service mailbox. This study is supported by a grant from The Pew Charitable Trusts. Questions or comments? Contact the National Survey of Student Engagement, Indiana University, Ashton Aley Hall, 1913 East Seventh Street, Bloomington IN 47405 or nsse@indiana.edu or www.indiana.edu/~nsse. Copyright pending.

STUDENT INSTRUCTIONAL REPORT II (SIR II)

SIR II Report Number

This questionnaire gives you the chance to comment anonymously about this course and the way it was taught. Using the rating scale below, mark the one response for each statement that is closest to your view. Fill in the appropriate circle to the right of the statement.

- (5) Very Effective
- (4) Effective
- (3) Moderately Effective
- (2) Somewhat Ineffective
- (1) Ineffective
- (0) Not applicable, not used in the course, or you don't know. In short, the statement does not apply to the course or instructor.

As you respond to each statement, think about each practice as it contributed to your learning in this course.

Rating columns: Very Effective, Effective, Moderately Effective, Somewhat Ineffective, Ineffective, Not applicable

A. Course Organization and Planning

1. The instructor's explanation of course requirements .... (5)...(4)...(3)...(2)...(1)......(0)
2. The instructor's preparation for each class period .... (5)...(4)...(3)...(2)...(1)......(0)
3. The instructor's command of the subject matter .... (5)...(4)...(3)...(2)...(1)......(0)
4. The instructor's use of class time .... (5)...(4)...(3)...(2)...(1)......(0)
5. The instructor's way of summarizing or emphasizing important points in class .... (5)...(4)...(3)...(2)...(1)......(0)

B. Communication

6. The instuctor's ability to make clear and understandable presentations .... (5)...(4)...(3)...(2)...(1)......(0)
7. The instructor's command of spoken English (or the language used in the course) .... (5)...(4)...(3)...(2)...(1)......(0)
8. The instructor's use of examples or illustrations to clarify course material .... (5)...(4)...(3)...(2)...(1)......(0)
9. The instructor's use of challenging questions or problems .... (5)...(4)...(3)...(2)...(1)......(0)
10. The instructor's enthusiasm for the course material .... (5)...(4)...(3)...(2)...(1)......(0)

C. Faculty/Student Interaction

11. The instructor's helpfulness and responsiveness to students .... (5)...(4)...(3)...(2)...(1)......(0)
12. The instructor's respect for students .... (5)...(4)...(3)...(2)...(1)......(0)
13. The instructor's concern for student progress .... (5)...(4)...(3)...(2)...(1)......(0)
14. The availability of extra help for this class (taking into account the size of the class) .... (5)...(4)...(3)...(2)...(1)......(0)
15. The instructor's willingness to listen to student questions and opinions .... (5)...(4)...(3)...(2)...(1)......(0)

D. Assignments, Exams, and Grading

16. The information given to students about how they would be graded .... (5)...(4)...(3)...(2)...(1)......(0)
17. The clarity of exam questions .... (5)...(4)...(3)...(2)...(1)......(0)
18. The exams' coverage of important aspects of the course .... (5)...(4)...(3)...(2)...(1)......(0)
19. The instructor's comments on assignments and exams .... (5)...(4)...(3)...(2)...(1)......(0)
20. The overall quality of the textbook(s) .... (5)...(4)...(3)...(2)...(1)......(0)
21. The helpfulness of assignments in understanding course material .... (5)...(4)...(3)...(2)...(1)......(0)

E. Supplementary Instructional Methods

Many different teaching practices can be used during a course. In this section (E), rate only those practices that the instructor included as part of this course.

Rate the effectiveness of each practice used as it contributed to your learning.

Rating columns: Very Effective, Effective, Moderately Effective, Somewhat Ineffective, Ineffective, Not used

22. Problems or questions presented by the instructor for small group discussions .... (5)...(4)...(3)...(2)...(1)......(0)
23. Term paper(s) or project(s) .... (5)...(4)...(3)...(2)...(1)......(0)
24. Laboratory exercises for understanding important course concepts .... (5)...(4)...(3)...(2)...(1)......(0)
25. Assigned projects in which students worked together .... (5)...(4)...(3)...(2)...(1)......(0)
26. Case studies, simulations, or role playing .... (5)...(4)...(3)...(2)...(1)......(0)
27. Course journals or logs required of students .... (5)...(4)...(3)...(2)...(1)......(0)
28. Instructor's use of computers as aids in instruction .... (5)...(4)...(3)...(2)...(1)......(0)

Questionnaire continued on the other side. ➡

For the next **two** sections (F and G), use the rating scale below. Mark the one response for each statement that is closest to your view. Fill in the appropriate circle to the right of each statement.

(5) **Much More** than most courses
(4) **More Than** most courses
(3) About the **Same** as others
(2) **Less** than most courses
(1) **Much Less** than most courses
(0) **Not Applicable**, not used in the course, or you don't know. In short, the statement does not apply to the course or instructor.

Much More than most courses
More Than most courses
About the Same as others
Less than most courses
Much Less than most courses
Not Applicable

F. Course Outcomes

29. My learning increased in this course .... ⑤...④...③...②...①.....⓪
30. I made progress toward achieving course objectives .... ⑤...④...③...②...①.....⓪
31. My interest in the subject area has increased .... ⑤...④...③...②...①.....⓪
32. This course helped me to think independently about the subject matter .... ⑤...④...③...②...①.....⓪
33. This course actively involved me in what I was learning .... ⑤...④...③...②...①.....⓪

G. Student Effort and Involvement

34. I studied and put effort into the course .... ⑤...④...③...②...①.....⓪
35. I was prepared for each class [writing and reading assignments] .... ⑤...④...③...②...①.....⓪
36. I was challenged by this course .... ⑤...④...③...②...①.....⓪

H. Course Difficulty, Work Load, and Pace

37. For my preparation and ability, the level of difficulty of this course was:

⑤ Very difficult   ④ Somewhat difficult   ③ About right   ② Somewhat elementary   ① Very elementary

38. The work load for this course in relation to other courses of equal credit was:

⑤ Much heavier   ④ Heavier   ③ About the same   ② Lighter   ① Much lighter

39. For me, the pace at which the instructor covered the material during the term was:

⑤ Very fast   ④ Somewhat fast   ③ Just about right   ② Somewhat slow   ① Very slow

I. Overall Evaluation

40. Rate the quality of instruction in this course as it contributed to your learning (try to set aside your feelings about the course content):

⑤ Very effective   ④ Effective   ③ Moderately effective   ② Somewhat Ineffective   ① Ineffective

J. Student Information

41. Which one of the following best describes this course for you?

① A major/minor requirement   ② A college requirement   ③ An elective   ④ Other

42. What is your class level?

① Freshman/1st year   ② Sophomore/2nd year   ③ Junior/3rd year   ④ Senior/4th year   ⑤ Graduate   ⑥ Other

43. Do you communicate better in English or in another language?

① Better in English   ② Better in another language   ③ Equally well in English and another language

44. Sex   ① Female   ② Male

45. What grade do you expect to receive in this course?

① A   ② A-   ③ B+   ④ B   ⑤ B-   ⑥ C   ⑦ Below C

K. Supplementary Questions   If the instructor provided supplementary questions and response options, mark your answers in this section. Mark only one response for each question.

46. ⑤④③②①Ⓝ Ⓐ   48. ⑤④③②①Ⓝ Ⓐ   50. ⑤④③②①Ⓝ Ⓐ   52. ⑤④③②①Ⓝ Ⓐ   54. ⑤④③②①Ⓝ Ⓐ
47. ⑤④③②①Ⓝ Ⓐ   49. ⑤④③②①Ⓝ Ⓐ   51. ⑤④③②①Ⓝ Ⓐ   53. ⑤④③②①Ⓝ Ⓐ   55. ⑤④③②①Ⓝ Ⓐ

L. Student Comments   If you would like to make additional comments about the course or instruction, use a separate sheet of paper. You might elaborate on the particular aspects you liked most as well as those you liked least. Also, how can the course or the way it was taught be improved? An additional form may be provided for your comments. **Please give these comments to the instructor.**

If you have any comments about this questionnaire, please send them to:
Student Instructional Report II, Educational Testing Service, Princeton, NJ 08541-0001.

Teaching Improvement Form -- Lecture Courses

Instructor: _____   Time to complete form _____

Course Title/Number: _____   Date of Evaluation: _____

Instructions: This section includes items about a variety of aspects of teaching. Please give an overall rating of each aspect of teaching and also check any of the specific strengths or concerns which match your experience in the course.

OVERALL RATING (Select one for each category)	**SPECIFIC STRENGTHS** (Check all that apply)	**SPECIFIC CONCERNS** (Check all that apply)

Course Organization

OVERALL RATING

❑ commendable
❑ fine
❑ needs improvement

SPECIFIC STRENGTHS

❑ good continuity
❑ lectures and assignments are coordinated well
❑ lectures and section meetings are coordinated well (if applicable)
❑ other strengths?

_____
_____

SPECIFIC CONCERNS

❑ course objectives weren't clear
❑ doesn't give big picture
❑ lectures don't prepare students for assignments/exams
❑ fell behind schedule often
❑ other concerns?

_____
_____

Lecturing

OVERALL RATING

❑ commendable
❑ fine
❑ needs improvement

SPECIFIC STRENGTHS

❑ useful syllabus
❑ stimulates interest
❑ engaging speaking style
❑ key ideas emphasized
❑ easy to take notes
❑ effective examples
❑ good summaries provided
❑ other strengths?

_____
_____

SPECIFIC CONCERNS

❑ speech is hard to understand
❑ pitched too high for students
❑ unclear explanations
❑ unclear board writing
❑ talks too fast
❑ not enough examples
❑ starts or ends late
❑ other concerns?

_____
_____

Interaction and Discussion

OVERALL RATING

❑ commendable
❑ fine
❑ need improvement
❑ not applicable

SPECIFIC STRENGTHS

❑ responds well to student questions
❑ encourages active participation
❑ right amount of interaction for this size and type of class
❑ student contributions valued
❑ useful in-class activities (e.g. groups, simulations, demonstrations)
❑ other strengths?

_____
_____

SPECIFIC CONCERNS

❑ not enough interaction
❑ too few participants
❑ speech is hard to understand
❑ not enough opportunities to participate
❑ instructor doesn't respond effectively to questions
❑ instructor's questions not stated clearly
❑ other concerns?

_____
_____

OVERALL RATING (Select one for each category)	SPECIFIC STRENGTHS (Check all that apply)	SPECIFIC CONCERNS (Check all that apply)

Visual Aids
(e.g. board work, transpariencies and computer projection)

❏ commendable
❏ fine
❏ need improvement
❏ not applicable

❏ well organized
❏ emphasize key points
❏ appropriately detailed
❏ very helpful to my learning
❏ well designed
❏ other strengths?
_____
_____

❏ too fast
❏ poor handwriting
❏ wordy
❏ not enough written explanation
❏ other concerns?
_____
_____

Texts and Readings

❏ commendable
❏ fine
❏ need improvement

❏ high quality (content or readability)
❏ match course goals well
❏ other strengths?
_____

❏ difficult to learn from
❏ not discussed enough in lecture
❏ too expensive
❏ difficult to obtain copies
❏ other concerns?
_____
_____

Handouts, Reserve or Online Materials

❏ commendable
❏ fine
❏ need improvement
❏ not applicable
❏ haven't used enough to evaluate

❏ very helpful
❏ motivating
❏ enhanced my learning
❏ other strengths?
_____
_____

❏ not enough
❏ too many
❏ not helpful
❏ other concerns?
_____
_____

Testing

❏ commendable
❏ fine
❏ need improvement
❏ not applicable

❏ good coverage of material
❏ appropriately challenging
❏ right length for amount of time given
❏ other strengths?
_____
_____

❏ unreasonably difficult
❏ poor coverage of materials
❏ too few tests/quizzes
❏ too many test/quizzes
❏ unclear grading criteria
❏ other concerns?
_____
_____

Assignments

❏ commendable
❏ fine
❏ need improvement
❏ not applicable

❏ appropriately challenging
❏ clear grading criteria
❏ helpful feedback
❏ appropriate number
❏ interesting and/or useful questions assigned
❏ other strengths?
_____
_____

❏ poor coverage of material
❏ inconsistent grading
❏ insufficient comments on returned assignments
❏ slow or no return
❏ other concerns?
_____
_____

OVERALL RATING
(Select one for each category)

SPECIFIC STRENGTHS
(Check all that apply)

SPECIFIC CONCERNS
(Check all that apply)

Attitude to Students

❑ commendable
❑ fine
❑ needs improvement

❑ personable & approachable
❑ help readily available out of class
❑ concerned about individual students' needs
❑ attentive to needs of diverse student populations
❑ other strengths?

❑ not sufficiently accessible to students out of class
❑ unresponsive to students' requests for help or review
❑ other concerns?

Classroom Control and Climate

❑ commendable
❑ fine
❑ need improvement

❑ students are respectful toward professor
❑ students are respectful toward each other
❑ other strengths?

❑ some students disruptive in class
❑ poor physical environment for this type of class
❑ other concerns?

Overall Evaluation (Circle one for each question.)

How heavy/light is the workload for this course compared with other courses you have taken this year?

Much lighter   Lighter   About the same   Heavier   Much Heavier

How is the pace in this course?

Too slow   A bit slow   Just right   A bit fastToo fast

How challenging do you find this course?

Too easy   A bit easy   Just right   A bit difficult   Too difficult

How much do you think you have learned in this course compared with other courses you have taken this year?

Almost nothing   Little   A fair amount   Much   A great deal

How well has this course met your expectations?

Not at all   Not very well   Adequately   Well   Very well

Overall, what contributed most significantly to your learning in this course? In other words, what are the important features to retain the next time this course is taught?

Overall, what made your learning in this course more difficult? In other words, what are the most important changes you would suggest for the next time this course is taught?

Any comments about this form?

<u>Student Information</u> (Circle one for each question.)

Main reason for taking course:		Required	Interested	Required and Interested	Other	
Class:	First-Year	Sophomore	Junior	Senior	Masters	Ph.D.	Other

Current Grade in the Course:

Undergraduate:	A	B	C	D	R	Don't Know
Graduate:	A	A-	B+	B	B-	Don't Know

% of Classes Attended for this Course:	0-20%	21-40%	41-60%	61-80%	81-100%

Teaching Improvement Form -- Laboratory Courses

Instructor: _____   Time to complete form _____

Course Title/Number: _____   Date of Evaluation: _____

Instructions: This section includes items about a variety of aspects of teaching. Please give an overall rating of each aspect of teaching and also check any of the specific strengths or concerns which match your experience in the course.

OVERALL RATING	SPECIFIC STRENGTHS	SPECIFIC CONCERNS
(Select one for each category)	(Check all that apply)	(Check all that apply)

Content

❑ commendable
❑ fine
❑ needs improvement

❑ appropriately challenging
❑ good breadth of topics and techniques
❑ other strengths?

_____

_____

❑ pitched too low for students
❑ pitched too high for students
❑ does not relate materials to learning in prior courses
❑ other concerns?

_____

_____

Organization

❑ commendable
❑ fine
❑ needs improvement
❑ not applicable

❑ useful syllabus
❑ instructor well prepared and organized
❑ logical order of experiments
❑ class time managed well
❑ other strengths?

_____

_____

❑ seems disorganized
❑ difficult to see purpose of some experiments
❑ not enough time allotted per experiment
❑ not enough time allotted to write reports
❑ other concerns?

_____

_____

Lectures/Presentations

❑ commendable
❑ fine
❑ need improvement
❑ not applicable

❑ excellent explanations
❑ provided good preparation for lab work
❑ good use of board or other visual aids
❑ dynamic, engaging style
❑ right amount of interaction for this size and type of class
❑ other strengths?

_____

_____

❑ speech is hard to understand
❑ language used is too complex
❑ unclear explanations
❑ poor use of visual aids
❑ other concerns?

_____

_____

Experiments

❑ commendable
❑ fine
❑ need improvement
❑ not applicable

❑ managed well
❑ clearly stated goals
❑ ample opportunities to ask questions
❑ thorough follow-through on questions
❑ other strengths?

_____

_____

❑ unclear instructions
❑ individual attention not available when needed
❑ underlying rationale for techniques not explained
❑ instructor or TAs not sufficiently familiar with experiments and equipment
❑ too few opportunities to interact with other students
❑ other concerns?

_____

_____

OVERALL RATING (Select one for each category)	SPECIFIC STRENGTHS (Check all that apply)	SPECIFIC CONCERNS (Check all that apply)

Course Materials
(e.g. laboratory manual, handouts)

❑ commendable
❑ fine
❑ need improvement
❑ not applicable

❑ good variety
❑ helpful
❑ clear directions given
❑ other strengths?

_____

❑ confusing
❑ need more procedural details
❑ need more connection to theory
❑ difficult to access needed information
❑ other concerns?

_____
_____

Assignments
(e.g. homework, notebooks, written exercises)

❑ commendable
❑ fine
❑ needs improvement
❑ not applicable

❑ appropriately challenging
❑ well specified assignments
❑ enhanced my learning
❑ other strengths?

_____
_____

❑ unclear instructions for assignments
❑ connection to course goals not apparent
❑ other concerns?

_____
_____

Feedback and Grading

❑ commendable
❑ fine
❑ needs improvement

❑ clear grading criteria
❑ reports returned in a reasonable time
❑ helpful feedback on reports
❑ other strengths?

_____
_____

❑ not enough feedback
❑ unclear or unhelpful feedback
❑ unfair grading
❑ unclear grading criteria
❑ connection to course goals not apparent
❑ other concerns?

_____
_____

Attitude to Students

❑ commendable
❑ fine
❑ needs improvement
❑ not applicable

❑ personable and approachable
❑ patient with students
❑ genuine interest in individual students
❑ welcomes student involvement
❑ provides individual attention
❑ other strengths?

_____
_____

❑ little encouragement provided
❑ unresponsive to student requests
❑ showed little concern about equipment failures or difficulties
❑ other concerns?

_____
_____

Overall Evaluation (Circle one for each question.)

How heavy/light is the workload for this course compared with other courses you have taken this year?

Much lighter   Lighter   About the same   Heavier   Much Heavier

How is the pace in this course?

Too slow   A bit slow   Just right   A bit fast Too fast

How challenging do you find this course?

Too easy   A bit easy   Just right   A bit difficult   Too difficult

How much do you think you have learned in this course compared with other courses you have taken this year?

Almost nothing   Little   A fair amount   Much   A great deal

How well has this course met your expectations?

Not at all   Not very well   Adequately   Well   Very well

Overall, what contributed most significantly to your learning in this course? In other words, what are the important features to retain the next time this course is taught?

Overall, what made your learning in this course more difficult? In other words, what are the most important changes you would suggest for the next time this course is taught?

Any comments about this form?

<u>**Student Information**</u> (Circle one for each question.)

Main reason for taking course: Required   Interested   Required and Interested   Other

Class: First-Year   Sophomore   Junior   Senior   Masters   Ph.D.   Other

Current Grade in the Course:

         Undergraduate: A   B   C   D   R   Don't Know

         Graduate: A   A-   B+   B   B-   Don't Know

% of Classes Attended for this Course: 0-20%   21-40%   41-60%   61-80%   81-100%

This form is adapted from the Teaching Improvement Form used at the City University of Hong Kong.

Teaching Improvement Form -- Discussion Courses

Instructor: _____   Time to complete form _____

Course Title/Number: _____   Date of Evaluation: _____

Instructions: This section includes items about a variety of aspects of teaching. Please give an overall rating of each aspect of teaching and also check any of the specific strengths or concerns which match your experience in the course.

OVERALL RATING (Select one for each category)	**SPECIFIC STRENGTHS** (Check all that apply)	**SPECIFIC CONCERNS** (Check all that apply)

Course Content

❏ commendable
❏ fine
❏ needs improvement

❏ good breadth
❏ good depth of treatment
❏ appropriately challenging
❏ other strengths?

_____

_____

❏ assumes too much prior knowledge
❏ does not relate materials to learning in prior courses
❏ pitched too low for students
❏ other concerns?

_____

_____

Organization

❏ commendable
❏ fine
❏ needs improvement

❏ useful syllabus
❏ instructor clearly well prepared
❏ logical order of topics
❏ managed class time well
❏ other strengths?

_____

_____

❏ course objectives weren't clear
❏ couldn't see big picture
❏ couldn't see continuity between classes
❏ started or ended late
❏ other concerns?

_____

_____

Discussion

❏ commendable
❏ fine
❏ needs improvement

❏ well managed
❏ clearly stated goals
❏ ample opportunities to ask questions
❏ thorough follow up to student questions
❏ good summaries by instructor
❏ other strengths?

_____

_____

❏ too controlled
❏ not controlled enough
❏ unclear goals
❏ inequitable distribution of participation
❏ too few opportunities to interact with other students
❏ contribution of students not always acknowledged
❏ other concerns?

_____

_____

Lectures/Presentations

❏ commendable
❏ fine
❏ need improvement
❏ not applicable

❏ excellent explanations
❏ good use of board or visual aids
❏ dynamic, engaging style
❏ interesting examples
❏ other strengths?

_____

_____

❏ speech is hard to understand
❏ language used is too complex
❏ unclear explanations
❏ lacks examples
❏ unhelpful examples
❏ other concerns?

_____

_____

OVERALL RATING (Select one for each category)	**SPECIFIC STRENGTHS** (Check all that apply)	**SPECIFIC CONCERNS** (Check all that apply)

Attitude to Students

❑ commendable
❑ fine
❑ needs improvement

❑ personable and approachable
❑ genuine interest in individual students
❑ welcomes student involvement
❑ attentive to needs of diverse student populations
❑ other strengths?

_____

_____

❑ willing to provide individual attention
❑ little encouragement provided
❑ unresponsive to student requests
❑ other concerns?

_____

_____

Course Materials
(e.g. text, readings, handouts)

❑ commendable
❑ fine
❑ need improvement

❑ well chosen
❑ engaging
❑ good variety
❑ appropriately challenging
❑ enhanced my learning
❑ other strengths?

_____

_____

❑ some not relevant to course goals
❑ too few readings
❑ too many readings
❑ some were a waste of time
❑ other concerns?

_____

_____

In-Class Activities
(e.g simulations, small groups, demonstrations)

❑ commendable
❑ fine
❑ need improvement
❑ not applicable

❑ well designed
❑ engaging
❑ good variety
❑ clearly related to course goals
❑ other strengths?

_____

_____

❑ too few
❑ too many
❑ some were a waste of time
❑ unclear instructions
❑ other concerns?

_____

_____

Assignments/Testing

❑ commendable
❑ fine
❑ needs improvement

❑ appropriately challenging
❑ well specified assignments
❑ helpful feedback
❑ appropriate number
❑ interesting and/or useful questions
❑ other strengths?

_____

_____

❑ slow or no return
❑ poor coverage of material
❑ too many assignments/tests
❑ not enough assignments/tests
❑ unclear grading criteria
❑ unclear feedback
❑ assignments not connected to what happens in class
❑ other concerns?

_____

_____

Overall Evaluation (Circle one for each question.)

How heavy/light is the workload for this course compared with other courses you have taken this year?

Much lighter   Lighter   About the same   Heavier   Much Heavier

How is the pace in this course?

Too slow   A bit slow   Just right   A bit fast   Too fast

How challenging do you find this course?

Too easy   A bit easy   Just right   A bit difficult   Too difficult

How much do you think you have learned in this course compared with other courses you have taken this year?

Almost nothing   Little   A fair amount   Much   A great deal

How well has this course met your expectations?

Not at all   Not very well   Adequately   Well   Very well

Overall, what contributed most significantly to your learning in this course? In other words, what are the important features to retain the next time this course is taught?

Overall, what made your learning in this course more difficult? In other words, what are the most important changes you would suggest for the next time this course is taught?

Any comments about this form?

<u>**Student Information**</u> (Circle one for each question.)

Main reason for taking course: Required   Interested   Required and Interested   Other

Class: First-Year   Sophomore   Junior   Senior   Masters   Ph.D.   Other

Current Grade in the Course:

        Undergraduate: A   B   C   D   R   Don't Know

        Graduate: A   A-   B+   B   B-   Don't Know

% of Classes Attended for this Course: 0-20%   21-40%   41-60%   61-80%   81-100%

This form is adapted from the Teaching Improvement Form used at the City University of Hong Kong.

Derek Bok Center for Teaching and Learning, Harvard University
Form 3

Mid-Course Evaluations

1. What do you like the most about this course?

2. What do you like the least about this course?

3. What would you like to see happen that isn't happening?

4. Please rate this course so far on a scale from 1 to 10:
   (poor) 1 —————————————————→ 10 (excellent)

Derek Bok Center for Teaching and Learning, Harvard University
Form 4

Class Evaluation

Please take a few moments to provide feedback to us on how you are finding the course, and any suggestions for improvement you may have. Written comments are especially helpful to us.
Please do NOT write your name on this form.

STUDENT PREPARATION FOR CLASS

Please circle:

1. Do you understand what is expected of you in preparation and participation for sections? — Yes   Sometimes   No

2. Do you review the lecture notes and readings before sections? — Yes   Sometimes   No

3. Do you attempt to do the homework before sections? — Yes   Sometimes   No

4. When you have the lecture notes ahead of time, do you read them before lectures? — Yes   Sometimes   No

5. Do you work on homework assignments with other students (this is allowed)? — Yes   Sometimes   No

6. Do you prepare questions on the material you don't understand before section? — Yes   Sometimes   No

7. Are you usually well prepared for class? — Yes   Sometimes   No

8. Do the assignments make sense to you? — Yes   Sometimes   No

9. Outside of lectures and sections, how many hours per week do you spend on reading, computing, homework, etc., for the class? — _____ Hours

7. How much of the reading assigned in the book have you done?   Comment.

8. What would help you to learn the material better?

EVALUATION OF INSTRUCTOR

	DISAGREE			AGREE	
1. The instructor is well prepared.	1	2	3	4	5
2. The instructor explains the material clearly.	1	2	3	4	5
3. The instructor answers questions well.	1	2	3	4	5
4. The instructor shows genuine concern for student learning and the quality of teaching.	1	2	3	4	5
5. The instructor is accessible outside of class.	1	2	3	4	5
6. The instructor effectively directs and stimulates participation.	1	2	3	4	5
7. The instructor adjusts the pace of the class to students' level of understanding.	1	2	3	4	5

8. Do you have any suggestions or comments for the instructor?

SURVEY FORM - STUDENT REACTIONS TO INSTRUCTION AND COURSES

IDEA CENTER

IMPORTANT!

USE NO. 2 PENCIL ONLY

Proper Marks Improper Marks

Institution:		Instructor:	
Course Number:		Time and Days Class Meets:	

Your thoughtful answers to these questions will provide helpful information to your instructor.

Describe the frequency of your instructor's teaching procedures, using the following code:

1=Hardly Ever	2=Occasionally	3=Sometimes	4=Frequently	5=Almost Always

The Instructor:

1. ① ② ③ ④ ⑤ Displayed a personal interest in students and their learning
2. ① ② ③ ④ ⑤ Found ways to help students answer their own questions
3. ① ② ③ ④ ⑤ Scheduled course work (class activities, tests, projects) in ways which encouraged students to stay up-to-date in their work
4. ① ② ③ ④ ⑤ Demonstrated the importance and significance of the subject matter
5. ① ② ③ ④ ⑤ Formed "teams" or "discussion groups" to facilitate learning
6. ① ② ③ ④ ⑤ Made it clear how each topic fit into the course
7. ① ② ③ ④ ⑤ Explained the reasons for criticisms of students' academic performance
8. ① ② ③ ④ ⑤ Stimulated students to intellectual effort beyond that required by most courses
9. ① ② ③ ④ ⑤ Encouraged students to use multiple resources (e.g. data banks, library holdings, outside experts) to improve understanding
10. ① ② ③ ④ ⑤ Explained course material clearly and concisely
11. ① ② ③ ④ ⑤ Related course material to real life situations
12. ① ② ③ ④ ⑤ Gave tests, projects, etc. that covered the most important points of the course
13. ① ② ③ ④ ⑤ Introduced stimulating ideas about the subject
14. ① ② ③ ④ ⑤ Involved students in "hands on" projects such as research, case studies, or "real life" activities
15. ① ② ③ ④ ⑤ Inspired students to set and achieve goals which really challenged them
16. ① ② ③ ④ ⑤ Asked students to share ideas and experiences with others whose backgrounds and viewpoints differ from their own
17. ① ② ③ ④ ⑤ Provided timely and frequent feedback on tests, reports, projects, etc. to help students improve
18. ① ② ③ ④ ⑤ Asked students to help each other understand ideas or concepts
19. ① ② ③ ④ ⑤ Gave projects, tests, or assignments that required original or creative thinking
20. ① ② ③ ④ ⑤ Encouraged student-faculty interaction outside of class (office visits, phone calls, e-mail, etc.)

Twelve possible learning objectives are listed below. For each, rate your progress in this course compared with your progress in other courses you have taken at this college or university. (Of course, ratings on objectives which were not addressed by the course will usually be low.)

In this course, my progress was:
- 1-Low (lowest 10 percent of courses I have taken here)
- 2-Low Average (next 20 percent of courses I have taken here)
- 3-Average (middle 40 percent of courses I have taken here)
- 4-High Average (next 20 percent of courses I have taken here)
- 5-High (highest 10 percent of courses I have taken here)

Progress on:

21. ① ② ③ ④ ⑤ Gaining factual knowledge (terminology, classifications, methods, trends)
22. ① ② ③ ④ ⑤ Learning fundamental principles, generalizations, or theories
23. ① ② ③ ④ ⑤ Learning to *apply* course material (to improve thinking, problem solving, and decisions)
24. ① ② ③ ④ ⑤ Developing specific skills, competencies, and points of view needed by professionals in the field most closely related to this course
25. ① ② ③ ④ ⑤ Acquiring skills in working with others as a member of a team
26. ① ② ③ ④ ⑤ Developing creative capacities (writing, inventing, designing, performing in art, music, drama, etc.)
27. ① ② ③ ④ ⑤ Gaining a broader understanding and appreciation of intellectual/cultural activity (music, science, literature, etc.)
28. ① ② ③ ④ ⑤ Developing skill in expressing myself orally or in writing
29. ① ② ③ ④ ⑤ Learning how to find and use resources for answering questions or solving problems
30. ① ② ③ ④ ⑤ Developing a clearer understanding of, and commitment to, personal values
31. ① ② ③ ④ ⑤ Learning to *analyze* and *critically evaluate* ideas, arguments, and points of view
32. ① ② ③ ④ ⑤ Acquiring an interest in learning more by asking my own questions and seeking answers

Mark Reflex® forms by NCS Pearson MM75864-4   654321   ED06   Printed in U.S.A.   Copyright © IDEA Center, 1998

Continued on back page

On the next three items, compare this course with others you have taken at this institution, using the following code:

| 1=Much Less than Most Courses | 2=Less than Most Courses | 3=About Average | 4=More than Most Courses | 5=Much More than Most Courses |

The Course:

33. ① ② ③ ④ ⑤ Amount of reading
34. ① ② ③ ④ ⑤ Amount of work in other (non-reading) assignments
35. ① ② ③ ④ ⑤ Difficulty of subject matter

Describe your attitudes and behavior in this course, using the following code:

| 1=Definitely False | 2=More False Than True | 3=In Between | 4=More True Than False | 5=Definitely True |

36. ① ② ③ ④ ⑤ I had a strong desire to take this course.
37. ① ② ③ ④ ⑤ I worked harder on this course than on most courses I have taken.
38. ① ② ③ ④ ⑤ I really wanted to take a course from this instructor.
39. ① ② ③ ④ ⑤ I really wanted to take this course regardless of who taught it.
40. ① ② ③ ④ ⑤ As a result of taking this course, I have more positive feelings toward this field of study.
41. ① ② ③ ④ ⑤ Overall, I rate this instructor an excellent teacher.
42. ① ② ③ ④ ⑤ Overall, I rate this course as excellent.

For the following items, blacken the space which best corresponds to your judgment:

| 1=Definitely False | 2=More False Than True | 3=In Between | 4=More True Than False | 5=Definitely True |

43. ① ② ③ ④ ⑤ As a rule, I put forth more effort than other students on academic work.
44. ① ② ③ ④ ⑤ The instructor used a variety of methods--not only tests--to evaluate student progress on course objectives.
45. ① ② ③ ④ ⑤ The instructor expected students to take their share of responsibility for learning.
46. ① ② ③ ④ ⑤ The instructor had high achievement standards in this class.
47. ① ② ③ ④ ⑤ The instructor used educational technology (e.g., Internet, e-mail, computer exercises, multi-media presentations, etc.) to promote learning.

EXTRA QUESTIONS

If your instructor has extra questions, answer them in the space designated below (questions 48-66):

48. ① ② ③ ④ ⑤
49. ① ② ③ ④ ⑤
50. ① ② ③ ④ ⑤
51. ① ② ③ ④ ⑤
52. ① ② ③ ④ ⑤
53. ① ② ③ ④ ⑤
54. ① ② ③ ④ ⑤
55. ① ② ③ ④ ⑤
56. ① ② ③ ④ ⑤
57. ① ② ③ ④ ⑤

58. ① ② ③ ④ ⑤
59. ① ② ③ ④ ⑤
60. ① ② ③ ④ ⑤
61. ① ② ③ ④ ⑤
62. ① ② ③ ④ ⑤
63. ① ② ③ ④ ⑤
64. ① ② ③ ④ ⑤
65. ① ② ③ ④ ⑤
66. ① ② ③ ④ ⑤

Your comments are invited on how the instructor might improve this course or teaching procedures. Use the space below for comments (unless otherwise directed). *Note: Your written comments may be returned to the instructor. You may want to PRINT to protect your anonymity.*

Comments: _____

_____

_____

_____

_____

_____

_____

_____

_____

_____

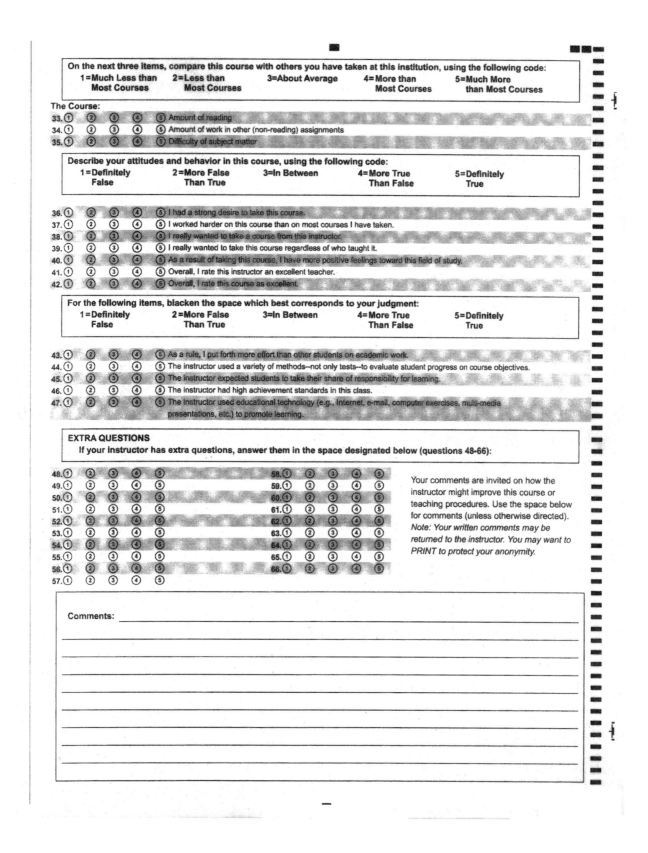

Faculty Information Form

IDEA CENTER

Institution: _____ Instructor: _____

Course Number: _____ Time and Days Class Meets: _____

IMPORTANT!

USE NO. 2 PENCIL ONLY

Proper Marks ● ● ● ● ● ●

Improper Marks ⊙ ⊘ ⊗ ⊚ ◕ ⊕

Last Name (Up to 11 letters) | **Init.**

[Bubble grid A–Z for name fields]

Objectives: (Scale - M = Minor or No Importance, I = Important, E = Essential)

M I E

1. ○○○ Gaining factual knowledge (terminology, classifications, methods, trends)
2. ○○○ Learning fundamental principles, generalizations, or theories
3. ○○○ Learning to *apply* course material (to improve thinking, problem solving, and decisions)
4. ○○○ Developing specific skills, competencies, and points of view needed by professionals in the field most closely related to this course
5. ○○○ Acquiring skills in working with others as a member of a team
6. ○○○ Developing creative capacities (writing, inventing, designing, performing in art, music, drama, etc.)
7. ○○○ Gaining a broader understanding and appreciation of intellectual/cultural activity (music, science, literature, etc.)
8. ○○○ Developing skill in expressing oneself orally or in writing
9. ○○○ Learning how to find and use resources for answering questions or solving problems
10. ○○○ Developing a clearer understanding of, and commitment to, personal values
11. ○○○ Learning to *analyze* and *critically evaluate* ideas, arguments, and points of view
12. ○○○ Acquiring an interest in learning more by asking questions and seeking answers

Days Class Meets
○ Mon
○ Tues
○ Wed
○ Thu
○ Fri
○ Sat
○ Sun

Department Code | **Time Class Begins** | **Course Number** | **Number Enrolled** | **Local Code**

[Numeric bubble grids 0–9]

Contextual Questions (Research Purposes):

The IDEA Center will conduct research on these optional questions in order to improve the interpretation of student ratings.

1. Which of the following represents the primary approach to this course? (Mark only one)

(1) = Lecture
(2) = Discussion/recitation
(3) = Seminar
(4) = Skill/activity
(5) = Laboratory
(6) = Field Experience
(7) = Studio
(8) = Multi-Media
(9) = Practicum/clinic
(0) = Other

2. If multiple approaches are used, which one represents the secondary approach?

(1) = Lecture
(2) = Discussion/recitation
(3) = Seminar
(4) = Skill/activity
(5) = Laboratory
(6) = Field Experience
(7) = Studio
(8) = Multi-Media
(9) = Practicum/clinic
(0) = Other

3. Describe this course in terms of its requirements with respect to the features listed below. Use the following code to make your responses:
N = None (or little) required
S = Some required
M = Much required

N S M
○○○ A. Writing
○○○ B. Oral communication
○○○ C. Computer applications
○○○ D. Group work
○○○ E. Mathematical/quantitative work
○○○ F. Critical thinking
○○○ G. Creative/artistic/design endeavor

Mark Reflex® forms by NCS Pearson MM75862-3   654321   ED05   Printed in U.S.A.   Copyright © IDEA Center, 1998

Continue on back page

Contextual Questions Continued:

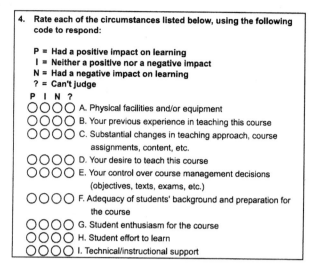

4. Rate each of the circumstances listed below, using the following code to respond:

P = Had a positive impact on learning
I = Neither a positive nor a negative impact
N = Had a negative impact on learning
? = Can't judge

P I N ?
○ ○ ○ ○ A. Physical facilities and/or equipment
○ ○ ○ ○ B. Your previous experience in teaching this course
○ ○ ○ ○ C. Substantial changes in teaching approach, course assignments, content, etc.
○ ○ ○ ○ D. Your desire to teach this course
○ ○ ○ ○ E. Your control over course management decisions (objectives, texts, exams, etc.)
○ ○ ○ ○ F. Adequacy of students' background and preparation for the course
○ ○ ○ ○ G. Student enthusiasm for the course
○ ○ ○ ○ H. Student effort to learn
○ ○ ○ ○ I. Technical/instructional support

5. Please identify the principal type of student enrolling in this course

① = Freshmen/sophomores seeking to meet a "general education" or "distribution" requirement
② = Freshmen/sophomores seeking to develop background needed for their intended specialization
③ = Upperclassmen non-majors taking the course as a "general education" or "distribution" requirement
④ = Upperclassmen majors (in this or a related field of study) seeking competence or expertise in their academic/professional specialty
⑤ = Graduate or professional school students
⑥ = Combination of two or more of the above types

6. Is this class:

a. Team taught?   ○ Yes   ○ No
b. Taught through distance learning?   ○ Yes   ○ No

Department Codes (Modified CIP Codes)

0100 Agricultural Business and Production	4506 Economics	5009 Music (Performing, Composing, Theory)
0200 Agricultural Sciences	1300 Education (EXCEPT Physical Education and Vocational-Technical Education)	5116 Nursing
0300 Conservation and Renewable Natural Resources		3801 Philosophy
0400 Architecture and Related Programs	1400 Engineering	1332 Physical Education/Health/Safety Education
0500 Area Ethnic and Cultural Studies	1500 Engineering-Related Technologies	4000 Physical Sciences (EXCEPT Physics and Chemistry)
5007 Art (Painting, Drawing, Sculpture)	2301 English Language and Literature	4008 Physics
2600 Biological Sciences/Life Sciences	5000 Fine and Applied Arts (EXCEPT Art and Music)	4510 Political Science and Government
5201 Business, General	1600 Foreign Languages and Literatures	4200 Psychology
5202 Business Administration and Management	5100 Health Professions and Related Sciences (EXCEPT Nursing)	4400 Public Administration and Services (EXCEPT Social Work)
5203 Business - Accounting	5199 Health Professions and Related Sciences (2-year program)	3900 Religion and Theological Studies
5208 Business - Finance	4508 History	5204 Secretarial Services
5212 Business Information and Data Processing Services	1900 Home Economics	4500 Social Sciences (EXCEPT Economics, History, Political Science, and Sociology)
5214 Business - Marketing	——— Industrial Arts (See Vocational-Technical Education)	4407 Social Work and Service
4005 Chemistry	2400 Liberal Arts & Sciences, General Studies and Humanities	4511 Sociology
0900 Communications	2200 Law	2310 Speech and Rhetorical Studies
1100 Computer and Information Sciences	2500 Library Science	1320 Vocational-Technical Education
1103 Data Processing Technology (2-year program)	2700 Mathematics and Statistics	9900 Other (to be used when none of the above codes apply)
	2900 Military Science/Technologies	

To see an expanded list of department codes go to www.idea.ksu.edu

The IDEA Report
Communications 0000 (MWF 11:30)
IDEA Center
www.idea.ksu.edu

| Faculty Name: SAMPLE, AX | Number Enrolled: 18 | Term: Fall 1998-1999 |
| Institution: ALPHA UNIVERSITY | Number Responding: 15 | % Responding: 83.3 |

Your results are considered fairly reliable; it is unlikely that re-rating by the same students would produce more than a moderate change in your report. The percentage of enrollees who provided ratings is high; results can be considered representative of the the class as a whole.

Sections and Purposes of the Report

Page	Section	Purpose
2	I. Overall Measures of Teaching Effectiveness	Primarily for **administrative use** in helping to make personnel recommendations. *Only this page and Page 6 are essential if this is the only use you plan to make of the report.*
3	II. Student Ratings of Progress on Specific Objectives	Primarily to identify the **teaching objectives** where improvement is most needed
4-5	III. Teaching Methods or Style Related to Student Rating of Progress	Primarily to help develop a **strategy for improving teaching** methods
6	IV. Course Description/Context	Primarily to **assist in interpreting** the results by considering the context in which the course was
7-8	V. Statistical Detail	Primarily to provide details which may help you or your consultants to **understand or interpret** the report accurately
8	VI. Processing Error Messages	Identifies errors resulting from incomplete information provided on the Faculty Information Form

---

Definitions

Raw Score: Results obtained by using students' numerical ratings, all of which are based on a scale of 1 (low) to 5 (high).

Adjusted Score: Ratings which have been statistically adjusted to take into account factors which affect ratings but which are beyond the instructor's control (size of class; student desire to take course regardless of who taught it; course difficulty not attributable to instructor; student effort not attributable to instructor; and other student motivational influences).

T Score: A statistically derived score which makes it easy to compare various measures. Unlike raw scores which have different averages and standard deviations (variabilities), T Scores all have an average of 50 and a standard deviation of 10. This means that 40% of all T Scores will be in the range of 45-55, while less than 2% will be below 30 or above 70.

Similar Classes: On Page 4, ratings of specific teaching methods are compared with national averages for classes of "similar size and level of student motivation." Your ratings are compared with those from one of 20 groups defined by considering both class size (less than 15; 15-34; 35-99; or 100 or more) and average student response to "I had a strong desire to take this course" (under 3.0; 3.0-3.4; 3.5-3.9; 4.0-4.4; or 4.5 or above).

Understanding the Graphs

Most results are presented on graphs. Unadjusted T Scores are shown by the symbol ✕; adjusted T Scores are shown by the symbol ◆. In most cases, we use a line on both sides of a symbol to indicate that ratings have a "margin of error"; the line represents ± one standard error of measurement, a statistical of the reliability of the measure.

A. Few Words of Caution

1. New items on the IDEA form are marked by an asterisk (*) because they have been tested on only 3,668 classes. Comparisons with the national database on these items will be less stable than for the items retained from the original IDEA form which are based on over 35,000 classes rated during the 1993-94 and 1994-95 academic years.

2. Student ratings can make a useful contribution to the appraisal of teaching effectiveness and to the development of improvement strategies. However, they have distinct limitations which need to be acknowledged before appropriate use can be made of them. Please read the enclosed *Overview of Student Ratings: Values and Limitations.*

Section I: Overall Measures of Teaching Effectiveness

This section compares your results with those for other instructors and courses in the national database on for OVERALL MEASURES OF TEACHING EFFECTIVENESS. **The primary value of this information is to aid in making administrative recommendations: if this is the only use you will make of the report, you need to consult only these results and the context provided by Part IV, page 6.** Please remember that most of the classes included in the database have been taught in a reasonably successful manner; therefore, a rating which is "below average" does not necessarily mean that the quality of instruction was unacceptable.

Overall Measure of Effectiveness	T-Score Unadj. **Adj.**	2% of all classes	28% of all classes	40% of all classes (Avg. range)	28% of all classes	2% of all classes	Your Average (5-Point Scale) Raw	Adjusted
1. Progress on Relevant (Essential and Important) Objectives	58 / **55**						NA[1]	NA[1]
2. Improved Student Attitude	50 / **46**						3.9	3.6
3. Overall Excellence of Teacher	51 / **52**						4.2	4.3
4. Overall Excellence of Course	51 / **44**						3.9	3.5

```
        20      30      40      50   55  60      70      80
```
T Score--Comparison will all Classes in National Database

⊢✕⊣ Unadjusted T Score ± one standard error of measurement

⊢◆⊣ Adjusted T Score ± one standard error of measurement (adjusted for class size; student desire to take course regardless of who taught it; course difficulty not attributable to instructor; student effort not attributable to instructor; and other student motivational influences)

You may wish to assign these ratings to categories like those which have been used historically with the IDEA system. Simply assign T Scores to categories as follows: **Low** (lowest 10%)=T Score below 37; **Low Average** (next 20%)=T Score 37-44; **Average** (middle 40%)=T Score 45-55; **High Average** (next 20%)=T Score 56-63; and **High** (highest 10%)=T Score above 63.

1. Progress on Relevant (Essential and Important) Objectives. Because student learning is the central purpose of teaching, and because you chose the objectives considered by this measure, this is probably the most vital measure of effectiveness. A double weight is given to student ratings of progress on objectives you chose as *Essential*, and a single weight to those chosen as *Important*; objectives identified as being of *Minor or No Importance* were ignored in developing this measure.

2. Improved Student Attitude. The graph shows the average response of students to item 16, "As a result of taking this course, I have more positive feelings toward this field of study." This rating is most meaningful for courses which are taken by many non-majors. Most teachers hope that such students will develop a respect and appreciation for the discipline even if they choose to take no additional courses in it.

3. Overall Excellence of Teacher. This shows the average response to item 17, "Overall, I rate this instructor an excellent teacher." Overall impressions of a teacher affect student attitudes, effort, and learning.

4. Overall Excellence of Course. This shows the average response to item 18, "Overall, I rate this course as excellent." This evaluation is likely determined by a number of factors (e.g., teaching style, student satisfaction with course outcomes, and characteristics such as organization, selection of readings and/or other influences).

---

[1]Based on a combination of ratings where an average on a 5-point scale is not comparable.

Section II: Student Ratings of Progress on Specific Objectives

This graph shows student progress ratings on the objectives you chose as *Essential* (Part A) and those you chose as *Important* (Part B). To the degree that students make progress on the objectives you stress, your teaching has been effective.

Part A. Essential Objectives	T-Score Unadj. Adj.	2% of all classes	28% of all classes	40% of all classes (Avg. range)	28% of all classes	2% of all classes	Your Average (5-Point Scale) Raw	Adjusted
24. Professional skills, viewpoints	52 **45**						4.1	3.7
28. Oral and written communication skills	61 **61**						4.5	4.6

Part B. Important Objectives								
26. Creative capacities	61 **56**						4.5	4.3
*31. Analysis and critical evaluation of ideas	62 **61**						4.1	4.1

```
20    30    40    45  50  55    60    70    80
```

T Score--Comparison will all Classes in National Database where the
Objective was Selected as "Essential" or "Important"

⊢—✕—⊣ Unadjusted T Score ± one standard error of measurement

⊢—◆—⊣ Adjusted T Score ± one standard error of measurement (adjusted for class size; student desire to take course regardless of who taught it; course difficulty not attributable to instructor; student effort not attributable to instructor; and other student motivational influences)

Similar to Section I, you may wish to assign ratings to categories. Simply assign T Scores to categories as follows: **Low** (lowest 10%)=T Score below 37; **Low Average** (next 20%)=T Score 37-44; **Average** (middle 40%)=T Score 45-55; **High Average** (next 20%)=T Score 56-63; and **High** (highest 10%)=T Score above 63.

It is recommended that priority attention be given to *Essential* objectives with progress ratings which are *below average*. The second priority might be directed to *Important* objectives for which progress ratings are *below average*. A third priority might be *Essential* or *Important* objectives for which progress ratings are in the *average* range. If all progress ratings are *above the average* range, it is suggested that your present methods of teaching are effective and changes in your teaching style or approaches do not appear to be needed in order to ensure that your teaching promotes student learning. If improvement is needed, strategies can be formulated by examining "Strengths" and "Weaknesses" associated with progress ratings on the objectives chosen for priority attention. These are identified in **Section III** of this report.

Note: Students in your class also rated their progress on the objectives which you classified as being of *Minor or No Importance*. These ratings are considered irrelevant in judging your teaching effectiveness. However, a review of student ratings on these objectives, found in **Section V** (Statistical Detail), may provide you with insights about some "unintended" or "additional" effects of your instruction.

* New item

Section III: Teaching Methods or Style Related to Student Ratings of Progress

This section focuses on specific teaching methods. Results are given in two parts. **Part One** graphically compares ratings of your teaching methods with those of others who teach classes similar to this one in terms of size and level of student motivation. **Part Two** identifies the teaching methods most closely related to attaining your ***Important*** and ***Essential*** objectives, providing a basis for developing improvement strategies. **Part Three** highlights potential areas to emphasize for improvement efforts and teaching strengths that should be retained.

<u>Part One</u>: The graphs below classify methods as "strengths" if your rating was at least 0.3 above average for classes of similar size and level of student motivation and as "weaknesses" if your rating was at least 0.3 below the average for such classes. Although effectiveness generally improves when weaknesses are overcome while maintaining strengths, not all teaching methods promote progress on every teaching objective. The methods which are especially relevant to each of your ***Essential*** and ***Important*** objectives are identified in **Part Two** (page 5).

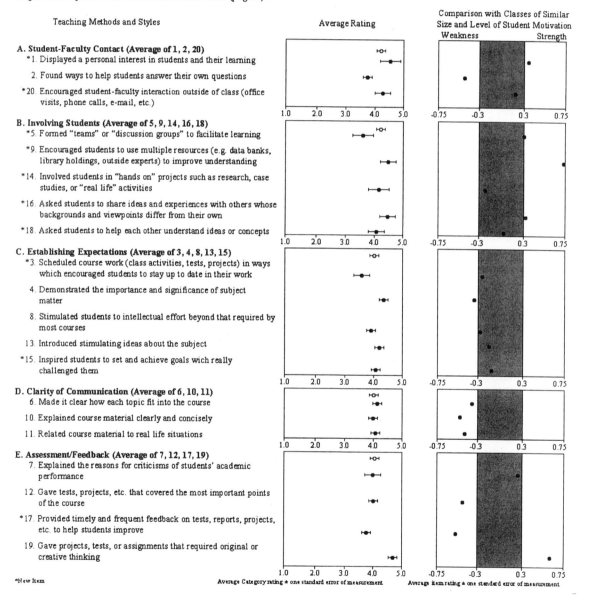

Teaching Methods and Styles

A. Student-Faculty Contact (Average of 1, 2, 20)
  *1. Displayed a personal interest in students and their learning

  2. Found ways to help students answer their own questions

  *20. Encouraged student-faculty interaction outside of class (office visits, phone calls, e-mail, etc.)

B. Involving Students (Average of 5, 9, 14, 16, 18)
  *5. Formed "teams" or "discussion groups" to facilitate learning

  *9. Encouraged students to use multiple resources (e.g. data banks, library holdings, outside experts) to improve understanding

  *14. Involved students in "hands on" projects such as research, case studies, or "real life" activities

  *16. Asked students to share ideas and experiences with others whose backgrounds and viewpoints differ from their own

  *18. Asked students to help each other understand ideas or concepts

C. Establishing Expectations (Average of 3, 4, 8, 13, 15)
  *3. Scheduled course work (class activities, tests, projects) in ways which encouraged students to stay up to date in their work

  4. Demonstrated the importance and significance of subject matter

  8. Stimulated students to intellectual effort beyond that required by most courses

  13. Introduced stimulating ideas about the subject

  *15. Inspired students to set and achieve goals wich really challenged them

D. Clarity of Communication (Average of 6, 10, 11)
  6. Made it clear how each topic fit into the course

  10. Explained course material clearly and concisely

  11. Related course material to real life situations

E. Assessment/Feedback (Average of 7, 12, 17, 19)
  7. Explained the reasons for criticisms of students' academic performance

  12. Gave tests, projects, etc. that covered the most important points of the course

  *17. Provided timely and frequent feedback on tests, reports, projects, etc. to help students improve

  19. Gave projects, tests, or assignments that required original or creative thinking

*New Item

Average Category rating ± one standard error of measurement

Average item rating ± one standard error of measurement

Section III: Teaching Methods or Style Related to Student Ratings of Progress (continued)

Part Two: Column 1 below again lists those objectives you listed as *Essential* or *Important*. Column 2 lists those teaching methods which in combination are most closely related to progress ratings on your chosen objectives. Column 3 separates out those teaching methods rated as "strengths" and those rated as "weaknesses" in comparison to the national average. (The numbers in Columns 2 and 3 refer to the teaching methods numbered 1-20 on the graphical presentations in **Part One, page 4**.)

Column 1 Chosen Objectives	Column 2 Most Relevant Teaching Methods	Column 3 Most Relevant Strengths/Weaknesses Strengths	Weaknesses
Essential Objectives			
24. Professional skills viewpoints	3,4,6,7,8,11,12,14,18		4,5,11,12
28. Oral and written communication skills	1,3,5,7,8,9,10,19	1,5,9,19	10
Important Objectives			
26. Creative capacities	1,5,6,7,13,19,20	1,5,19	6
*31. Analysis and critical evaluation of ideas	3,5,8,13,18,19,20	5,19	

Part Three: This section summarizes teaching methods to consider for improvement strategies and methods which are effective and should be retained.

Potential Areas for Improvement Efforts

Generally, improvement efforts are most successful if they focus on no more than three teaching strategies at a time. These results suggest that your improvement strategies might best be chosen from the following teaching methods:

6. Made it clear how each topic fit into the course
4. Demonstrated the importance and significance of the subject matter
10. Explained course material clearly and concisely
11. Related course material to real life situations
12. Gave tests, projects, etc. that covered the most important points of the course

Strengths to Retain

In doing so, you should take care to retain the methods which are currently effective, including:

*5. Formed "teams" or "discussion groups" to facilitate learning
19. Gave projects, tests or assignments that required original or creative thinking
*1. Displayed a personal interest in students and their learning
*9. Encouraged students to use multiple resources (e.g. data banks, library holdings, outside experts) to improve understanding

---

* New Item

Section IV: Course Description/Context

This section describes several aspects of your course. Some of the description summarizes information you supplied when you administered the IDEA form, and some of the information comes from student responses. Information on this page provides the context in which the class was taught and in which interpretation of the ratings should be made. The IDEA Center will conduct additional research on these data to determine more precisely how they can improve interpretation of the report.

Course Description:

Primary Instructional Type:	*Discussion/recitation*	Team Taught:	*Not reported*
Secondary Instructional Type:	*Other/Not Indicated*	Distance Learning:	*Not reported*
Principal Type of Student:	*Underclassmen, general*		

Instructor's Ratings of Special Circumstances:

Positive Impact on Learning	Neither Positive nor Negative Impact	Negative Impact on Learning
Previous experience teaching course	*Physical facilities and/or equipment*	*Adequacy of students' background/preparation*
Desire to teach course	*Changes in teaching approach*	
	Control over course management decisions	
	Student enthusiasm	
	Student effort	
	Technical/instructional support	

Instructor's Ratings of Course Requirements:

Much Required	Some Required	None (or little) Required
Writing		*Computer applications*
Oral communication		*Group work*
Critical thinking		*Mathematical/quantitative work*
Creative/artistic/design endeavor		

Student Ratings of the Course:

	Number of Students Saying:*					Average	T Score
	1	2	3	4	5		
33. Amount of reading	2	3	7	1	0	2.5	43
34. Amount of work in other (non-reading) assignments	0	1	3	7	2	3.8	57
35. Difficulty of subject matter	0	0	7	4	2	3.6	56

*1 = Much less than most courses   2 = Less than most courses   3 = About average   4 = More than most courses   5 = Much more than most courses

Similar to Sections I and II, you may wish to assign ratings to categories. Simply assign T Scores to categories as follows: **Low** (lowest 10%)=T Sore below 37; **Low Average** (next 20%)=T Score 37-44; **Average** (middle 40%)=T Score 45-55; **High Average** (next 20%)=T Score 56-63; and **High** (highest 10%)=T Score above 63.

Section V: Statistical Detail: Item Frequencies, Averages, and Standard Deviations

Items 1-20: Teaching Methods

Key: 1=Hardly Ever   2=Occasionally   3=Sometimes
     4=Frequently   5=Almost Always

	1	2	3	4	5	Omit	Avg.	s.d.
1.	0	0	0	6	9	0	4.6	0.5
2.	0	1	5	4	5	0	3.9	1.0
3.	0	1	3	5	6	0	4.1	1.0
4.	0	1	2	4	8	0	4.3	1.0
5.	2	0	5	2	6	0	3.7	1.4
6.	0	1	4	3	7	0	4.1	1.0
7.	1	1	1	4	7	1	4.1	1.3
8.	0	2	5	3	5	0	3.7	1.1
9.	0	0	1	5	9	0	4.5	0.6
10.	0	1	5	3	6	0	3.9	1.0
11.	1	1	1	5	7	0	4.1	1.2
12.	0	2	2	5	6	0	4.0	1.1
13.	0	0	4	4	7	0	4.2	0.9
14.	0	2	4	0	9	0	4.1	1.2
15.	0	1	5	4	5	0	3.9	1.0
16.	0	0	3	2	10	0	4.5	0.8
17.	1	2	4	2	6	0	3.7	1.3
18.	0	3	1	3	8	0	4.1	1.2
19.	0	0	0	5	10	0	4.7	0.5
20.	0	0	4	2	9	0	4.3	0.9

Items 21-32: Progress on Objectives

Key: 1=Low   2=Low Average   3=Average   4=High Average
     5=High

	1	2	3	4	5	Omit	Avg.	s.d.
21.	0	1	2	4	8	0	4.3	1.0
22.	1	2	1	5	6	0	3.9	1.3
23.	1	0	4	3	7	0	4.0	1.2
24.	**0**	**2**	**2**	**4**	**7**	**0**	**4.1**	**1.1**
25.	1	0	3	5	6	0	4.0	1.1
26.	**0**	**1**	**1**	**2**	**11**	**0**	**4.5**	**0.9**
27.	2	0	3	3	7	0	3.9	1.4
28.	**0**	**0**	**2**	**3**	**10**	**0**	**4.5**	**0.7**
29.	0	0	3	4	8	0	4.3	0.8
30.	2	1	3	4	5	0	3.6	1.4
31.	**0**	**0**	**5**	**3**	**7**	**0**	**4.1**	**0.9**
32.	0	1	5	2	7	0	4.0	1.1

Bold items were selected as *Essential* or *Important*.

Items 33-35: The Course

Key: 1=Much Less than Most Courses   2=Less than Most Courses
     3=About Average   4=More than Most Courses
     5=Much More than Most Courses

	1	2	3	4	5	Omit	Avg.	s.d.
33.	2	3	7	1	0	2	2.5	0.9
34.	0	1	3	7	2	2	3.8	0.8
35.	0	0	7	4	2	2	3.6	0.8

Items 43-47: Experimental

Key: 1=Definitely False   2=More False Than True
     3=In Between   4=More True Than False
     5=Definitely True

	1	2	3	4	5	Omit	Avg.	s.d.
43.	1	4	1	5	3	1	3.4	1.3
44.	0	2	2	6	4	1	3.9	1.0
45.	0	0	1	9	4	1	4.2	0.6
46.	0	1	2	7	4	1	4.0	0.9
47.	1	1	6	5	1	1	3.3	1.0

Items 36-42: Self Ratings

Key: 1=Definitely False   2=More False Than True
     3=In Between   4=More True Than False
     5=Definitely True

	1	2	3	4	5	Omit	Avg.	s.d.
36.	1	0	1	1	11	1	4.5	1.2
37.	0	2	4	6	2	1	3.6	0.9
38.	1	2	6	0	5	1	3.4	1.3
39.	1	0	3	4	6	1	4.0	1.2
40.	2	1	0	4	7	1	3.9	1.5
41.	0	1	2	4	7	1	4.2	1.0
42.	0	1	4	4	5	1	3.9	1.0

Section V: Statistical Detail: Continued

Items 48-66: Extra Questions

	1	2	3	4	5	Omit	Avg.	s.d.
48.	0	0	4	18	6	0	4.1	0.6
49.	1	3	11	13	0	0	3.3	0.8
50.	3	7	14	4	0	0	2.7	0.9
51.	0	11	7	10	0	0	3.0	0.9
52.	23	0	2	0	3	0	1.6	1.3
53.	4	12	10	2	0	0	2.4	0.8
54.	5	4	9	6	4	0	3.0	1.3
55.	0	0	0	0	0	28	N/A	N/A
56.	0	0	0	0	0	28	N/A	N/A
57.	0	0	0	0	0	28	N/A	N/A

	1	2	3	4	5	Omit	Avg.	s.d.
58.	0	0	0	0	0	28	N/A	N/A
59.	0	0	0	0	0	28	N/A	N/A
60.	0	0	0	0	0	28	N/A	N/A
61.	0	0	0	0	0	28	N/A	N/A
62.	0	0	0	0	0	28	N/A	N/A
63.	0	0	0	0	0	28	N/A	N/A
64.	0	0	0	0	0	28	N/A	N/A
65.	0	0	0	0	0	28	N/A	N/A
66.	0	0	0	0	0	28	N/A	N/A

Section VI: Processing Error Messages

Hampshire College
Student Course Evaluation

Part 1 Progress on Course Objectives

On each of the objectives listed below, rate the progress you have made as a result of taking this course by filling in the appropriate circle on the following scale:

None	Little	Some	Much	Very Much
○	○	○	○	○

In rating your progress, consider each objective carefully. Because the objectives are stated in general terms, interpret each of them in the context of this course; for instance, if an objective includes a list of items, consider the objective only in terms of the relevant item(s). Also, because most courses do not attempt to achieve all of these objectives, there are likely to be some objectives on which you have made no progress. Thus, an answer of "None" may simply mean that the objective in question was not one the course sought to achieve.

	None	Little	Some	Much	Very Much
1. Gaining knowledge of facts, terms, classifications, works, major figures, etc.	○	○	○	○	○
2. Gaining an understanding of theories, fundamental concepts, or other important ideas.	○	○	○	○	○
3. Learning to understand professional/scholarly literature.	○	○	○	○	○
4. Learning to interpret primary texts or works.	○	○	○	○	○
5. Developing skill in critical thinking.	○	○	○	○	○
6. Developing skill in problem solving.	○	○	○	○	○
7. Developing skill in critical/analytical writing.	○	○	○	○	○
8. Developing creative capacities.	○	○	○	○	○
9. Learning techniques and methods for gaining new knowledge in this subject.	○	○	○	○	○

Hampshire College Student Course Evaluation, Part I, page 2

10. Developing the ability to conceive and carry out independent work.
    ○   ○   ○   ○   ○

11. Developing the ability to work collaboratively with others.
    ○   ○   ○   ○   ○

12. Developing skill in expressing ideas orally.
    ○   ○   ○   ○   ○

13. Developing skill in expression through art, music, media, writing, design, or performance.
    ○   ○   ○   ○   ○

14. Developing specific skills or competencies, such as artistic techniques, production methods, laboratory methods, quantitative techniques, computer applications, or fieldwork methods.
    ○   ○   ○   ○   ○

15. Gaining an understanding of the relevance of the subject matter to real-world issues.
    ○   ○   ○   ○   ○

16. Gaining an understanding of the historical and social context in which the subject has developed.
    ○   ○   ○   ○   ○

17. Gaining an understanding of different views and perspectives on the subject.
    ○   ○   ○   ○   ○

18. Discovering the implications of the course material for understanding myself (interests, talents, preconceptions, values, etc.).
    ○   ○   ○   ○   ○

Hampshire College
Student Course Evaluation

Part 2 General Questions

Indicate your level of agreement with each of the next twelve statements by filling in the appropriate circle on the following scale:

Strongly Disagree	Disagree	Neutral	Agree	Strongly Agree
○	○	○	○	○

	Strongly Disagree	Disagree	Neutral	Agree	Strongly Agree
Questions 19–21 refer to this course's instructor or, if the course has two instructors, to: _____ .					
19. I really wanted to take a course from this instructor.	○	○	○	○	○
20. I would like to take another course from this instructor.	○	○	○	○	○
21. Overall, I rate this instructor an excellent teacher.	○	○	○	○	○
Answer questions 22–24 only if this course has two instructors, these questions refer to: _____ .					
22. I really wanted to take a course from this instructor.	○	○	○	○	○
23. I would like to take another course from this instructor.	○	○	○	○	○
24. Overall, I rate this instructor an excellent teacher.	○	○	○	○	○
Please answer all of the remaining questions.					
25. I really wanted to take this course, regardless of who taught it.	○	○	○	○	○
26. As a result of taking this course, I have a new or increased interest in this subject.	○	○	○	○	○

27. I put considerable effort into this
course.   O   O   O   O   O

28. I had an adequate background
for this course.   O   O   O   O   O

29. Overall, I rate this an excellent
course.   O   O   O   O   O

30. Overall, I learned a great deal
in this course.   O   O   O   O   O

31. Please indicate how this course fits into your educational program (choose only one)

   O Course-based Division I exam
   O Project-based Division I exam
   O Division II concentration
   O Division III
   O Other (please specify) _____

32. Please indicate any other reason(s) you had for taking this course (choose all that apply).

   O Curiosity
   O Recommendation of student or faculty member
   O Acquisition of particular skills
   O Graduate or professional school requirement
   O Prerequisite for another course
   O Other (please specify) _____

Hampshire College
Student Course Evaluation

Course Number _____

Part 3 General Comments

33. Please comment on what you did and did not get out of this course, given your expectations for the course.

Hampshire College
Instructor Objectives Report

Course Number _____
(please print clearly)

Course Objectives

On each of the objectives listed below, rate the importance of this objective in your course by filling in the appropriate circle on the following scale:

Minor Importance
○

Moderate Importance
○

Essential
○

The rating "Minor Importance" should be understood to mean "of no more than minor importance."

	Minor Importance	Moderate Importance	Essential
1. Gaining knowledge of facts, terms, classifications, works, major figures, etc.	○	○	○
2. Gaining an understanding of theories, fundamental concepts, or other important ideas.	○	○	○
3. Learning to understand professional/ scholarly literature.	○	○	○
4. Learning to interpret primary texts or works.	○	○	○
5. Developing skill in critical thinking.	○	○	○
6. Developing skill in problem solving.	○	○	○
7. Developing skill in critical/analytical writing.	○	○	○
8. Developing creative capacities.	○	○	○
9. Learning techniques and methods for gaining new knowledge in this subject.	○	○	○
10. Developing the ability to conceive and carry out independent work.	○	○	○

Hampshire College Instructor Objectives Report, page 2

11. Developing the ability to work
collaboratively with others.   ○   ○   ○

12. Developing skill in expressing
ideas orally.   ○   ○   ○

13. Developing skill in expression through art,
music, media, writing, design, or performance.   ○   ○   ○

14. Developing specific skills or competencies,
such as artistic techniques, production methods,
laboratory methods, quantitative techniques,
computer applications, or fieldwork methods.   ○   ○   ○

15. Gaining an understanding of the relevance
of the subject matter to real-world issues.   ○   ○   ○

16. Gaining an understanding of the historical
and social context in which the subject has
developed.   ○   ○   ○

17. Gaining an understanding of different
views and perspectives on the subject.   ○   ○   ○

18. Discovering the implications of the course
material for understanding myself (interests,
talents, preconceptions, values, etc.).   ○   ○   ○

Appendix C

Examples of Questions for Conducting Peer Evaluations of Teaching

This report has emphasized the importance of using multiple approaches in evaluating teaching effectiveness. As discussed in Chapters 4 and 5, feedback from faculty colleagues can be a highly useful source of information for improving teaching and learning. However, research has indicated that faculty colleagues can be far more effective in this role if they are trained in how to conduct peer evaluations and if they work from an accepted set of criteria.

The forms included in this appendix serve as examples of peer evaluation surveys. French-Lazovik's (1981) form is designed to assist faculty in evaluating their colleagues on the basis of written materials that are provided in a dossier. The forms from Syracuse University and The University of Texas outline behaviors that colleagues can observe directly when they visit their colleagues' classrooms.

SUGGESTED FORM FOR PEER REVIEW OF UNDERGRADUATE TEACHING BASED ON DOSSIER MATERIALS

QUESTION	DOSSIER MATERIALS	SUGGESTED FOCUS IN EXAMINING DOSSIER MATERIAL
1. What is the quality of materials used in teaching?	Course outline Syllabus Reading list Text used Study guide Description of non-print materials Hand-outs Problem sets Assignments	Are these materials currents? Do they represent the best work in the field? Are they adequate and appropriate to course goals? Do they represent superficial or thorough coverage of course content?
Peer Reviewer's Rating: Low _____ Very High		
Comments _____		
2. What kind of intellectual tasks were set by the teacher for the students (or did the teacher succeed in getting students to set for themselves), and how did the students perform?	Copies of graded examinations Examples of graded research papers Examples of teacher's feedback to To students on written work Grade distribution Descriptions of student performances, e.g., class presentations, etc. Examples of completed assignments	What was the level of intellectual performance achieved by the students? What kind of work was given an A? a B? a C? Did the students learn what the department curriculum expected for this course? How adequately do the tests or assignments represent the kinds of student performance in the course objective?
Peer Reviewer's Rating: Low _____ Very High		
Comments _____		
3. How knowledgeable is this faculty member in subjects taught?	Evidence in teaching materials Record of attendance at regional or national meetings Record of colloquia or lecture given	Has the instructor kept in thoughtful contact with developments in his or her field? Is there evidence of acquaintance with the ideas and findings of other scholars? (This question addresses the scholarship necessary to good teaching. It is not concerned with scholarly research publication.)
Peer Reviewer's Rating: Low _____ Very High		
Comments _____		

4. Has this faculty member assumed responsibilities related to the department's or University's teaching mission?

Record of service on department curriculum committee, honors program, advising board of teaching, special committees (e.g., to examine grading policies, admission standards, etc.
Description of activities in supervising graduate students learning to teach.
Evidence of design of new courses

Has he or she become departmental or college citizen in regard to teaching responsibilities?
Does this faculty member recognize problems that hinder good teachings and does he or she take a responsible part in trying to solve them?
Is the involvement of the faculty member appropriate to his or her academic level? (e.g., assistant professors may sometimes become over-involved to the detriment of their scholarly and teaching activities.)

Peer Reviewer's Rating: Low   Very High
Comments

5. To what extent is this faculty member trying to achieve excellence in teaching?

Factual statement of what activities the faculty member has engaged in to improve his or her teaching.
Examples of questionnaires used for formative purposes.
Examples of changes made on the basis of feedback.

Has he or she sought feedback about teaching quality, explored alternative teaching methods, made changes to increase student learning?
Has he or she sought aid in trying new teaching ideas?
Has he or she developed special teaching materials or participated in cooperative efforts aimed at upgrading teaching quality?

Peer Reviewer's Rating: Low   Very High
Comments

Peer Reviewer's Signature _____

Date _____

SOURCE: French-Lazovik (1981).

Syracuse University
Resource B: Sample Forms

Classroom Observation Worksheet

Instructor _____   Course _____

Date _____   Observer _____

Directions: Below is a list of instructor behaviors that may occur within a given class or course. Please use it as guide to making observations, not as a list of required characteristics. When this worksheet is used for making improvements to instruction, it is recommended that the instructor highlight the areas to be focused on before the observation takes place.

Respond to each statement using the following scale:

	Not observed	More emphasis	Accomplished very well
	1	2	3

Circle the number at the right that best represents your response. Use the comment space below each section to provide more feedback or suggestions.

Content Organization	Not Observed	More emphasis Recommended	Accomplished very Well
	1	2	3
1. Made clear statement of the purpose of the lesson.	1	2	3
2. Defined relationship of this lesson to previous lessons	1	2	3
3. Presented overview of the lesson	1	2	3

	1	2	3
4. Presented topics with a logical sequence	1	2	3
5. Paced lesson appropriately	1	2	3
6. Summarized major points of lesson	1	2	3
7. Responded to problems raised during lesson	1	2	3
8. Related today's lesson to future lessons	1	2	3

Comments:

Reflective Faculty Evaluation

Presentation	Not Observed	More emphasis Recommended	Accomplished very Well
9 Projected voice so easily heard	1	2	3
10. Used intonation to vary emphasis	1	2	3
11. Explained things with clarity	1	2	3
12. Maintained eye contact with students	1	2	3
13. Listened to student questions and comments	1	2	3
14. Projected nonverbal gestures consistent with intentions	1	2	3
15. Defined unfamiliar terms, concepts, and principles	1	2	3

	Not Observed	More emphasis Recommended	Accomplished very Well
16. Presented examples to clarify points	1	2	3
17. Related new ides to familiar concepts	1	2	3
18. Restated important ideas at appropriate times	1	2	3
19. Varied explanations for complex and difficult material	1	2	3
20. Used humor appropriately to strengthen retention and interest	1	2	3
21. Limited use of repetitive phrases and hanging articles.	1	2	3

Comments:

Resource B: Sample Forms

Instructor-Student Interactions	Not Observed	More emphasis Recommended	Accomplished very Well
22. Encouraged student questions	1	2	3
23. Encouraged student discussion	1	2	3
24. Maintained student attention	1	2	3
25. Asked questions to monitor students' progress	1	2	3
26. Gave satisfactory answers to student questions	1	2	3
27. Responded to nonverbal cues of confusion, boredom, and curiosity	1	2	3

	Not Observed	More emphasis Recommended	Accomplished very Well
28. Paced lesson to allow time for note taking	1	2	3
29. Encouraged students to answer difficult questions	1	2	3
30. Asked probing questions when student answer was incomplete	1	2	3
31. Restated questions and answers when necessary	1	2	3
32. Suggested questions of limited interest to be handled outside of class	1	2	3

Comments:

Reflective Faculty Evaluation

Instructional Materials and Environment	Not Observed	More emphasis Recommended	Accomplished very Well
33. Maintained adequate classroom facilities	1	2	3
34. Prepared students for the lesson with appropriate assigned readings	1	2	3
35. Supported lesson with useful classroom discussions and exercises	1	2	3
36. Presented helpful audio-visual materials to support lesson organization and major points	1	2	3

37. Provided relevant written assignments

	Not Observed	More emphasis Recommended	Accomplished very Well
37. Provided relevant written assignments	1	2	3

Comments:

Content Knowledge And Relevance

	Not Observed	More emphasis Recommended	Accomplished very Well
38. Presented material worth knowing	1	2	3
39. Presented material appropriate to student knowledge and background	1	2	3
40. Cited authorities to support statements	1	2	3
41. Presented material appropriate to stated purpose of course	1	2	3
42. Made distinctions between fact and opinion	1	2	3
43. Presented divergent viewpoints when appropriate	1	2	3
44. Demonstrated command of subject matter	1	2	3

Comments:

Resource B: Sample Forms

45. What overall impressions do you think students left this lesson with in terms of content or style?

46. What were the instructor's major strengths as demonstrated in this observation?

47. What suggestions do you have for improving upon this instructor's skills?

Checklist of Teaching Skills*

Instructor: _____ Class: _____
Observer: _____ Date: _____

Directions: Respond to each of the following statements by checking the blank which corresponds to your observation.

Yes = Observed   **No** = Not observed; would have been appropriate   **NA** = Not applicable

	Yes	Some-times	No	NA	Comments
Importance and Suitability of Content					
1. Students seemed to have the necessary background to understand the lecture material	___	___	___	___	
2. The examples used drew upon student experiences.	___	___	___	___	
3. When appropriate, a distinction was made between factual material and opinions.	___	___	___	___	
4. When applicable, appropriate authorities were cited to support statements.	___	___	___	___	
5. When appropriate, divergent viewpoints were presented.	___	___	___	___	
6. An appropriate amount of material was included in the lecture	___	___	___	___	
Organization and Clarity					
7. Stated the purpose of the class session.	___	___	___	___	
8. Presented a brief overview of the content.	___	___	___	___	
9. Made explicit the relationship between today's and other aspects of the course.	___	___	___	___	
10. Defined new terms, concepts and principles.	___	___	___	___	
11. Arranged and discussed the content in a systematic and organized fashion.	___	___	___	___	
12. Asked questions periodically to determine whether too much or too little information was being presented.	___	___	___	___	
13. Presented clear and simple examples to clarify very abstract and difficult ideas.	___	___	___	___	
14. Used alternate explanations when necessary.	___	___	___	___	
15. Explicitly stated the relationships among various ideas.	___	___	___	___	
16. Periodically summarized the most important ideas.	___	___	___	___	
17. Slowed the word flow when ideas were complex and difficult.	___	___	___	___	
18. Did not often digress from the main topic.	___	___	___	___	
19. Summarized the main ideas.	___	___	___	___	
20. Related the day's material to upcoming sessions.	___	___	___	___	
Activities					
21. Used a variety of activities in the class.	___	___	___	___	
22. Activities used were appropriate for this class.	___	___	___	___	
23. Instructions for activities were clear.	___	___	___	___	
24. Sufficient time was given to complete the activities.	___	___	___	___	
25. The students were actively involved.	___	___	___	___	
26. Debriefing of the activity was student-centered.	___	___	___	___	

Use of Questions	**Yes**	**Some-times**	**No**	**NA**	**Comments**
31. Asked questions to see what the students knew about the lecture topic.	___	___	___	___	
32. Addressed questions to individual students as well as the group at large.	___	___	___	___	
33. Used questions to gain students' attention.	___	___	___	___	
34. Paused after all questions to allow students time to think of an answer.	___	___	___	___	
29. Encouraged students to answer difficult questions by providing cues or rephrasing.	___	___	___	___	
30. When necessary, asked students to clarify their questions.	___	___	___	___	
31. Asked probing questions if a student's answer was incomplete or superficial.	___	___	___	___	
32. Repeated answers when necessary so the entire class could hear.	___	___	___	___	
33. Received student questions politely and enthusiastically.	___	___	___	___	
34. Requested that very difficult, time-consuming questions of limited interest be discussed before or after class or during office hours.	___	___	___	___	

Interaction

	Yes	**Some-times**	**No**	**NA**	
35. Established and maintained eye contact with the class.	___	___	___	___	
36. Listened carefully to student comments and questions.	___	___	___	___	
37. Facial and body movements did not contradict speech or expressed intentions (e.g., waited for responses after asking for questions).	___	___	___	___	
38. Noted and responded to signs of puzzlement, boredom, curiosity, etc.	___	___	___	___	
39. Encouraged student questions.	___	___	___	___	

Use of Media

	Yes	**Some-times**	**No**	**NA**	
27. Writing on board/overhead/slides was legible.	___	___	___	___	
28. Information presented on board/overhead/slides was organized and easy to follow.	___	___	___	___	
29. The AV-materials used added to the students' comprehension of the concept(s) being taught.	___	___	___	___	
30. The AV-materials were handled competently (e.g., the instructor did not walk in front of the image for overhead or slide projector; the instructor spoke to the class, not the screen or board; etc.).	___	___	___	___	

Individual Style

	Yes	**Some-times**	**No**	**NA**	
40. Voice could be easily heard.	___	___	___	___	
41. Voice was raised or lowered for variety and emphasis.	___	___	___	___	
42. Speech was neither too formal nor too casual.	___	___	___	___	
43. Speech fillers (e.g., "ok now", "ahmm", etc.) were not distracting.	___	___	___	___	
44. Rate of speech was neither too fast nor too slow.	___	___	___	___	
45. Wasn't too stiff and formal in appearance.	___	___	___	___	
46. Wasn't too casual in appearance.	___	___	___	___	
47. Varied the pace of the lecture to keep students alert.	___	___	___	___	
48. Spoke at a rate which allowed students time to take notes.	___	___	___	___	

Comments:

---

* Adapted from material in *Improving Your Lectures* from the University of Illinois at Urbana-Champaign. Used by permission.

Appendix D

Biographical Sketches of Committee Members

Marye Anne Fox, *Co-chair,* is chancellor of North Carolina State University. Prior to assuming the chancellorship in 1998, Dr. Fox served as Vice President for Research and the M. June and J. Virgil Waggoner Regents Chair in chemistry at the University of Texas at Austin. Her recent research activities include organic photochemistry, electrochemistry, and physical organic mechanisms. She is a former editor of the *Journal of the American Chemical Society.* Previously, she was the director for the Center for Fast Kinetics Research, vice chair of the National Science Board, and a member of the Task Force on Alternative Futures for the Department of Energy National Laboratories (the Galvin Committee). Dr. Fox is a member of the National Academy of Sciences (NAS) and serves on several NAS and National Research Council (NRC) committees. In addition to her role as cochair of the Committee on

Undergraduate Science Education, she serves on the Committee on Science, Engineering, and Public Policy and as cochair of the Government–University–Industry Research Roundtable. Dr. Fox is a former member of the Commission on Physical Sciences, Mathematics, and Applications; the NAS Council; and the NRC Governing Board. She also served on the Committee on Criteria for Federal Support of Research and Development.

Norman Hackerman, *Co-chair*, served as president of Rice University from 1970 to 1985 and holds the positions of president emeritus and distinguished professor emeritus of chemistry at Rice University. Prior to coming to Rice, Dr. Hackerman spent 25 years at The University of Texas, Austin, Texas, where he joined the faculty as an assistant professor of chemistry in 1945 and became president in 1967. He is now professor emeritus of chemistry at The University of Texas at Austin. He taught chemistry at Loyola College and Virginia Polytechnic, and worked as a research chemist for Colloid Corporation, Kellex Corporation, and the U.S. Coast Guard. Dr. Hackerman was a member of the National Science Board from 1968 to 1980 and chairman from 1957 to 1980. He was editor of the *Journal of the Electrochemical Society* from 1969 to 1989. He is a member of the NAS, the American Philosophical Society, and the American Academy of Arts and Sciences and belongs to numerous scientific organizations. He is author or coauthor of 225 publications. In addition to several previous awards, Dr. Hackerman received the American Institute of Chemists Gold Medal in March 1978, the Mirabeau B. Lamar Award of the Association of Texas Colleges and Universities in 1981, the Distinguished Alumnus Award from The Johns Hopkins University in 1982, the Edward Goodrich Acheson Award of the Electrochemical Society in 1984, the Alumni Gold Medal for distinguished service to Rice University in 1984, the Charles Lathrop Parsons Award of the American Chemical Society in 1987, the AAAS-Philip Hauge Abelson Prize in 1987, the Vannevar Bush Award of the National Science Board in 1993, and the National Medal of Science in 1993. Dr. Hackerman serves as Chairman of the

Scientific Advisory Board of the Robert A. Welch Foundation.

Trudy Banta is vice chancellor for planning and institutional improvement, Indiana University–Purdue University at Indianapolis. She has edited five published volumes on assessment, contributed 15 chapters to other published works, and written more than 80 articles and reports. *Making a Difference: Outcomes of a Decade of Assessment in Higher Education* was published by Jossey-Bass in October 1993. Dr. Banta's most recent work, *Assessment in Practice: Putting Principles to Work on College Campuses*, was published by Jossey-Bass in early 1996. She is the founding editor of *Assessment Update*, a bimonthly periodical published by Jossey-Bass. Dr. Banta has developed, coordinated, and addressed conferences worldwide on assessing quality in higher education and matters related to outcome assessment. She has consulted with faculty and administrators on campuses and at statewide conferences in 37 states. In 1997, she was recognized by the American Productivity and Quality Center for leadership of one of the seven most effective programs in the world for using management information in decision making.

John Centra is a research professor and professor emeritus at Syracuse

University. He is a former chair of the Higher Education Program at the university. Prior to coming to Syracuse in 1985, he was a research psychologist at the Educational Testing Service, where he conducted studies on college teaching, faculty development, student learning, the effects of colleges on students, and other topics. He is the author of *Determining Faculty Effectiveness* (1979) and *Reflective Faculty Evaluation* (1993), and coauthor of *Tenure, Promotion, and Reappointment: Legal and Administrative Implications* (1995) and more than 85 articles, monographs, and books. He has consulted or given talks at well over a hundred colleges in the United States and abroad. Dr. Centra's current research is on assessing the scholarship of teaching. In 1993 he received a career achievement award from the American Educational Research Association's Special Interest Group on Faculty Evaluation and Development.

Barbara Gross Davis is assistant vice chancellor, Student Life and Educational Development, University of California-Berkeley. Dr. Davis' primary interests are in instructional improvement, assessment and accreditation, faculty development and evaluation, and program and curriculum evaluation in higher education. She has conducted workshops and seminars for faculty on topics related to teaching, learning, and evaluation; has written about these topics in a number of articles, book chapters, and evaluation reports (including a chapter on assessment in the NRC report *Science Teaching Reconsidered*); and authored or coauthored five books.

Denice Denton is dean of engineering and a professor in the Department of Electrical Engineering at the University of Washington. Her current interests include plasma deposition of polymers and the use of micromachining in solid state actuator design. Professor Denton was codirector of the National Institute for Science Education 1995–1996. She is a recipient of the National Science Foundation Presidential Young Investigator Award (1987–1992), the American Society of Engineering Education AT&T Foundation Teaching Award (1991), the WM. Keck Foundation Engineering Teaching Excellence Award (1994), the American Society of Electrical Engineers George Westinghouse Award (1995), and the Institute of Electronic and Electrical Engineering Harriet B. Rigas Teaching Award (1995).

Diane Ebert-May is director of Lyman Briggs School, a residential, liberal arts science program within the College of Natural Sciences at Michigan State University, and is a professor of botany and plant pathology. She provides national leadership in promoting professional development opportunities for faculty, postdoctoral teaching fellows, and graduate students who participate actively not only in their own discipline-based research, but also in creative scholarship and research on teaching and learning. She chairs the Education Committee of the National Long Term Ecological Research Network and is chairperson of the Education Section of the Ecological Society of America. Her current research in biology education is based on an empirically based model she developed to test the effectiveness of active learning in a large introductory biology course for nonmajors and an ecology course for majors. From this she has developed models for using argument structure to develop assessments for critical thinking. Dr. Ebert-May's recent publications describe the inquiry-based instructional strategies she uses in a course with large class meetings (lectures) and multiple laboratory sections. Her research, funded by the National Science Foundation, the National Institutes of Health, and Howard Hughes Medical Institute, focuses on alternative assessments for large science courses, including student self-reflection as a form of student evaluation. Her ecological research continues on Niwot Ridge, Colorado, where she has conducted long-term

ecological research on alpine tundra plant communities since 1971.

Timothy Goldsmith is professor of molecular, cellular, and developmental biology at Yale University. He has experience in the classroom and is actively involved with other educational activities at Yale, the NRC, and elsewhere. Dr. Goldsmith has served on numerous NRC boards and committees, including the Commission on Life Sciences, the Board on Biology, and the Board on International Comparative Studies in Education. He was a member of the advisory board for the NRC's Center for Science, Mathematics, and Engineering Education. He also serves as chair of the board of directors for the Biological Sciences Curriculum Study and is a member of the American Academy of Arts and Sciences. Among his other teaching responsibilities, Dr. Goldsmith teaches an undergraduate course for nonmajors, for which he is also writing (with W. F. Zimmerman) a textbook entitled *Biology, Evolution, and Human Nature*. His research involves physiological and behavioral aspects of photopigments and photoreception in invertebrate and vertebrate animals.

Manuel Gomez is vice president for research and academic affairs at the University of Puerto Rico. He has overseen the implementation of an assessment plan that is driving the reform of undergraduate science, technology, engineering, and mathematics (STEM) education at the University of Puerto Rico, a multicampus system with 68,000 students, eight 2- and 4-year colleges, and three campuses offering the Ph.D. degree. Dr. Gomez is a theoretical physicist, specializing in solid state and condensed matter physics. Upon his graduation, he received a research fellowship from the NRC to work on the optical properties of solids at the Naval Research Laboratory in Washington, DC. He served as professor of physics and chairperson of the physics department at the University of Puerto Rico. He was then appointed dean of the College of Natural Sciences and later became the director of the Resource Center for Science and Engineering. Dr. Gomez has been director of the Puerto Rico EPSCoR program since its inception in 1986. He also served as a member of the NRC's Coordinating Council for Education.

Eileen Lewis is professor of chemistry at Cañada College (California). Her academic training is in chemistry and cognition, and her research interests include conceptual change in students' understanding of science, curricular designs that support knowledge integration, and systemic reform issues. Dr.

Lewis has served in a variety of capacities at the University of California-Berkeley, including visiting professor in the Graduate School of Education, director of assessment and evaluation and then project director for the ModularCHEM Consortium, and currently principal investigator for the Multi-Initiative Dissemination Project in the Department of Chemistry. She has also served as a National Institute of Science Education Fellow at the University of Wisconsin, Madison, and as editor of FLAG (Field-Tested Learning Assessment Guide). She serves on the editorial boards of the *International Journal of Science Education* and the *Journal of Science Education and Technology*.

Jeanne L. Narum is director of the Independent Colleges Office and Project Kaleidoscope (PKAL). PKAL is a consortium of colleges and universities across the United States that for the past 10 years has sought to discover and disseminate best practices in undergraduate STEM education. A major component of PKAL is the "Faculty for the 21st Century," which has as its goal identifying and providing professional development for up to 1,000 pretenured STEM faculty members from a variety of types of postsecondary institutions who have been recognized as potential leaders and educational innovators on their campuses. As a result of her leadership in PKAL, Ms. Narum has extensive background in and knowledge of university science curricula, issues related to the improvement of college teaching, and the culture of higher education.

Cornelius J. Pings is immediate past president, Association of American Universities (AAU), and thoroughly knowledgeable about the culture of and issues surrounding higher education. In addition to his recent presidency of the AAU, he held positions as provost and senior vice president for academic affairs at the University of Southern California and as professor of chemical engineering, vice provost, and dean of graduate studies at the California Institute of Technology. He also has considerable expertise in the corporate sector, having served as director of the Farmers Group, Nations Funds, Maxtor Corporation, and the Hughes Aircraft Company. Dr. Pings has been a member and chair of the National Academies' Committee on Science, Engineering, and Public Policy.

Michael Scriven is professor of psychology at Claremont Graduate University. His academic training is in mathematics and the philosophy of mathematical logic. He has taught in the United States and Australia in departments of mathematics, philosophy, psychology, the history and philosophy of science, and education. He has held fellowships from the Educational Testing Service, the Center for Advanced Studies in the Behavioral Sciences in Palo Alto, and the National Science Foundation, among others. His more than 300 publications are mainly in the areas of critical thinking, technology and computer studies, and evaluation. Dr. Scriven is well known for his expertise in evaluation. He is credited with coining the terms "formative" and "summative" to describe different kinds of personnel and program evaluations. He is an ex-president of the American Educational Research Association and the American Evaluation Association, and is the 2000 recipient of the McKeachie Award for lifetime contribution to the methodology of faculty evaluation.

Christine Stevens is professor of mathematics at St. Louis University. She has extensive experience with educational issues. She is the recipient of both statewide and national awards for distinguished college and university teaching from the Mathematical Association of America. Dr. Stevens also has served as associate program director for the National Science Foundation's Teacher Enhancement Program. She is involved extensively with Project NExT, a professional development program for new and recent Ph.D.s in the mathematical sciences that addresses issues in the teaching and learning of undergraduate mathematics. Dr. Stevens has authored articles on the implications of the National Council of Teachers of Mathematics standards for undergraduate education, an assessment of calculus reform efforts, and the history of mathematics. She has served on several committees of the Mathematical Association of America and the Society for Industrial and Applied Mathematics dealing with education, science policy, and minority participation in mathematics. Her scholarly interests are concerned with topological groups.

Dennis Weiss is dean of natural science and mathematics at The Richard Stockton College of New Jersey. He was previously dean of science at the City College of New York (CCNY). Dr. Weiss's research deals with bottom and subbottom mapping of New York's coastal zones, including the waterways in and around New York City and the continental shelf lying off the coast of New York City. This work is being done in conjunction with archaeologists who are seeking to locate sites of prehistoric settlements in the New York area. As a dean of science, Dr. Weiss has been active in overseeing educational reform in departments and programs under his purview. He has attended Project Kaleidoscope workshops on science and mathematics at Urban and Commuter Institutions and Science for All Students and an A.C.E. Workshop on Chairing the Academic Department. He was a convenor for a university-wide faculty development workshop on mentoring students and served on CCNY's President's Task Force on Advising and Mentoring. At CCNY he was the principal investigator for a grant from National Science Foundation to establish a Faculty Development Center at CCNY. He has taught numerous courses in the earth sciences to both undergraduate and graduate students. While at CCNY, a campus with a strong union, Dr. Weiss is working on his campus to change evaluation procedures for faculty.

Index

Course materials
  evaluation of, 63
Cultures of research and teaching, 18, 40-50
  balancing preparation for careers in research and teaching, 43-46
  developing and implementing improved means for evaluating effective teaching and learning, 50
  increasing support for effective teaching by professional organizations, 46-49
Curriculum design
  becoming inseparable from teaching and learning, 25
  the collective responsibility of faculty in all departments, 2, 15, 116

D

Data sources for evaluation, 54-67
  of course materials, 63
  faculty colleagues, 61-63
  graduating seniors and alumni, 60
  institutional data and records, 66-67
  instructional contributions, 63
  of knowledge and enthusiasm for subject matter, 102
  of professional involvement and contributions, 107
  of professionalism with students within and beyond the classroom, 106
  of proficiency in assessment, 104
  self-assessment by faculty, 64-66
  of skill in and experience with appropriate pedagogies and technologies, 103
  students in classroom observations, 63-64
  teaching assistants, 60-61
  undergraduate student evaluations, 54-60
Department heads
  providing personnel recommendations containing separate ratings on teaching, research, and service, 7, 125
Departmental and institutional records, 53
  number and levels of courses taught and number of students enrolled in each course or section taught by the instructor over time, 53
  number of graduate students mentored in their preparation as teaching assistants or future faculty members and their effectiveness in teaching, 53

number of undergraduate students advised, mentored, or supervised by the faculty member, 53
number of undergraduate students guided in original or applied research by the faculty member, 53
Departmental undergraduate programs. *See* Evaluation of departmental undergraduate programs
Departments. *See also* Graduate school faculties
  contributing to campus-wide awareness of the premium placed on improved teaching, 6-7, 125
  establishing panels on teaching effectiveness and expectations, 98
  evidence about student learning from, 3
  periodically reviewing their mission statement to include appropriate emphasis on teaching and student learning, 6, 124
  practicing the scholarship of teaching, 88
  providing funds to faculty to enhance teaching skills and knowledge, 7, 125-126
  supporting faculty moving to greater emphasis on instruction or educational leadership, 7, 126
Disciplinary-focused centers for teaching and learning
  providing opportunities for ongoing professional development, 5-6, 122-123
Discussion
  encouraging, 29
Diversity
  seen as asset-based, 25

E

Educational community
  involving representatives from across, 34
Educational Resources Information Center, 54n
Educational Testing Service, 145, 151-152
Educational values
  beginning with, 33
Effective undergraduate teaching, 18, 25-39. *See also* Teaching effectiveness
  challenges to, 32-39
  characteristics of, 27-31
  engaging students in original research, 38-39
  ensuring availability for all students, 2, 15, 116
  improving the assessment of learning outcomes, 32, 35-36

Evidence of faculty member's effectiveness
    adaptation of instructional techniques to
        improve student learning, 54
    participation in efforts to strengthen
        departmental or institutional curricula, 54
Evidence of student learning, 1-4
    from combined sources of evidence, 3
    from departments and other colleagues, 3
    from faculty members being evaluated, 3
    from graduate students, 3
    from institutional data and records, 3-4
    from the instructor's willingness to seek
        external support to improve teaching and
        learning, 3
    from student portfolios, 52
    from undergraduates and graduate teaching
        assistants, 3
Expectations
    of student learning outcomes for an individual
        course of study, 73
    of teaching assistants, appropriateness of, 93
    for those being evaluated to respond to
        evaluation results, 143-144

F

Facilitation of learning
    through metacognitive strategies that identify,
        monitor, and regulate cognitive practices,
        21
    through socially supported interactions, 22
    when new and existing knowledge is
        structured around major concepts and
        principles of the discipline, 20
Faculty. *See also* Colleagues; Evaluation of
        individual faculty; Graduate school
        faculties; Self-assessment
    encouraging to develop curricula that
        transcend disciplinary boundaries through
        a combination of incentives, 6, 124
    evidence about student learning from, 3
    expecting to contribute to a balanced program
        of undergraduate teaching, 6, 124-125
    guiding information searches, 28
    having a genuine interest in what is being
        taught, 28
    involvement in a larger set of conditions that
        promote change, 34-35
    involvement in enhancing teaching and
        learning, 31, 106-107

making clear how results of student
    evaluations will be used, 141
meeting all classes and labs, posting and
    keeping regular office hours, and holding
    exams as scheduled, 31
meeting responsibilities to students and to the
    public, 35
participation in seeking external support for
    activities that further the teaching mission,
    54
publicly recognizing and rewarding those who
    have excelled in teaching, 6, 123-124
rewarding for consistent improving of
    learning by both major and nonmajor
    students, 5, 120-121
supporting and mentoring those working with
    undergraduates throughout their careers,
    2
supporting in their obligation to improve their
    teaching skills through departmental and
    institutional reinforcement, 5, 121
using outcomes of effective formative and
    summative assessments of student
    learning to improve their teaching, 17
willingness to seek external support to
    improve teaching and learning, 3
Faculty Code of Conduct Manual, 31n
Faculty Information Form for Student
    Evaluations, 168-169
Faculty teaching portfolios, 54
    evidence of adaptation of instructional
        techniques to improve student learning, 54
    evidence of participation in efforts to
        strengthen departmental or institutional
        curricula, 54
    including in valid summative assessments of
        teaching, 4-5, 119-120
    sharing of, 97-98
    showing participation in seeking external
        support for activities that further the
        teaching mission, 54
Feedback
    for both instructors and students, 72
    from graduating seniors and alumni, 98
Formative evaluation by faculty colleagues, 83-86,
    93-96
    ad hoc committees on teaching effectiveness,
        93-95
    colleagues' evaluation questionnaires, 95-96
    discussions between the department chair
        and individual faculty members, 97
    observation, 84-85

Harvard University Derek Bok Center for Teaching and Learning, 163-165
  End-of-Semester Course Evaluation Form, 164-165
  Mid-Course Evaluation Form, 163
How People Learn: Brain, Mind, Experience, and School, 14
Howard Hughes Medical Institution, 48

I

Implementation of evaluation methodologies, 96-99
  departmental panels on teaching effectiveness and expectations, 98
  feedback from graduating seniors and alumni, 98
  formative discussions between the department chair and individual faculty members, 97
  helpful policies and procedures, 96-97
  legal considerations, 98-99
  oversight committee to monitor departmental curriculum and instruction, 98
  regular meetings between new faculty members and the department chair, 97
  sharing faculty-generated teaching portfolios, 97-98
Independent research
  encouraging students to engage in, 113-114
Informal conversations, 80
Input from students and peers, 52-53
  evidence of learning from student portfolios, 52
  faculty from "user" departments for service courses and from related disciplines for interdisciplinary courses, 52-53
  informed opinions of other members of the faculty member's department, 52
  summary of professional attainments of undergraduate students engaging in research under the faculty member being evaluated, 53
  undergraduate and graduate students, 53
  undergraduate and graduate teaching assistants, 53
Institutional data and records, 66-67
  data for evaluating teaching quality and effectiveness from, 66-67
  evidence about student learning from, 3-4

grade distributions, course retention, and subsequent enrollment figures, 66-67
  quality and performance of undergraduate research students, 67
Instructional contributions
  data for evaluating teaching quality and effectiveness from, 63
Instructor Objectives Report, 183-184
Integrated learning, 33
Intellectual development of individual students
  contributions to ongoing, 31
Interdepartmental cooperation
  in improving undergraduate STEM education, 114
International Technology Education Association (ITEA), 110
ITEA. *See* International Technology Education Association

J

Just-in-time teaching, 79

K

Kansas State University IDEA Center, 166-177
  Faculty Information Form for Student Evaluations, 168-169
  Sample Results of Student Evaluations, 170-177
  Student Reactions to Instruction and Courses, 166-167
Knowing What Students Know: The Science and Design of Educational Assessment, 15
Knowledge of subject matter, 27-28, 101
  answering students' questions and guiding information searches, 28
  data sources and forms of evaluation for evaluating, 102
  helping students learn and understand the general principles of their discipline, 28
  providing students with an overview of the whole domain of the discipline, 28
  staying current through an active research program or through scholarly reading, 28

L

Learners
bringing different strategies, approaches, patterns of abilities, and learning styles, 21
motivation to learn and sense of self affecting what and how much is learned and how much effort is put into learning, 21-22
using what they already know to construct new understandings, 20
Learning process. *See also* Facilitation of learning; Principles of learning
as multidimensional, integrated, and revealed in performance over time, 33
promoting active, 29
viewing as a joint venture with the students, 29
Legal considerations, 98-99
Limitations
on faculty knowledge of research on effective teaching, 39
on the use of rating forms, 144

M

Making Teaching Community Property: A Menu for Peer Collaboration and Peer Review, 86
Master Faculty Program, 85
Mathematical Association of America, 46, 109
Mentoring
of faculty by other faculty, 85
Mid-Course Evaluation Form, 163
Minute papers, 79
Miracosta Community College, 81n
Multidimensional learning, 33

N

National Center for Education Statistics, 35
National Center for Public Policy and Higher Education, 12
National Council of Teachers of Mathematics (NCTM), 46, 110
National Council on Measurement in Education (NCME), 55
National Institute for Science Education, 30, 72, 76

National Research Council (NRC), 1, 11, 15, 26, 35
National Science Board, 11
National Science Education Standards, 35, 37n
National Science Foundation (NSF), 11, 29n
Assessment of Student Achievement in Undergraduate Education, 48
Centers for Learning and Teaching program, 127n
Course, Curriculum, and Laboratory Improvement program, 54n
Shaping the Future, 108
National Survey of Student Engagement: The College Student Report, 77
National Teaching and Learning Forum, 81n
NCME. *See* National Council on Measurement in Education
NCTM. *See* National Council of Teachers of Mathematics
New faculty members
regular meetings with the department chair, 97
New scholarship on teaching, 25
NRC. *See* National Research Council
NSF. *See* National Science Foundation

O

Observation, 84-85
Outcomes assessment, 73-76
adjusting expected learning outcomes as appropriate, 73
benefits of, 75-76
determining when in a student's education specific knowledge and skills should be developed, 73
developing expected student learning outcomes for an individual course of study, 73
incorporating specified learning outcomes in statements of objectives for courses, 73
scoring, 74-75
selecting appropriate assessment strategies to test student learning of specified knowledge, 73
using to provide formative feedback to individual students, 73
Outside evaluators, 81
Oversight committee
to monitor departmental curriculum and instruction, 98

P

Pedagogical content knowledge, 16n
Pedagogies and technologies
  ability to recognize students not achieving to their fullest potential and assisting them in their academic difficulties, 29
  contextually appropriate, 29n
  data sources and forms of evaluation for evaluating skill in and experience with, 103
  enabling teaching, 25
  encouraging discussion and promoting active learning strategies, 29
  organized and clear communication to students of expectations for learning and academic achievement, 29
  persistently monitoring students' progress toward achieving learning goals, 29
  skill, experience, and creativity with a range of appropriate, 28-30, 101-103
  viewing the learning process as a joint venture with the students, 29
Peer reviews of teaching
  including in valid summative assessments of teaching, 4-5, 119-120
  providing both objective and subjective assessment of a faculty member's commitment to quality teaching, 7, 125
Pew Charitable Trust, 48
Pew Forum on Undergraduate Education, 147-150
Pew Forum on Undergraduate Learning, 77, 145
Portfolio Clearinghouse, The, 65
Portfolios. *See* Faculty teaching portfolios
Predictions about undergraduate teaching, 25
  changes in evaluation and documentation of teaching, 25
  changing appearance of higher education facilities, 25
  curriculum and program design becoming inseparable from teaching and learning, 25
  diversity seen as asset-based, 25
  focus of teaching shifting away from content transmission, 25
  nature and quality of assessment, 25
  a new scholarship of teaching, 25
  pedagogies students experienced prior to college changing their expectations about good teaching, 25
  teaching becoming more public than ever before, 25
  technology enabling teaching, 25

Preparation
  adequacy of, 87
  of future teachers, 32
Preparing for Peer Evaluation, 95
Primary trait analysis
  in scoring outcome assessments, 74-75
Principles of good practice for assessing student learning, 33-35
  educational values, 33
  illuminating questions people really care about, 34
  involving a larger set of conditions that promote change, 34-35
  involving representatives from across the educational community, 34
  meeting responsibilities to students and to the public, 35
  ongoing, not episodic, 34
  paying attention to outcomes and equally to the experiences leading to them, 33
  programs with clear, explicitly stated purposes, 33
  understanding learning as multidimensional, integrated, and revealed in performance over time, 33
Principles of learning, 20-22
  effect of learners' motivation to learn and sense of self on what and how much is learned and how much effort is put into learning, 21-22
  effect of the practices and activities engaged in while learning on what is learned, 22
  enhancement of learning through socially supported interactions, 22
  facilitation of learning through metacognitive strategies that identify, monitor, and regulate cognitive practices, 21
  facilitation of learning with understanding when new and existing knowledge is structured around major concepts and principles of the discipline, 20
  learners' different strategies, approaches, patterns of abilities, and learning styles coming from their heredity and prior experiences, 21
  learners' use of what they already know to construct new understandings, 20
Professional interactions with students, 30-31, 104-106
  advising students experiencing problems with course material, 31
  contributing to the ongoing intellectual development of individual students, 31

Q

R

departmental and institutional reinforcement, 5, 121

faculty who have excelled in teaching should be publicly recognized and rewarded, 6, 123-124

funding agencies and research sponsors should undertake a self-examination by convening expert panels to examine agency policy regarding quality undergraduate teaching, 7, 127

funding agencies should support programs to enable an integrated network of national and campus-based centers for teaching and learning, 7-8, 126-127

graduate school faculties should be required to show evidence they are effectively mentoring their teaching assistants and advising them about their duties to undergraduate students, 6, 124

for granting and accrediting agencies, research sponsors, and professional societies, 7-8, 126-127

individual faculty members should be expected to contribute to a balanced program of undergraduate teaching, 6, 124-125

individual faculty should be rewarded for consistent improving of learning by both major and nonmajor students, 5, 120-121

normal departmental professional developmental activity should include informing faculty about research findings that can improve student learning, 7, 125

one or more senior university-level administrators should be assigned responsibility for encouraging faculty to adopt effective means to improve instruction, 6, 123

only deans and department chairs willing to emphasize student learning and to make allocations of departmental resources in support of teaching should be appointed, 6, 124

overall, 4-5, 118-121

peer reviews and teaching portfolios should be included in valid summative assessments of teaching, in addition to student evaluations, 4-5, 119-120

for presidents, overseeing boards, and academic officers, 5-6, 122-124

professional societies should encourage publication of peer-reviewed articles on

evolving educational issues in STEM, 7, 127

professional societies should offer opportunities to discuss undergraduate education issues during annual and regional meetings, 7, 127

quality teaching and effective learning should be ranked highly in institutional priorities, 5, 122

scholarly activities focusing on improving teaching and learning should be recognized and rewarded, 4, 118-119

teaching effectiveness should be judged by the quality and extent of student learning, 4, 118

Reflective critiques, 87

Reliability
of undergraduate student evaluations, 55-56

Research. *See also* Applications of research; Cultures of research and teaching
education through, 38

Respect
for students as individuals and for their privacy, 31

Responsiveness
to students' concerns, 82

Role of colleagues in "formal" formative evaluation, 85-86
faculty mentoring faculty, 85
formative evaluation by faculty colleagues from other institutions, 85-86
projects of the American Association for Higher Education (AAHE), 86

S

Sample Results of Student Evaluations form, 170-177

Scholarly activities
focusing on improving teaching and learning, 4, 118-119

Scholarly standards
upholding and modeling for students the best in, 31

Scholarship on teaching, 9-67. *See also* Evaluation of the scholarship on teaching
according the same administrative and collegial support as for other research and service endeavors, 2, 15-16, 116

U

V

W